P9-DEA-428

THE NAMES OF WASHINGTON, D.C.

Who Were They?

Why Are Their Names Honored Here?

by

Dex Nilsson

Twinbrook Communications
Rockville, MD

THE NAMES OF WASHINGTON, D.C.
Copyright © 1998 by John Dexter Nilsson.
All rights reserved.
Printed in the United States of America.

1st Printing, March, 1999
2nd Printing, March, 2000

Published by
Twinbrook Communications
PO Box 730, Twinbrook Station
Rockville, MD 20848-0730

Copies may be ordered directly from the publisher
for $14.95 plus $3 for mailing ($17.95 total).
Maryland residents must also add $0.75 sales tax ($18.70 total).

Library of Congress Catalog Card Number
98-090927

ISBN 0-9629170-5-2

TABLE OF CONTENTS

About This Book........1

Bridges and Islands........3

Circles, Squares, and Parks........9

Federal Buildings........24

Fountains........37

Metro Stations........41

Military Reservations........44

Museums and Galleries........46

Neighborhoods........55

Other Places and Names........66

Points........91

Schools and Universities........93

Statues........101

Streets........139

Theaters and Auditoriums........144

Washington Himself........158

Bibliography........164

Index........168

PHOTO CREDITS

Of the photographs shown on pages 81 through 88, those of Paul Dunbar, the Eckington & Soldiers Home streetcar, and Octagon House are reproduced from the collections of the Library of Congress. The pictures of Congressional Cemetery, the John Ericsson memorial, Ford's Theater, Frances Perkins, the Albert Pike statue, Rawlins Park, and the Gen. Sheridan and "Boss" Shepherd statues are from the collection in the Washingtoniana Room of the Martin Luther King Library. Other photos are by the author.

THE AUTHOR

Dex Nilsson was born in Washington, D.C., a long time ago. Although he grew up in the Midwest and spent a dozen years in Huntsville, AL, he returned to the Washington area in the 1960s. He's lived in nearby Rockville, MD, for the last 30-plus years.

Dex has been a writer since his teens. Most recently and for more than 20 years, he managed the writing and publishing activities at GE Information Services. For ten years he served on and/or chaired the Committee on Editing for the U.S. Department of Agriculture Graduate School. He is a fellow of the Society for Technical Communication.

Fascinated with the names of things, in 1991 and again in 1995, he wrote and published *Discover Why It's Called ...*, stories about how 190 towns and locations on the Maryland Eastern Shore got their names.

ABOUT THIS BOOK

Who were they? Why are they and their names honored here?

If you live in or near Washington, you know that friends and relatives come to visit a lot. This is a great city to visit. I knew my way around the city and I knew a little about the main memorials, and I liked to show our visitors. But sooner or later someone would point to a statue - a Burke or a Shevchenko - and ask, "Who's that?" And I'd say, "I'm not sure." That's Washingtonian for "I have no idea."

The same happened with the names of buildings and theaters and parks and other places. I too got to wondering. Metro would stop at Tenleytown, and I'd wonder who Tenley was. Or Van Ness or Totten. I went to a concert at Lisner Auditorium, and no one there knew who Lisner was.

I asked others questions like "What Dupont is Dupont Circle named for?" "Is Farragut the one who said 'Don't give up the ship' or was he the one who defeated the Barbary pirates?" "Who was the Willard of the Willard Hotel?" A lot of people answered the last question by telling me he was a TV weather man. That clinched it.

I knew that other Washingtonians, to say nothing of nearby Marylanders, Virginians, and visitors, didn't know what they were talking about when it came to names and places - names they saw on the streets, places they traveled to and discussed, almost daily. We all needed a quick reference book of such information. So here it is.

You can now be a source of remarkable information as you travel through the city showing your visitors around. Or, if you're a visitor, you can cut out the unknowing middleman and read for yourself.

There are three good ways to use the book: When you see one of the country's distinguished characters commemorated in stone or park or building, look him or her up in the index, find the referenced entry, and enjoy a brief history of the person's accomplishments, plus perhaps a few remarks about the thing you are viewing. Or you can use the book backwards. That is, having discovered an interesting description of someone's memorial or statue, you can use its location and go there to see it. Or you can simply read the book. I've tried to put something special in each little biography.

I had to stop at just over 275 write-ups and 175 pages or cost and price would become too high. I restricted the book to only those names that exist in Washington today (although it would have been fun to write about the likes of old Griffith Stadium, Woodward & Lothrop's store, Harvey's Restaurant). And for pictures, instead of the popular scenes of the Washington monument and Capitol, I chose about a baker's dozen of seldom seen photos representing some of the more unusual name stories, statues, and sites.

Some of the information for the book was readily available in local libraries. But much was difficult to find. It certainly has never been compiled in this form before. For some of the more obscure material, I wish to thank the very responsive people I met throughout the city:

Special thanks go to Matthew Gilmore, reference librarian in the Washingtoniana Room of the Martin Luther King Memorial Library, who got for me school files, neighborhood information, clip files, and numerous references - and then reviewed my draft manuscript. To Gail Redmann, library director at the Historical Society of Washington, D.C., who helped me with references I could find nowhere else. And to the Historical Society's Robert Truax, who carefully reviewed the finished manuscript.

For the pictures in this book I'm indebted to Mary Ternes, the photo librarian in the Washingtoniana Room, and Mary Ison, in the Photo Reading Room of the Library of Congress, both of whom showed me where to look and helped me in my search for photographs.

Thanks too to Karen Blackman-Mills, a second librarian in the Washingtoniana Room who found for me still more clip files and biographies. At the Library of Congress, Betty Culpepper helped get me started with the Library's biographical collection, and Wayne Shirley found sources for me in the music reading room. At the Adams School Linda Jones pointed out the source of the Adams-Morgan name and showed me the old Morgan school. At the Klutznick B'nai B'rith Jewish Museum it was Harvey Berk, director of communications, and Marjorie Goldman who helped with information about Philip Klutznick. At the Smithsonian Archives, William Cox headed me in the right direction to find out about the Smithsonian's lesser known patrons. At the Smithsonian's Freer Gallery, Colleen Hennessey provided the sources for much of my information about Eugene and Agnes Meyer. And in the Octagon House, Dorothy Ryder told me the stories about the building's eight angles and niches.

Final thanks go to my wife, Nancy, herself a writer and editor, who carefully read through the manuscript, tolerated my many hours running around the city and typing at the computer, and had to listen to my excited tales each time I successfully discovered a name and an origin.

May you too now discover some of the names of Washington.

Dex Nilsson, Rockville, MD

BRIDGES

Washington is tied by bridges to Virginia across the Potomac River on the west and to Maryland across the Anacostia River to the east. Almost all the bridges have been named to serve as memorials. This section describes 15 of them.

Most misnamed is the 14th Street Bridge, name generally given to the group of bridges where I-395 and U.S. 1 cross the Potomac. But across the Potomac, the southernmost eastbound vehicle bridge is the Arland Williams, and the other eastbound one is the Rochambeau. The westbound one is the George Mason. Further east, I-395 crosses the Washington Channel on the Francis Case. To its north, U.S. 1 goes over water that runs between the Tidal Basin and Channel. That little bridge is the only one now officially named the "14th Street Bridge."

FRANCIS CASE MEMORIAL BRIDGE
I-395 as it crosses the Washington Channel

The water between East Potomac Park and the Maine Avenue waterfront is called the Washington Channel. Interstate 395 crosses it just southeast of the Jefferson Memorial on a short nondescript bridge. The bridge has been named as a memorial to Francis Higbee Case, former long-time U.S. representative (1937-51) and senator (1951-62) from South Dakota. Case excelled in domestic issues, including water conservation.

CHAIN BRIDGE
Crossing the Potomac from the north end of Canal Road to Virginia

The bridge is not named for a person. It was originally built of wood in 1797 and has been rebuilt several times. In the 1810 rebuilding, chains were used for reinforcement, hence its name.

FREDERICK DOUGLASS MEMORIAL BRIDGE. (See **Cedar Hill.**)
South Capitol Street crossing the Anacostia River

This bridge was built in 1949 and logically called the South Capitol Street Bridge. The name was changed in 1965 to honor abolitionist Frederick Douglass.

DUKE ELLINGTON MEMORIAL BRIDGE. (See **Duke Ellington School of the Arts.**)
On Calvert Street, crossing over Rock Creek Park

The Calvert Street Bridge was built in 1935. It was renamed in honor of the Washington jazz musician Edward Kennedy "Duke" Ellington in 1975.

Bridges

FRANCIS SCOTT KEY BRIDGE. (See also **Woodley Park.**)

Linking Georgetown with Rosslyn, VA, across the Potomac River. The north end meets M Street and the Whitehurst Freeway.

Francis Scott Key was born in what is now Carroll County, MD, in 1799. He graduated from St. John's College in Annapolis, studied law, and began practice in Frederick, MD. In 1802 he moved to Georgetown, and in 1806 took over his uncle's law business there. From about 1805 to 1830 he lived in a house just next to the bridge. About that time, an aqueduct bridge spanned the river. The current bridge was built at the same site in 1923, but Key's house was torn down in 1948 for one of the ramps to the Whitehurst Freeway when a bill to preserve it wasn't signed by President Truman.

Key is the author of *The Star Spangled Banner*. In 1814, during the War of 1812, friends of a doctor held by the British asked Key to help free him. In doing so, Key was held on a ship behind British lines on the night of September 13-14 during the bombardment of Baltimore. At daybreak, when he saw the American flag still flying over Fort McHenry, he wrote the poem that became the words of the anthem. It was called *The Defense of Fort McHenry.* A friend had it printed, and newspapers picked it up. It was adapted to the melody of an English song, *To Anacreon in Heaven.* The Army and Navy bands began to play it regularly. In 1931 Congress voted *The Star Spangled Banner* the official national anthem.

Key was U.S. attorney for the District of Columbia from 1833 to 1841. In 1834 he published a book, *The Power of Literature and Its Connection with Religion.* Although he never considered himself a poet, he wrote other verse, and a collection was published posthumously in 1857. He died in Baltimore in 1843.

KUTZ BRIDGE

Independence Avenue as it crosses the northern tip of the Tidal Basin

During the early 1940s Independence Avenue between the Lincoln Memorial and 15th Street was widened to its present size and made into a divided highway. This extra width required running part of the avenue over the northern tip of the Tidal Basin, which in turn meant a bridge had to be constructed. The bridge was completed in 1943 under the supervision of Brig. Gen. Charles W. Kutz. Kutz had spent over 40 years in military service when he retired in 1929. He had been Engineer Commissioner 1914 to 1917 and 1918 to 1921, and was called to serve as such again during World War II from 1941 to 1945.

LONG BRIDGE

Crossing the Potomac south of the so-called 14th Street Bridge

Here's another bridge not named for a person. It was originally built as a draw bridge in 1834 and was then the longest span across the river, others at the time being the Aqueduct Bridge (later named the Key Bridge) and the Chain Bridge. After the Civil War, railroad tracks were added. When the "14th Street Bridge" was built in 1905, Long Bridge became exclusively a railroad bridge.

GEORGE MASON BRIDGE

The northern span of the "14th Street Bridge," crossing the Potomac River, for west-bound traffic

Born of a land-owning family in nearby Fairfax County in 1725, George Mason received no formal education. He always considered himself a private citizen, and his public service was undertaken reluctantly and with distaste because of his low esteem for politicians. During the conflict between the colonies and England in the 1760s and 1770s he wrote many papers defending the colonial position. These included the Fairfax Resolves, adopted by the Continental Congress. In 1776 he drafted Virginia's first constitution including a Declaration of Rights, which Thomas Jefferson later used in writing the Declaration of Independence. Mason was a member of the Virginia House of Delegates from 1776 to 1788, and in 1787 attended the Constitutional Convention in Philadelphia. He felt the constitution gave too much power to central government, and left the convention early, opposing ratification. His objections and his previous Declaration of Rights were largely responsible for the first ten amendments to the constitution - the Bill of Rights. Mason died in 1792 at his Virginia plantation home, Gunston Hall.

ROCHAMBEAU BRIDGE. (See **Jean Rochambeau.**)

The center span of the "14th Street Bridge," for east-bound traffic crossing the Potomac River

This is named for Jean Rochambeau, who commanded France's troops during America's Revolutionary War.

JOHN PHILIP SOUSA BRIDGE. (See also **Congressional Cemetery.**)

Pennsylvania Avenue across the Anacostia River

John Philip Sousa was one of America's most famous bandmasters and composer of over 100 marches, including *Semper Fidelis* and *The Stars and Stripes Forever*. He was known as "The March King."

Sousa was born in Washington in 1854, son of a Portuguese father and German mother. He studied violin, orchestration, harmony, and wind instruments, and by 14 was playing in the Marine Band. He played in theater orchestras, and in 1876 was violinist in the special Philadelphia orchestra conducted by Offenbach during his U.S. tour. In 1880 he was appointed conductor of the Marine Band. About 1890 he developed a bass tuba with an upright bell, appropriately named the sousaphone. In 1892, he formed his own band, which played at the Chicago

World's Fair in 1893, Paris Exposition in 1900, made four European tours with increasing popularity, and finally in 1910-11, made an around-the-world tour. During the Spanish-American War he was musical director of the Sixth Army Corps. During World War I he was director of all navy bands and served as a lieutenant in the Naval Reserve. He continued annual tours with his own band almost to the time of his death, in 1932.

Lesser known Sousa marches include *In Memoriam* (1881) (for the assassinated President Garfield), *Boy Scouts of America March* (1916), *Marquette University March* (1924) (upon his receiving an honorary doctor's degree), *The National Game* (1925) (for the 50th anniversary of baseball's National League), and *Century of Progress* (1931) (for the Chicago World's Fair). In addition to the marches, Sousa wrote ten operettas (of which *El Capitan* is the best known). He compiled patriotic songs of other nations for the Navy Department. He authored three novels, and wrote manuals for the trumpet and drum. And on top of all this, he is credited with suites for band, overtures, orchestral works, and over 75 more songs, ballads, and hymns.

The bridge that serves as his memorial was built in 1940.

TAFT BRIDGE
Connecticut Avenue over Rock Creek Park

The bridge was built between 1897 and 1906, was the first in the country to be constructed of precast concrete, and when finished was known as the Million Dollar Bridge. After the death of President Taft in 1930, the bridge was renamed in his memory.

Few people can match a career as distinguished as his: William Howard Taft was born in Ohio in 1857, son of Alphonse Taft, who had been secretary of war and attorney general under President Grant. By the time he was 30, he was judge on the Superior Court of Ohio. President Harrison called him to be U.S. solicitor general. In 1900, President McKinley appointed him president of a commission to establish civil government in the Philippines. This was done in 1901, and Taft was made governor. Within four years he accomplished miracles of reforms in the Philippines that solved problems there and lasted decades. President Theodore Roosevelt appointed him secretary of war, he became governor of Cuba, then recommended the reorganization that made the Panama Canal possible. In 1908 the Republican Party nominated him for president, and he defeated William Jennings Bryan.

As president, his accomplishments were numerous and important, but he was not liberal, popular with business, or congenial toward Congress. The eventual split in his Republican Party, when Theodore Roosevelt formed his own Progressive (Bull Moose) Party, cost him the election against Woodrow Wilson.

Still, Taft didn't leave the public arena, but went on to be professor of law at Yale, president of the American Bar Association, and chairman of the American Red Cross. In 1921, President Harding appointed him chief justice of the United States. At the time of his death, Taft was held in high regard throughout the country. He is buried in Arlington National Cemetery. He and John F. Kennedy are the only presidents to be buried there.

OFFICER KEVIN J. WELSH MEMORIAL BRIDGE
Part of the 11th Street Bridge crossing the Anacostia River and connecting the Southeast-Southwest Freeway (I-395) with the Anacostia Freeway (I-295)

Kevin J. Welsh served almost eight years as a District of Columbia police officer. In 1986 a woman jumped from the bridge, and Welsh jumped after her. She was rescued, but Welsh drowned. The memorial serves not only to remember him, "but all police officers who risk their lives every day in the performance of their duty."

ARLAND D. WILLIAMS, JR., BRIDGE
The southern span of the "14th Street Bridge," for east-bound traffic crossing the Potomac River

In January 1982 an Air Florida plane left National Airport in bad weather, failed to rise properly after takeoff, and crashed into this span of the bridge. A total of 79 persons were killed in the crash; only six survived. In the icy waters of the Potomac River, Williams twice passed a life line to others before he drowned.

This span had been known as the Rochambeau Memorial Bridge. In 1994, it was renamed for Williams. At the same time, the center span of the bridge, which had been unnamed, was named the Rochambeau Bridge.

WOODROW WILSON BRIDGE (See also **Woodrow Wilson House**.)
On Route I-495 (the eastern half of the Beltway) crossing the Potomac

This bridge joins Maryland and Virginia and isn't really a District of Columbia bridge. It's included here because it serves as the main area memorial to President Wilson, and is certainly regularly in the traffic news.

Woodrow Wilson was born in Staunton, VA, in 1856, and grew up in Augusta, GA. As a boy he witnessed Southern troops during the Civil War and Southern poverty that followed during reconstruction, events that would later shape his opinions.

He attended Davidson College, then Princeton University. Law practice in Atlanta bored him, so he went to Johns Hopkins University in Baltimore for a Ph.D. About 25 years of college teaching followed, ending at Princeton, where he was quite a popular lecturer. In 1902 he became president of Princeton. By 1910 he was recognized as a man with keen judgment in political matters and became governor of New Jersey. At the Democratic Convention in Baltimore in 1912 he was chosen to head the ticket. The rift between William Howard Taft and Theodore Roosevelt split the Republicans, and Wilson was elected president.

As president, Wilson lowered tariffs, initiated an income tax, established the Federal Reserve bank system. In foreign policy he prepared to make the Philippines ready for self-government, sent troops to Haiti, broke off relations with Mexico. He tried to keep the U.S. out of World War I, but had to declare war in 1917 after German U-boat threats to U.S. shipping escalated. In 1918 he proposed peace be secured through a League of Nations. No one paid much attention. Also in 1918 he proposed 14 points on which a treaty of peace might be based. The Germans accepted these as a basis for surrender, but in the subsequent Treaty of Versailles, the points were ignored - planting the seeds of discontent that grew into World War II. Entry of the U.S. into the League of Nations became a major theme of the next election. He was overwhelmingly defeated by Republican Warren Harding.

Afterwards, Wilson continued to live in Washington, in ill health and retired from political affairs, until his death in 1924.

The bridge that has his name extends for a mile across the Potomac River. On the center traffic tower, facing traffic in each direction, are five-foot medallions, each bearing his profile.

WHITNEY YOUNG MEMORIAL BRIDGE.
East Capitol Street over the Anacostia River, at the east side of RFK Stadium

Whitney Moore Young, Jr., was born in Kentucky in 1921. He was educated at Kentucky State College, MIT, and University of Minnesota, where he obtained his master's degree. He served in the army, then worked for urban leagues in St. Paul and Omaha. In 1954 he was appointed dean of the graduate school of social work at Atlanta University. In 1961 he became executive director of the National Urban League. During the civil rights movement of the 1960s, he dramatically broadened the programs of the League, securing millions of dollars in corporate donations, and always trying to turn legal victories by blacks into actual improvements in housing, jobs, and education. He favored cooperation rather than confrontation with whites, withstanding severe criticism from black militants. He served on various commissions under President Kennedy, and later many of Young's proposals became part of President Johnson's antipoverty program. Young died suddenly in 1971 on a trip to an Afro-American conference in Nigeria.

CIRCLES, SQUARES, AND PARKS

Pierre L'Enfant's and Andrew Ellicott's plans for the city included a grid of streets intersected at angles by wide avenues and dotted with public open spaces. As Washington traffic grew, circles were added., and most of the original circles, squares, and little parks have been successfully retained. Almost all bear names and serve as memorials. Here are over 30 such places. They range from tiny Robert Latham Owen Park to 100-acre Glover-Archbold Park.

One park has two names. Many have statues in them, but there are two squares that don't have the same names as their statues. There's one circle that's not named for a person, but instead for the home of the developer's sister. And there's one square that isn't square at all.

BENJAMIN BANNEKER PARK

The circle overlooking Maine Avenue south of L'Enfant Plaza, and the park land at Maine Avenue and 9th Street, S.W.

Banneker was born a free Negro in 1731 in Ellicott City, MD. He spent most of his life as a tobacco planter. Except for elementary school, he was self-taught, yet mastered mathematics and astronomy. He made all the astronomical and tide calculations and weather predictions for a yearly almanac published between 1792 and 1797. More than 29 editions were published. And in 1791 he assisted Maj. Andrew Ellicott in the original survey of the 10-mile square for what was then the Territory of Columbia, in which the national capital was planned.

BRYCE PARK

At the intersection of Wisconsin and Massachusetts Avenues, and Garfield Street, N.W.

This little landscaped triangle has been given the name of Bryce Park in honor of James Bryce, ambassador to the United States from Great Britain from 1907 to 1913.

Bryce was born in Glasgow, graduated from Oxford, became professor of law there, was a member of Parliament, and served as chief secretary for Ireland before becoming ambassador. He authored several books on a variety of subjects from the flora of Arran to the Holy Roman Empire, trademark registration, and South Africa. He was the recipient of many honorary degrees and awards.

The area and view - before tall trees and high rise buildings - up Massachusetts Avenue from the British Embassy, was his favorite. Among his concerns was the future development of Washington. Here are suggestions from a speech he gave before Washington's Committee of One Hundred in February, 1913:

Circles, Squares, and Parks

"In considering the beautifying of streets, something should be done to take into account the possibilities in the little open space triangles that you have here in Washington at the intersection of streets and avenues. They are very pleasant places in the summer because they are green; but surely more might be made in a decorative way of them. You need not perhaps put up any more statues, but treat these corners in some ornamental fashion, so as to give them a greater landscape value."

And: "May I mention another point of view that is now threatened and perhaps almost gone? You all know the spot at which Wisconsin Avenue (up which the cars run to Tennallytown and the District line) intersects Massachusetts Avenue. At that point of intersection, just opposite where the Episcopal Cathedral is to stand, there is one spot commanding what is one of the most beautiful general views of Washington.... Can it be saved?... There may be other views of Washington that are as good, but there is none better."

Thus the little triangle has been made beautiful and bears his name, although the fine view no longer quite exists.

ANNA J. COOPER CIRCLE

3rd and T Streets, N.W.

Not a big circle, but a small one, in the center of the LeDroit Park neighborhood. It honors Anna Julia Cooper, who taught in D.C. schools for almost 40 years.

Anna Haywood was born to slave parents in Raleigh, NC, in 1858. She married George Cooper, an Episcopal clergyman and professor of Greek. He died when she was 21, and she never remarried. She graduated from Oberlin College in 1884, got her master's there in 1887, and later at the Sorbonne added her doctorate - much later: when she was 67. Cooper taught Latin and mathematics. She served as principal (1900-1906) of M Street High School, predecessor of Dunbar High School, only academic high school for blacks in the District. From 1930 to 1940 she was president of Frelinghuysen University, a group of evening schools with volunteer faculty for employed colored persons. (Its name honored F. T. Frelinghuysen, secretary of state under President Arthur.) Cooper wrote many published works including an autobiography and the words to the Dunbar alma mater. When she died in 1964, she was 105.

DUPONT CIRCLE. (See also **Dupont Memorial Fountain.**)

The intersection of Massachusetts, Connecticut, and New Hampshire Avenues at 19th Street, N.W.

The family of du Pont de Nemours has been part of national and local politics, public service, and philanthropy for over 150 years. Of all the Duponts, Samuel

Francis Dupont was not the most successful or the most well known, but it is from him that Dupont Circle gets its name.

Samuel Francis was born in Bergen Point, NJ, in 1803 and when only 12 years old was appointed to the Navy by President Madison. By 1842 he was a commander. In 1845 he helped organize administration of the newly formed U.S. Naval Academy. Later that year he served in the Pacific, then commanded a ship along the California coast during the Mexican War. In 1861 he commanded the squadron blockading the South Atlantic. A year later he was made rear admiral. In 1863, however, he was the officer in charge when the Union's naval attack on Charleston failed. He was relieved of command. He died in 1865. After his death it was proved he had advised against the Charleston attack, but had been ordered to proceed anyway.

In 1880, the circle was called Pacific Circle, because it was then in the westernmost part of the city. The Dupont family, to help re-establish the admiral's reputation, erected a statue of him at the site in 1884, and the circle's name changed. Later the family moved the statue to Wilmington, DE. The family then commissioned sculptor Daniel Chester French to design a fountain instead. The fountain was dedicated in 1921. Its three allegorical figures represent the arts of ocean navigation, and the admiral's name is around its base.

FARRAGUT SQUARE

K and 17th Streets, N.W.

David G. Farragut, born at Stony Point in the East Tennessee valley, joined the U.S. Navy at the age of ten, fought in the War of 1812 and the Mexican War. In the Civil War he captured New Orleans, fought his way up the Mississippi River to Vicksburg, and opened the river to Union navigation. He went on to attack Mobile Bay, destroy the Confederate fleet, take the forts, and close the port to blockade runners. He's best known for urging his fleet into the bay with the words, "Damn the torpedoes! Full speed ahead!" - torpedoes being what mines were then called. He became the first admiral of the U.S. Navy, the rank created by Congress especially for him.

After his death, his wife commissioned Vinnie Hoxie, a well-known woman sculptor, to do a bust of her husband. The bust became a 10-foot statue on which the sculptor worked for six years, in a studio set up in the Washington Navy Yard. The completed model was cast from the propeller of the *USS Hartford*, Farragut's ship. Dedicated in 1881, it was the first in Washington to honor a naval war hero.

FRANKLIN SQUARE. (Also known as **Franklin Park.**)(See **John Barry** and **Benjamin Franklin.**)
Between I and K, and 13th and 14th Streets, N.W.

Unlike other squares named for the persons they honor and the statues they contain, this one does not have a statue of Benjamin Franklin, and may not even be named for him.

The area was once Port Royal, land held by one Samuel Davidson. It was the fresh water spring on the site that attracted the government. By 1822, pipes tied the spring to White House water supplies, and the square became known, for obvious reasons, as Fountain Square. There once was a row of houses along the K Street side known as Franklin Row - origin unknown - and by 1830, the square was called Franklin Square. Some sources say that Benjamin Franklin owned a house in the area, but the National Park Service has never found documentation as to where the house might have been or that the park was really named after him. Indeed the statue in the park is that of Commodore John Barry, and why the square isn't thus named Barry Square is a mystery.

GARFIELD PARK. (See **James Garfield.**)
South of Capitol Hill about F and 2nd Streets, S.E.

The assassinated president deserves something better than this relatively hidden park - now obscured by a power plant on one side and the Southeast (Eisenhower) Freeway on another. Indeed the real Garfield Memorial is directly at the base of the Capitol.

GLOVER-ARCHBOLD PARK. (See also **Riggs National Bank.**)
North from the Potomac River across New Mexico and Massachusetts Avenues to Van Ness Street, between Foxhall Road and Wisconsin Avenue, N.W.

This narrow woodland park was a 1924 gift to the city by Charles Glover, who gave 77 acres along Foundry Creek, and Mrs. Anne Archbold, who gave 28 acres from her Reservoir Road property.

Charles Glover was born in rural North Carolina in 1846, attended Rittenhouse Academy in Washington. He was first a bookstore clerk, then at 19 became a clerk at Riggs & Co., bankers. By the time he was 27, he was a partner. In 1896, when the firm became the Riggs National Bank, Glover became its president. Later he also became chairman of the board, serving until 1921. Washington owes a lot to Glover: He inaugurated and successfully carried through Congress projects establishing Rock Creek Park, what is now the National Zoo, buildings at American University, the Corcoran Art Gallery, and the Washington Cathedral. He died in Washington in 1936.

Anne Archbold was born in Titusville, PA, in 1873, daughter of John Dustin Archbold, who later became president of Standard Oil of New Jersey. Anne became a world traveler and was the first Western woman to enter Tibet. She married, went to East Africa for her honeymoon, shot game, and provided information for one of the trips President Theodore Roosevelt later made. She divorced and in 1923 came to Washington where she purchased her Hillandale estate. Further trips included a flight across the Pacific when aviation was in its infancy, and, when she was 70, one in a Chinese junk to Melanesia to gather plant specimens. In addition to Washington, she had residences in England, Bar Harbor, Virginia, and Nassau. In Nassau, at 84, she caught a record 64-pound wahoo mackerel! She died there in 1968.

GOMPERS SQUARE. (See **Samuel Gompers.**)
Massachusetts Avenue and 10th Street, N.W.

This is the site of the memorial statue to Samuel Gompers, founder of the American Federation of Labor. The statue was put up in 1933. The little triangle/trapezoid of land it is on was officially named Gompers Square in 1951. Only in Washington would a triangle or a trapezoid be called a square.

GRANT CIRCLE. (See **Ulysses S. Grant.**)
At the intersection of New Hampshire and Illinois Avenues and 5th and Varnum Streets

Named for the 18th U.S. president, this is the center of the Petworth residential neighborhood. This large circle features no statue, but instead walks and attractive landscaping around two very old pine trees.

LAFAYETTE PARK. (See **Gilbert Lafayette.**)
In front of the White House, bordered by Pennsylvania Avenue, Jackson and Madison Places, and H Street, N.W.

In 1791, President Washington proposed acquiring the site, then known as Pierce Farm, as a park, first known as President's Park. Blair House was the first building in the area in 1810, Decatur House was built in 1819, and then others began to form a square. The park's name became Lafayette Square; it was changed to Lafayette Park during the 1930s.

In the center of the park is the equestrian figure of Andrew Jackson, and at each corner is a statue of a man of foreign lands who contributed to Revolutionary America: Lafayette and Rochambeau of France, Kosciuszko of Poland, and von Steuben of Germany. It was in 1853 that Jackson's statue was erected, after the Civil War that Congress officially named the area after Lafayette, in 1891 that the Lafayette statue was unveiled, and in the 1900s before the others were erected.

Circles, Squares, and Parks

LINCOLN SQUARE. (Also known as **Lincoln Park.**) (See **Abraham Lincoln,** the **Emancipation Monument,** and **Mary McLeod Bethune Memorial.**)

One mile east of the Capitol, between 11th and 13th Streets, N.E., intersected by Massachusetts, North Carolina, Tennessee, and Kentucky Avenues

This square was one of the 17 such open areas in L'Enfant's initial layout of Washington. The site appears to have been nameless until 1867, when Congress authorized it to be Lincoln Square in honor of the recent president.

LOGAN CIRCLE

Where Vermont Avenue, N.W., and 13th and P Streets intersect

This space, a major intersection within the Shaw neighborhood, was known as Iowa Circle until the memorial to Maj. Gen. Logan was dedicated in 1901. It contains his elaborate equestrian bronze statue.

John Alexander Logan was born in Illinois, studied law, got elected to the House of Representatives. At the start of the Civil War, when 35 years old, "Black Jack" (because of his long, jet-black hair) Logan entered the Union Army as colonel of a volunteer regiment that he organized. He played a major role in the capture of Vicksburg and was appointed military governor of that district, and later commander of the Army of the Tennessee. He left the army in 1865 and was again elected to Congress, serving three terms as U.S. senator. He helped organize the Grand Army of the Republic, the principal organization of Union veterans after the Civil War. He is most honored for conceiving the idea of Memorial Day, first celebrated on May 30, 1868.

MALCOLM X PARK. (See also **Meridian Hill Park.**)

Between 15th and 16th Streets, just north of Florida Avenue, N.W.

During the 1960s, Meridian Hill Park became a rallying place for civil rights groups. It was renamed to honor black leader Malcolm X. The renaming was unofficial: The park is run by the Interior Department, the renaming was done by the District of Columbia, and there is a question whether the D.C. government can rename federal property. The park is still commonly known by its Meridian Hill name.

Malcolm X was born Malcolm Little in Omaha, NE, in 1925. His father was a Baptist minister and an organizer of the Universal Negro Improvement Association. The family was run out of town by white vigilantes. When Malcolm was six, his father was murdered in Michigan by a Ku Klux Klan styled terrorist group. Malcolm dropped out of school, lived in Boston and Harlem, hustled drugs and prostitutes, finally served six years in prison for burglary and larceny.

In prison Malcolm learned about the Lost-Found Nation of Islam led by Elijah Muhammad and known popularly as the Black Muslims. He joined, and he took the Muslim "X" in place of his former "slave name." Upon release in 1952, he was ordained a Nation of Islam minister, and over the next 12 years, he was its most effective evangelist, heading its Harlem mosque and growing its national membership from 400 to 10,000. In 1964, Malcolm denounced Muhammad, split with the Nation of Islam, and formed his own organization. He became increasingly belligerent, denounced integration, ridiculed Martin Luther King's civil rights movement, declared whites enemies, and cheered hurricanes, airplane crashes, even President Kennedy's assassination - anything that might cause whites anguish or pain. Although shrill, he brought the 1960s fight for "Black Power" into the public consciousness like no other person. In 1965 unidentified attackers firebombed his home, and a week later, in New York, he was shot and killed. Perhaps Malcolm X's biggest impact came later, with posthumous publication of his *Autobiography*, which showed he was indeed a prophetic figure in a tumultuous time.

JOHN MARSHALL PARK. (See also **John Marshall.**)
Just north of Pennsylvania Avenue at 4th Street, N.W.

This narrow park next to the U.S. Court House honors the nation's fourth chief justice, considered the country's first great one.

John Marshall was born in a log cabin in what is now Fauquier County, VA, in 1755. He was a third cousin to Thomas Jefferson. He served in the Virginia House of Delegates at various times from 1782 to 1796. Unlike his fellow Virginians Jefferson, Madison, and Monroe, Marshall believed in a strong central government.

Marshall turned down more offers of high position than most people have been offered: Because of financial problems, he turned down president Washington's request that he be attorney general, then rejected appointment as ambassador to France. In 1797 he became a special envoy to France and achieved both popularity and enough money to satisfy his financial problems. Still, the next year, he turned down appointment as an associate justice of the Supreme Court. He got elected to the U.S. House of Representatives in 1799, then in 1800 turned down an offer to be secretary of war. However, that same year he finally agreed to be secretary of state under President John Adams.

A year later Adams made Marshall chief justice of the United States - mostly to get him away from the political scene where he was an embarrassment to those who wanted less federal government. They underestimated both Marshall and the power of the young judiciary. Marshall wrote significant opinions establishing the right of federal courts to pass on the validity of congressional legislation, and that the federal government could exercise not only those functions authorized by the Constitution but those implicitly suggested. All Marshall court rulings were in favor of national power as opposed to that of the states, and in extension of judicial power at the expense of the executive and legislative branches.

Marshall served as chief justice until 1835. When he died, in Philadelphia, the Liberty Bell was rung. It was then that it cracked.

MCPHERSON SQUARE

On 15th Street between I and K Streets, N.W.

James Birdseye McPherson was born in Green Creek Township, OH, in 1828. He attended West Point and graduated first in his class in 1853. He served with the Army Engineers and became Chief Engineer to Gen. Grant in 1862. During the Civil War he commanded the right wing of Grant's army at Vicksburg, took command of the Army of the Tennessee, fought at Chattanooga, participated with Gen. Sherman in the Georgia campaign, outflanked the Confederates at the Battle of Kennesaw Mountain, and led his troops into the Battle of Atlanta, where he was killed. He was considered the "most promising of Sherman's generals." Sherman wept unashamedly when his body was brought to him.

McPherson Square was originally Scott Square, changed when McPherson's statue was erected in it. The statue is on a high pedestal, because it was originally intended that McPherson be buried inside. That didn't happen. The statue itself is made from cannon captured at Atlanta. It was dedicated in 1876 with many notables present, including President Hayes and Gen. Sherman.

MERIDIAN HILL PARK. (See also **Malcolm X Park, James Buchanan, Dante,** and **Joan of Arc.**)

Between 15th and 16th Streets, just north of Florida Avenue, N.W.

Meridian Hill was originally Peter's Hill, after Robert Peter, mayor of Georgetown, who had his estate there in 1760. The land was later owned from the 1870s to the 1930s by Mary Henderson, wife of Missouri Senator John Brooks Henderson. Known as the "Queen of 16th Street," she had many of the area's buildings - and the park - built.

In 1816 a meridian - the north-south line representation that goes from pole to pole - was surveyed at this site. It was hoped that a new prime meridian in Washington for use by Americans would replace that of the English Greenwich. That didn't happen, but it gave the area its name. The park is also right at the fall line - the point at which land drops from the Piedmont Plateau to the Atlantic coastal plain. Much of Florida Avenue follows this line; it was once called Boundary Street.

The park combines its land features with gardens and statues. Toward the north, it features a large esplanade. Toward its south, there's a cascade of fountains. The hill once afforded a fine view, but high-rise buildings are now in the way.

MT. VERNON SQUARE. (See also **Shepherd Park.**)

At 7th and 9th Streets, N.W., cutting off 8th Street and Massachusetts and New York Avenues

The square is one of the 17 open areas set aside by Congress in 1791 as part of the L'Enfant plan for Washington. As Washington grew, most squares became parks, and houses surrounded them. But not this square.

By 1840, the noisy North Liberties Fire Department faced the square. Massachusetts and New York Avenues crossed the square with paved carriage roadways. By 1846, the square was the site of the North Liberty Market. Given lack of sewers in that time, rotting vegetables thrown onto the street, refuse from the butcher shops, and waste from the animals that pulled carts and carriages made the area unbearable, especially in summer. It took Boss Shepherd to clean it up in 1872 - in a raid with questionable authority but with approval of nearby citizens. By 1882 the carriage roadways were closed, and the square finally became a park, with over 200 trees and 600 shrubs, even fountains.

But not for long. In 1899, Andrew Carnegie was visiting President McKinley at the White House. B. H. Warner, vice president of the Washington Public Library, happened to call. In the course of conversation, need for a new library came up, and Carnegie in "a matter of a few minutes" offered to donate $250,000. Congress speedily accepted the gift. Mt. Vernon Square was selected as the site. Some objected, but others objected to Congress paying high land prices for a site elsewhere, and frugality won. When the library opened, Carnegie was so pleased, he donated more funds, for decorating the interior and for book shelves. (Indeed, he went on to donate $60 million to over 3,000 libraries.) The library lasted until the 1960s, when greater space was needed.

In 1969, the square and its building were turned over by the federal government to the District of Columbia, for Federal City College. Even now, the area directly to its north is to be site of a new convention center. Mt. Vernon Square continues to be an area never intended for the uses to which it has been put.

EDWARD R. MURROW PARK

The triangle formed by Pennsylvania Avenue, 20th Street, and H Street, N.W.

Born near Greensboro, NC, in 1908, Edward R. Murrow joined the Columbia Broadcasting System (CBS) in 1935 and became its European director in 1937. As a CBS correspondent in World War II he became famous with his dramatic broadcasts during the Battle of Britain that began with "This ... is London."

After the war, he produced on radio *Hear It Now* and between 1948 and 1960 on television *See It Now, Person to Person,* and *Small World.* In 1961 he was appointed director of the U.S. Information Agency by President Kennedy. Illness caused him to resign in 1964 ; he died in 1965.

ROBERT LATHAM OWEN PARK
Virginia Avenue and C Street, N.W.

This hidden little park, established in 1974, with its attractive pool and fountain, bears an explanatory plaque: Robert Latham Owen, Teacher, Lawyer, Banker, Businessman, and Statesman. Member, Cherokee Indian Nation. U.S. Senator from Oklahoma, 1907-25. Proponent and the First Chairman of the Senate Banking and Currency Committee. A principal advocate and co-sponsor of the Glass-Owen Bill creating the Federal Reserve System.

The park is appropriately located between the main Federal Reserve Building and the Department of Interior buildings that contain the Bureau of Indian Affairs.

PERSHING PARK
Formed by Pennsylvania Avenue and E, 14th, and 15th Streets, N.W.

Pershing Park is in front of the Willard Hotel. In the next block, in front of the National Theater, is Freedom Plaza. Pershing Park contains the statue of Gen. John J. Pershing. Freedom Plaza contains the statue of Count Pulaski.

John Joseph Pershing was born at Laclede, MO, in 1860. He went to school in Kirksville, taught at a country school, entered a contest that won him appointment to West Point, and graduated there in 1886. He fought Indians in New Mexico, Arizona, and South Dakota, then became military instructor at the University of Nebraska, where he earned a bachelor of laws degree. He taught at West Point, but when the Spanish-American War began in 1897, he joined the action. He earned a Silver Star for gallantry.

In the early 1900s, Pershing subdued the Moros in the Philippines and was made governor of Moro Province. He was a military attaché in Manchuria during the Russo-Japanese War when President Theodore Roosevelt promoted him from captain to brigadier general over 800 other officers - a wise choice but one that understandably caused bitter feelings among fellow officers.

In 1916 President Wilson ordered Pershing to disperse the army of Mexican outlaw Pancho Villa, which had just raided in New Mexico. He never caught Villa, but in ten months of campaigning did disperse his followers. During this time, there was a personal tragedy: Pershing's wife and three daughters died in a fire at the Presidio, in San Francisco; his son Warren was sole survivor.

When the U.S. entered World War I in 1917, Pershing, by now a major general, was sent to France to form the American Expeditionary Force (AEF). There was constant haggling: U.S. forces were to be independent; the Allies (France, Britain, Italy) wanted them solely as replacements. The AEF, however, proved to be a considerable force, and Allied commander Marshall Foch of France finally approved its tactical use. Divisions of the AEF stopped the Germans at the Marne, and then in September, 1918, launched an offensive at St. Mihiel. In 48 hours, 16,000 Germans were captured. During the next seven weeks the AEF consumed German divisions as fast as the enemy could send them. On November 11, the armistice came, and the war ended. In only 18 months, Pershing had built a U.S. army of over 2,000,000 and, as the first U.S. officer to lead an American army on European soil, had played a decisive role in ending the conflict.

In 1919 Pershing became the first general of the armies. In 1924, at age 64, he retired. In 1948 he died in Washington. He is buried in Arlington National Cemetery.

RANDLE CIRCLE. (See **Randle Highlands.**)

The intersection of Massachusetts, Minnesota, and Branch Avenues, S.E.

This is the only traffic circle east of the Anacostia River. It bears the name of Colonel Arthur E. Randle, who lived in the area in the late 1800s. A major benefactor to Washington, Randle is credited for giving to the city enough streets, free of cost, which if put in a straight line would extend from Washington all the way to Baltimore.

RAWLINS PARK

On E Street between 18th and 19th Streets, N.W.

John Aaron Rawlins was born in Galena, IL, in 1831. During the 1849 gold rush, he went to California, but returned home and studied law. In 1854, he was admitted to the Illinois bar. In 1857, he became Galena city attorney. As the Civil War began, in 1861 he helped organize the 45th Illinois Infantry and became its major. Later that year his neighbor, then-Col. Ulysses S. Grant, asked Rawlins to serve as his aide-de-camp. Rawlins became Grant's most trusted advisor, even to editing all of Grant's papers. He was promoted throughout the war, in 1865 reaching the rank of major general. After the war, Rawlins traveled to Wyoming, attempting to recover from tuberculosis. One of his camp sites became the town of Rawlins, WY. In 1869, back in Washington, Grant made him secretary of war. He lived only a few months more.

His statue shows him standing, in uniform, field glasses in one hand, sword in the other. His one-block park has trees that bloom early each spring, walks, benches, and a reflecting pool.

SCOTT CIRCLE

Where Massachusetts and Rhode Island Avenues intersect at 16th Street, N.W.

Winfield Scott was born near Petersburg, VA, in 1786. He attended William and Mary College, but joined the Army in 1808. In the War of 1812, he served in Canada and led the attack on Fort George. In 1814, as a brigadier general, he was the hero of the Battle of Lundy's Lane. Congress gave him a gold medal and rank of major general. In 1825 he prepared the Army's first manual on military tactics. In the 1830s he led troops in the Black Hawk War in Illinois, then served in the Seminole and Creek Indian campaigns in Florida and supervised removal of the Cherokees to their reservations out West. He received 57 votes on the first ballot as a candidate for president at the Whig convention of 1839. In 1841, Scott was named general in chief of the Army. In the Mexican War, he won victory after victory, and received another gold medal from Congress. The defeated Mexicans were so impressed, they asked him to remain as dictator. In 1852, he ran for president as a Whig, but was defeated by the Democrat's Franklin Pierce. At the outbreak of the Civil War, Scott planned the defense of Washington. His age caused him to retire in 1862. He died at West Point in 1866.

Scott served as an officer in the Army for over 50 years, from President Jefferson to President Lincoln. Perhaps it is fitting that he have two statues in Washington instead of one. Scott Circle contains his equestrian statue. It's made of cannon captured during the Mexican War, and shows Scott as a lieutenant general, then an honorary rank given by President Pierce. The U.S. Soldiers Home, at 2nd and Upshur Streets, N.W., has on its grounds his standing statue. There he wears his full dress uniform, the kind that earned him the nickname "Fuss and Feathers." The location is appropriate. It was Scott who founded the home with part of the money the U.S. received from the defeated Santa Anna at the end of the Mexican War.

SEWARD SQUARE

Three blocks southeast of the Capitol, where Pennsylvania and North Carolina Avenues, S.E., cross

This pleasant and relatively quiet square honors William H. Seward, secretary of state under Presidents Lincoln and Andrew Johnson. Some benches provide rest for walkers, there are trimmed hedges and a few trees. There's not one of those statues of someone on a horse. There's not even a statue of Seward.

Seward was born in Florida, a town in New York state, in 1801. He studied law, started practice, then got into politics. In 1830 he was elected to the New York Senate, and in 1838 became the first Whig governor of New York. He was re-elected in 1840, then in 1849 was elected to the U.S. Senate, where he became one of President Taylor's main advisors. By 1860, Seward was the most prominent Republican candidate for presidential nomination, and on the first ballot at the Chicago convention, he received more votes than Lincoln. When Lincoln was nominated, Seward campaigned hard for him, and was rewarded with appointment as secretary of state. It was a wise choice. He handled the department capably throughout the Civil War and after.

In 1865 Seward was thrown from his carriage, and his arm and jaw were fractured. While he was recovering, someone entered his room and struck him with a knife in the face and neck. It was the same night that Lincoln was assassinated, and part of the same conspiracy. But Seward recovered and continued as secretary of state throughout President Andrew Johnson's administration.

By 1867, Seward had arranged for the purchase of Alaska from Russia for $7 million. It was called "Seward's folly" by detractors, and the acquisition of the biggest state in the U.S. barely passed Congress. Indeed, showing foresight missing in others, Seward also negotiated for the purchase of all of the West Indies and control of the Isthmus of Panama - but both failed to pass the Senate.

In 1869 Seward retired, and the next year toured Alaska. In 1872, he died in Auburn, New York.

Sculptor John Cavanaugh "wished to commemorate a member of Seward's family," and selected as his unlikely subject Olive Risley Seward, William's foster daughter - for whom no photograph existed. His resultant 1971 statue is of a young Victorian lady. It is not placed in Seward Square, but is instead about a block away, where she appears to be looking toward the square. Afterwards a photograph was found. She and the statue look considerably alike.

SHERIDAN CIRCLE

Massachusetts Avenue at 23rd Street, N.W.

The circle features the sculpture of Gen. Philip H. Sheridan on his horse *Rienzi*, supposedly during one of the Civil War battles of Virginia's Shenandoah Valley.

Sheridan, born at Albany, NY, in 1831, became West Point graduate and was a captain when the Civil War began. He obtained a command and defeated the Confederates at Booneville, MS, which brought him promotion to general. He led troops at Chickamauga, Missionary Ridge at Chattanooga, and Richmond, before commanding all Union forces in the Shenandoah, where he ultimately drove Confederate forces from the valley. After the war he served as military governor of Texas and Louisiana, and became the foremost frontier general and Indian fighter in the country. He eventually succeeded Gen. Sherman as general of the Army. Sheridan died in 1888.

The sculpture is by Gutzon Borglum, who did the faces at Mount Rushmore, SD. Mrs. Sheridan selected the site. The memorial was dedicated in 1908, and the statue was unveiled by 2nd Lt. Philip H. Sheridan, Jr., with President Theodore Roosevelt looking on.

SHERMAN CIRCLE
At the intersection of Kansas and Illinois Avenues and 7th and Crittenden Streets

Named for Civil War general William Tecumseh Sherman, this large circle is at the north end of the Petworth residential neighborhood. It has no statue, but attractive landscaping, walkways, and four very old pine trees.

STANTON SQUARE. (See also **Nathaniel Greene.**)
At Massachusetts and Maryland Avenues, N.E.

Edwin McMasters Stanton was born in Steubenville, OH, in 1814. He attended Kenyon College and became a lawyer, starting practice in 1836. He became an expert in patent law, land title cases, and criminal law. For example, by 1850, he had pioneered the temporary insanity defense in a case in which a husband killed his wife's lover.

In 1860, Stanton left his very successful law practice to serve as attorney general under President Buchanan. In 1862 he was made secretary of war by President Lincoln, and innovatively and effectively controlled the armed forces of the Union throughout the Civil War. Stanton was present when Lincoln died, and is perhaps best known for his remark, "Now he belongs to the ages." Under President Johnson, it fell to Stanton and the Army to execute Reconstruction policy. He and the president, who attempted to obstruct many of the policies set by Congress, so differed in views that Johnson removed Stanton from the cabinet. Stanton stayed anyway, finally resigned in 1868. A year later President Grant appointed Stanton to the U.S. Supreme Court, and the Senate quickly confirmed him. But Stanton died at home in Washington before he could assume office.

A busy square just northeast of the Capitol, it doesn't contain a reference to Mr. Stanton, but instead contains the statue of Nathaniel Greene. How this strange mixture occurred is not clear, except that in 1877 Congress apparently just needed a place in which to put the statue.

THOMAS CIRCLE
At Massachusetts Avenue and 14th Street, N.W.

The circle contains the equestrian statue honoring Maj. Gen. George H. Thomas. He was born in Southhampton County, VA, in 1816. He graduated from West Point and served in the Florida and Mexican campaigns. Although a Virginian, at the start of the Civil War he elected to stay with the Union. He was the heroic general who defended Chickamauga at Lookout Mountain, Tennessee, in 1863, holding off a Confederate army of 71,000. After Chickamauga he was given command of the Army of the Cumberland and led victories at Missionary Ridge, in Gen. Sherman's campaigns toward Atlanta, and against Gen. Hood at Nashville. After the war, Thomas commanded the Division of the Pacific and was doing so when he died in San Francisco in 1870. The statue was erected in 1879 as a gift of the Army of the Cumberland Society and accepted for the American people by President Hayes.

WARD CIRCLE

Where Nebraska and Massachusetts Avenues, N.W., meet

In 1927, Harvard offered a gift to Washington for a statue of Gen. Artemas Ward, a Harvard alumnus. Congress approved it in recognition of the services by Gen. Ward during the Revolutionary War. The circle was built especially for the statue.

Artemas Ward (1727-1800) was governor of Massachusetts in 1775 when the American Revolution began. He commanded the Massachusetts military forces during the siege of British-held Boston until Gen. Washington, who had just been given command of all Continental forces, arrived. Ward was made major general by Washington, but stepped down soon thereafter because of ill health. He did continue in public affairs, serving in the Continental Congress and later as a member of the national Congress.

Ward Circle has nothing to do with Arte*mus* Ward, pseudonym for Charles Farrar Browne, the American humorist.

WESTMORELAND CIRCLE

On Massachusetts Avenue at Western Avenue, N.W., at the Maryland state line

This circle was constructed half by the District and half by Montgomery County, MD, and completed in 1932. It is named for Westmoreland County, VA, birthplace of the sister of Albert Walker of Walker & Dunlop, the firm that developed the area.

FEDERAL BUILDINGS

Here are 23 buildings, 22 of which are named for people and serve as memorials. Eight of the buildings are on or close to Capitol Hill and are used by the Senate or the House of Representatives. Four are in the Federal Triangle, that area of land bordered by 15th Street and Pennsylvania and Constitution Avenues. Three belong to the Library of Congress. One is named for a losing general. The one not named for a person takes its name from its most prominent site.

ADAMS BUILDING. (See also **Jefferson Building.**)
At 2nd Street and Independence Avenue, S.E.

The main building of the Library of Congress is known as the Jefferson Building. By 1939, the Library needed additional facilities, and an annex was constructed behind the main building. This second building is named for the second president of the United States, John Adams.

John Adams was born in 1735 at Braintree, now Quincy, MA, to a family already well established in New England. He attended Harvard, graduated at 20. He became well known as a lawyer, was elected to the Massachusetts legislature. In 1764 he married Abigail Smith; they had two daughters and three sons (one of whom, John Quincy Adams, would later become the sixth U.S. president). In 1774 Adams was sent to the First Continental Congress in Philadelphia, where he tried to ready participants for the war he saw coming. He managed to get the Second Continental Congress to call together volunteers - the minutemen. He also prompted the nomination of George Washington as commander in chief of the colonial forces.

Five men - Thomas Jefferson, Benjamin Franklin, Roger Sherman, Robert Livingston, and Adams - were selected to draw up the Declaration of Independence. Jefferson drafted it. Adams led the debate about it. It has been said that, if Adams never did another thing, Americans should be grateful for what he accomplished in controlling the debate and bringing it to its successful conclusion.

During the Revolutionary War Adams was sent to Paris with Franklin and John Jay to work on a peace treaty. They were to do nothing without agreement of the French, but Adams and Jay worked mainly in consultation with Britain. One result was establishment of the western boundary of the United States way out to the Mississippi River despite French interests there. In 1785, Adams was made minister to Great Britain, first to represent the U.S. at the Court of St. James.

In 1789, in the first presidential election, George Washington got 69 electoral votes, Adams 34. As runner-up, Adams became vice president. (It wasn't until the 12th Amendment to the Constitution that presidents and vice presidents were voted on separately.) In 1792, Washington and Adams were re-elected. In 1796, after Washington declined a third term, Adams was elected president. His administration was marked by political differences between those wanting more central government, still led by Alexander Hamilton, and those advocating more individual rights, led by Jefferson and James Madison. But it was during Adams' presidency that the government moved to Washington, and Adams became the first president to live in the White House. In the law he signed that moved the government, he included a provision for purchase of books and a place for them. In 1800 Jefferson defeated Adams' bid for re-election. Adams returned to Massachusetts and lived until 90.

In one of the great coincidences of history, Adams and Jefferson both died on the same day - July 4, 1823, exactly 50 years after the signing of the Declaration of Independence.

THE APEX BUILDING

Constitution and Pennsylvania Avenues at 6th Street, N.W.

Here's the one building in this section not named for a person. It houses the Federal Trade Commission, appointed by the President to prevent unfair competition, things like price-fixing and false advertising. It takes its name from its location at the apex or point of the Federal Triangle, where Constitution and Pennsylvania Avenues meet.

ARIEL RIOS BUILDING

Pennsylvania Avenue and 12th Street, N.W.

In 1985, President Reagan had this 1934 building renamed the Ariel Rios Building in recognition of Rios' dedicated service. Rios (1954-1982) was a special agent for the Bureau of Alcohol, Tobacco, and Firearms (ATF) and had been assigned to the vice-president's southern Florida anti drug smuggling task force. He was working undercover on an illicit narcotics and firearms investigation when killed. According to a plaque just inside the entrance, the renamed building is to serve as a reminder of the dedication and sacrifice by all men and women in federal law enforcement who help protect the American public. To some, especially to the ATF, the name is also a grim reminder of 1980s budget cutbacks - Rios reportedly had a layoff notice in his pocket when he was shot.

The building once was to house ATF headquarters, but that never came about. Instead it currently houses part of the Environmental Protection Agency, provides entry to the Federal Triangle Metro stop, and on its Pennsylvania Avenue side, houses the Benjamin Franklin post office.

Federal Buildings

CANNON BUILDING

Southeast of the Capitol, on Independence Avenue between New Jersey and 1st Streets, S.E.

The three office buildings for members of the House of Representatives (Cannon, Longworth, and Rayburn) are all named after former speakers of the House, this one for Joseph Gurney Cannon, known as "Uncle Joe."

Cannon was born in New Garden, NC, in 1836, but he eventually settled in Danville, IL. In 1872 he was elected to the House and held his seat (except for 1891-3 and 1913-5) until he retired in 1923. He was elected speaker in 1903. He ran the House with an iron hand, appointed committee chairmen, ran the Committee on Rules that then controlled the flow of all legislation, and arbitrarily recognized or ignored members on the floor. He was an arch conservative, and finally in 1910, moderates from his own Republican party as well as insurgent Democrats combined to enlarge the rules committee and have its chairman elected, even eliminating the speaker from being a member. Democrats took over the House in 1912, ending Cannon's rule as speaker, but he was still highly thought of and lived the role of elder statesman during his remaining years in office. He died in Danville in 1926.

DIRKSEN BUILDING

Just Northeast of the Capitol, on Constitution Avenue, between 1st and 2nd Streets, N.E., and next to the Russell Building

In 1972 Congress changed the name of the Old Senate Office Building to the Richard B. Russell Senate Office Building and that of the New Senate Office Building to the Everett M. Dirksen Senate Office Building.

Dirksen, Republican from Illinois, served in the House of Representatives from 1932 to 1949, and in the Senate from 1950 until his death in 1969. He became Senate minority leader and was adept at compromise. He was especially known for colorful speeches made with deep voice and dramatic flair - including many praising the marigold, which he wanted to become the national flower. He also authored a number of plays, five novels, and many short stories - none of which have apparently ever been published. His most well-known remark was made during debate on the budget: "A billion here, a billion there, and pretty soon you're talking about real money."

FORD BUILDING

D and 2nd Streets, S.W.

In 1990, two House of Representatives annexes used as offices were named for former members of Congress. Annex 1 became the Thomas P. O'Neill Office Building, and Annex 2 became the Gerald R. Ford Office Building.

Gerald Rudolph Ford was born Leslie King, Jr., at Omaha, NE, in 1913. His parents divorced when he was two, and when his mother remarried, he took the name of his stepfather. He grew up in Grand Rapids, MI, and graduated from the University of Michigan. There he played on two national-championship football teams and was the team's most valuable player. He became an assistant coach at Yale and while there earned his LL.B. degree. He started to practice law, but World War II interrupted. Ford spent four years in the Navy as an aviation operations officer and became a lieutenant commander.

In 1948 Ford was elected to Congress. He received national attention as chairman of the House Republican Conference in 1963. Two years later, Ford took over as minority leader and held that position until 1973.

In 1973, after Spiro Agnew resigned, President Nixon named Ford to succeed him. In 1974, when Nixon had to resign over the Watergate affair, Ford became the 38th president and the only one to occupy the White House without being elected either vice president or president. Ford proved open, decent, and honest, and his integrity helped heal the wounds of Watergate. He was both conservative and generally internationalist. He was also cautious and vetoed 48 bills in 21 months. He oversaw the end of the wars in Vietnam and Cambodia, and allowed over 100,000 Vietnamese refugees to enter and resettle in the U.S. In 1974, Ford pardoned Nixon. His caution over the economy, which slowed in 1976, and opposition to his pardon contributed to his losing the 1976 election to Georgia Gov. Jimmy Carter, and ended his 27 years of public service in Washington.

FORRESTAL BUILDING

On Independence Avenue at 10th Street, S.W.

James Vincent Forrestal was president of the Wall Street firm Dillon, Read and Company when he became President Franklin Roosevelt's administrative assistant and undersecretary of the Navy in 1940. He was instrumental in building up the Navy prior to World War II, and became secretary of the Navy in 1944. When President Truman decided on unifying the three armed services in 1947, Forrestal was named the country's first secretary of defense. He took a hard line against the Soviet Union and advocated stronger armed forces, but failed to halt seeming Air Force insubordination over appropriations and held unpopular pro-Arab anti-Israel views. In 1949 Forrestal resigned and entered Bethesda naval hospital for treatment of nervous exhaustion and depression. Soon thereafter he leaped to his death from a high window in the hospital.

This federal government office building was named in his honor. A bronze bust of Forrestal stands, not in this building, but more appropriately at the mall entrance to the Pentagon, in which are today's offices of the department of defense.

HART BUILDING

Constitution Avenue and 2nd Street, N.E., adjacent to the Dirksen Building

The third Senate office building (in addition to the Dirksen and Russell ones) is named for Philip Aloysius Hart.

Hart was born in Bryn Mawr, PA, in 1912. He graduated from Georgetown University and University of Michigan Law School. He practiced law in Detroit until World War II. He served as an infantry officer, attaining the rank of lieutenant colonel; he was wounded in the D-Day assault on Normandy. Hart then served as U.S. attorney, legal adviser to Gov. G. Mennen Williams, and lieutenant governor of Michigan, before being elected U.S. senator. He served in the Senate from 1959 until he died. A Democrat, he influenced civil rights, consumer, and antitrust legislation, and spoke out against the Vietnam War. He was floor manager of the Voting Rights Act. He died in Washington in 1976.

HERBERT HOOVER DEPARTMENT OF COMMERCE BUILDING

Between E Street and Constitution Avenues and between 14th and 15th Streets, N.W.

The north end of the building houses a Visitors Center where tickets to White House visits are obtained. Visitors are usually surprised by the large exhibit, not of the current president, but of President Herbert Hoover. That's because, as president when the building was built and as former secretary of commerce, the building bears his name. It is one of the biggest buildings in Washington, with over 3,000 rooms, 8 miles of hallways, and National Aquarium in its basement.

Herbert Clark Hoover was born in West Branch, IA, in 1874 in a Quaker family. His father was a blacksmith. His parents died when he was young, so he went to live in Oregon with an uncle. He attended Stanford University, graduating in 1895 with an engineering degree. He worked as a mining engineer in California's gold mines, then in Western Australia. He married, then went to work in China in 1899. The couple arrived there just as the Boxer Revolution began. They lived through the siege of Tientsin by the anti foreign Chinese, and it was Hoover's first experience with war, refugees, and war relief. In 1901 he was hired by a London firm with worldwide interests and traveled extensively. By the time he was 34, he had circled the globe five times, become wealthy, gained a worldwide reputation, and obtained chairmanship of several of mining companies. In 1909 he published *Principles of Mining,* and in 1912 became a trustee of Stanford.

Hoover was in London when World War I began and was asked to aid stranded Americans and direct the American Relief Committee. The committee helped 120,000 Americans get home. He then headed the Commission for Relief in Belgium, which eventually cared for some 10 million civilians. By this time he was famous throughout the world. In 1917, President Wilson appointed Hoover

U.S. food administrator. He increased food production and cut waste. After the war ended, Allied leaders appointed him director of relief, responsible for relieving Europe's food shortage. By 1920, Hoover had managed to feed and clothe 200 million people, and in subsequent years, millions more.

President Harding named Hoover secretary of commerce, where he served seven years under two presidents. In 1928, he secured the Republican nomination for president, campaigned by making only seven speeches, stressed farm relief, supported tariffs, favored prohibition, and repudiated religious bigots. His opponent, Roman Catholic Alfred E. Smith, favored repeal of prohibition and made religion an issue. Hoover won by the largest majority any president had ever received.

In 1929 Hoover got passed the Agricultural Marketing Act, to help poor farmers become prosperous. Later he obtained a bill that increased agricultural tariffs, again to aid farmers. But also in 1929, an economic depression began, and the stock market crashed. Hoover believed aid to the hungry and unemployed should come from local and not federal government. Still, he established the Reconstruction Finance Corp., with a capital of $500 million to provide relief by lending money to companies, banks, farm organizations, railroads, and local governments in order to stimulate jobs and economic activity. Opponents viewed this as aid to big business and called it "trickle down." By 1932, the Great Depression was the single subject of the election campaign, and Democrat Franklin D. Roosevelt easily defeated Hoover.

Hoover established his home in Palo Alto and his library at Stanford. He opposed President Roosevelt's New Deal and foreign policies. But after World War II, President Truman called Hoover back to government, making him chairman of the Commission on Organization of the Executive Branch. Hoover served until 1955 when a second commission ended its work, and retired at age 80. He then wrote *The Ordeal of Woodrow Wilson*, first book written by one president about another, and considered the best of his several books. When he was 84, he surpassed John Adams in living longest past his term as president. Hoover died in 1964 at age 90.

J. EDGAR HOOVER FBI BUILDING

Pennsylvania Avenue between 9th and 10th Streets, N.W.

John Edgar Hoover was born in Washington in 1895. He received LL.B. and master's degrees from George Washington University and joined the department of justice, serving as a special assistant to the attorney general. In 1924, Hoover became the first director of the FBI (Federal Bureau of Investigation). He eliminated politics from FBI appointments, improved recruiting and training, set high standards of conduct and appearance for agents, consolidated and automated the nation's fingerprint files, established a National Crime Reporting

Program making available in seconds data concerning wanted persons and criminal acts. For nearly 50 years he was in the news arresting gangsters, finding spies during World War II, tracking down communists during the Cold War. Sometimes, he and the FBI were criticized for exceeding their jurisdiction, manipulating data, and persecuting those who opposed them, yet he was confirmed as director by every president from Coolidge to Nixon. Hoover died in 1972. He lay in state in the Capitol rotunda and was buried in Congressional Cemetery.

Plans for the present building were underway while he was alive, and its cold Pennsylvania Avenue appearance and limited access were intentional. The building was finished in 1974 and given his name.

HUBERT H. HUMPHREY BUILDING, DEPARTMENT OF HEALTH AND HUMAN SERVICES

Independence Avenue and 3rd Street, S.W.

Hubert Horatio Humphrey was born in Wallace, SD, in 1911, and grew up in Doland, SD. He dropped out of the University of Minnesota because of the Depression, received a degree from the Denver College of Pharmacy, later returned to the University and graduated *magna cum laude*. He added a master's degree from Louisiana State University, then taught at both universities and at Macalester College.

Entering politics, Humphrey helped unite the Minnesota Farmer-Labor and Democratic parties. In 1945 he was elected mayor of Minneapolis, championed the country's first municipal fair employment practices ordinance, formed the liberal Americans for Democratic Action organization, and in 1947 was re-elected. The following year he was a delegate to the Democratic national convention and gained notice through his liberal, evangelical, and often cheerful oratory. The same year he was elected to the U.S. Senate. His first legislative proposal was for medical care for the aged (which would get enacted 17 years later). He was re-elected in 1954 and again in 1960. In 1956 he unsuccessfully sought the vice-presidential nomination, and in 1960 the presidential one, but by the time Lyndon Johnson became president in 1963, Humphrey was the logical choice for vice president, and in 1964, ran successfully with Johnson.

As vice president, Humphrey was a major spokesman for the administration's social legislation, civil rights programs, and attempts to reduce poverty. However, he supported Johnson's positions on the war in Vietnam, alienating many of his former liberal supporters. In 1968, Johnson announced he would not run for re-election, so Humphrey announced his candidacy. The Democratic party was torn over the war, and the convention in Chicago was marred by protests. Humphrey, with vice-presidential candidate Sen. Edmund Muskie, tried to reunite the party, but Alabama Gov. George Wallace became a third-party candidate, and

Humphrey lost to Republican Richard Nixon. Humphrey went back to teaching, then in 1970 regained his Senate seat and in 1976 was re-elected. Cancer struck him the next year, he was elected deputy president pro tem of the Senate - a position created just for him - and died at his home in Waverly, MN, in 1978.

JEFFERSON BUILDING. (See also **Jefferson Memorial.**)

1st Street, between East Capitol Street and Independence Avenue, S.E.

In 1800 Congress allotted $5,000 for a reference library. It was housed in a room in the Capitol building. It was lost, along with the building, when the British burned Washington in 1814. Soon thereafter, Thomas Jefferson, who needed the money, sold his collection of more than 6,000 books to the government. Thus the government restored its library with a single purchase, and for decades later, the library was informally referred to as "Mr. Jefferson's Library." Unfortunately, in 1851 a subsequent fire destroyed two-thirds of Jefferson's original collection. In 1897, the Library of Congress moved to its own building. At that time it was the largest and costliest library in the world. Its Great Hall is spectacular with marble columns, murals, mosaics, statues, and stained glass depicting themes of learning, knowledge, and civilization.

The buildings weren't originally named for people. When the first annex was built, it was generally known as the Thomas Jefferson Building. But when the third building was opened in 1980, the buildings were rechristened with the main building called the Thomas Jefferson Building, the annex the John Adams Building, and the third building the James Madison Building.

LONGWORTH BUILDING

On the Southeast side of the Capitol, on Independence Avenue between South Capitol Street and New Jersey Avenue, between the Rayburn and Cannon Buildings

Nicholas Longworth graduated from Harvard and Cincinnati Law School, served in Ohio as a representative and senator, then entered Congress in 1902 and was re-elected except for one term until his death in 1931. In 1906 he married Alice Lee Roosevelt, President Theodore Roosevelt's daughter. Although it was awkward, Longworth, a conservative Republican, supported President Taft in 1912 while his father-in-law ran for president on a third-party ticket (the Progressive "Bull Moose" Party). That party split resulted in Longworth's only defeat. He returned to Congress at the next opportunity, in 1915, and became majority leader in 1923 and speaker of the House in 1925.

The building that bears his name was built in 1930 and is one of the three House office buildings, the others being the Cannon and Rayburn buildings.

Federal Buildings

MADISON BUILDING. (See also **Jefferson Building, Dolley Madison House,** and **Mary Pickford Theater.**)
Independence Avenue between 1st and 2nd Streets, S.E.

The Library of Congress has spread into two former annexes, now the Adams and Madison buildings. Built in 1980, the Madison Building houses "special-format items" - photographs, prints, maps, drawings, and films. It contains the Pickford Theater for showings of its films. The building bears the name of the fourth president of the U.S., James Madison, and is his official memorial.

Madison was born at Port Conway, VA, in 1751. He was schooled at what is now Princeton University, graduating in 1771. In 1776 he was elected to the Virginia convention that voted for independence and that drafted a constitution for the new state. During 1778 and 1779 he served on the council of state under governors Patrick Henry and Thomas Jefferson. In 1779 he was elected to the Continental Congress. By the time he retired from Congress in 1783 he was thought of as its most effective legislator. He had also become the first sponsor of the idea of a library for Congress. By 1786 he was convinced that the Articles of Confederation were too weak to bind the states together, and led the call for a constitutional convention, which did meet the following year in Philadelphia. There Madison was an advocate of a strong central government, strong executive, independent court system, and bicameral legislature, with built-in checks and balances. He's known as the "father of the constitution" and is credited with wording much of it.

In 1794 Madison married Dolley Todd and wanted to retire, but he just couldn't let go of politics and rejoined the Virginia legislature. He returned to Washington when he was appointed secretary of state by President Jefferson in 1801. Madison, Jefferson, and Albert Gallatin, secretary of the treasury, led the country for eight years. He was then elected president in 1808, re-elected in 1812. There was a war between France and Britain, both heavily damaging American shipping, with Britain stopping American ships and impressing sailors on the high seas. For three years, Madison's diplomacy was ineffective. Under pressure from hawks in Congress, especially Henry Clay and John C. Calhoun, Madison declared war on Britain in 1812. The war was not waged successfully - instead of taking over Canada, one American army surrendered at Detroit and another army was defeated in Maryland as the British captured Washington and burned the White House. But then the British were defeated in Baltimore harbor, their invasion of New York was stopped at Lake Champlain, and Andrew Jackson won a major victory at New Orleans. A peace treaty was signed at Ghent in 1814, giving the U.S. an equal place with France and Britain in the world and giving Madison a last chance to implement a few domestic policies. He retired in 1817 to Montpelier, his Virginia estate, where he served President Monroe as a foreign policy advisor and helped Jefferson found the University of Virginia. He died in 1836.

THURGOOD MARSHALL JUDICIARY BUILDING

Next to Union Station, facing 2nd Street, N.E.

Thurgood Marshall was born in 1902 in Baltimore, MD. He graduated from Lincoln University (PA) and in 1933 from Howard University Law School. He was admitted to the bar and entered private practice. In 1936 he became special assistant counsel of the National Association for the Advancement of Colored People (NAACP), and by 1940 head of its legal services division. Over the next 20 years, Marshall argued 32 cases before the U.S. Supreme Court and helped form much of the civil rights progress made during that time. In 1962, President Kennedy appointed Marshall to the U.S. Court of Appeals, and in 1965, President Johnson named him solicitor general. Two years later, he named him to the U.S. Supreme Court. Marshall was a member of the liberal group on the court and championed a definition of equality that would assure full rights of citizenship for black Americans. He retired in 1991 and died in Bethesda, MD, in 1993. The building bearing his name was constructed and named in 1997.

NASSIF BUILDING, DEPARTMENT OF TRANSPORTATION

7th Street, between D and E Streets, S.W.

This is really a commercial building, but for the 28 years since it opened, it has been leased almost exclusively by the Department of Transportation. It is named for its builder, a real estate developer of Lebanese descent. One of its features is that its exterior is built with the same Italian marble as the Kennedy Center, which was under construction about the same time.

O'NEILL BUILDING

C Street and New Jersey Avenue, S.E.

In 1990, two House of Representatives annexes used as offices were named for former members of Congress. Annex 1 became the Thomas P. O'Neill Office Building, and Annex 2 became the Gerald R. Ford Office Building.

Thomas Philip O'Neill, Jr., was born in Cambridge, MA, in 1912. He graduated from Boston College in 1936 and was elected to the state House of Representatives. He became known as "Tip" O'Neill, getting his nickname from baseball player James "Tip" O'Neill. His constituents were hurt by the Depression, and O'Neill became a strong advocate of New Deal liberalism. He served as speaker of the state House from 1949 to 1952.

When John Kennedy gave up his seat in the House to run for the Senate in 1952, O'Neill was elected in his place. He continued his liberalism throughout his political life, supporting civil rights bills, antipoverty programs, Medicare, and federally funded health care. In 1971 he became assistant majority leader, and in 1973, majority leader. In 1977 he was elected speaker. In 1981, after Ronald

Reagan became president, O'Neill was his party's highest-ranking official. After the 1986 elections, O'Neill retired. He had served the public for 50 years.

FRANCES PERKINS BUILDING, DEPARTMENT OF LABOR

Constitution Avenue at 3rd Street, N.W.

Frances Perkins was the first woman to serve in the cabinet of a U.S. president. She was born in Boston in 1880. She graduated from Mount Holyoke College and Columbia University. In 1913 she married Paul Wilson but retained her maiden name. She became executive secretary of the Consumers' League of New York and of the city's Committee on Safety, and an expert on the health and safety of working women and children. During the administrations of New York governors Alfred Smith and Franklin Roosevelt, she was a major player in the American labor-reform movement. During the Great Depression, she became an expert on unemployment insurance and statistics. Before he even took office, President Roosevelt chose Perkins as his secretary of labor, and she served in that capacity during all four of his terms until his death in 1945. She helped form the Social Security Act and the Fair Labor Standards Act. She later was a member of the Civil Service Commission. She died in New York City in 1965.

RAYBURN BUILDING

On the Southwest side of the Capitol, on Independence Avenue between 1st and South Capitol Streets, next to the Longworth Building

Samuel Taliaferro Rayburn was a member of the House of Representatives from Texas from 1912 until his death in 1961. He thus served 49 consecutive years. For 17 years he was speaker, more than anyone else in history. He supported the New Deal, and was recognized throughout his career for his ability to get needed legislative votes by quiet persuasion. The building that bears his name was built in 1964 as the House badly needed more office space. It received much criticism because of its size, pompous design, and enormous cost. But it has been said it befits the big Democrat from Texas - even if he was originally from Tennessee.

RONALD REAGAN BUILDING

13th Street and Pennsylvania Avenue, N.W.

Officially the Ronald Reagan Building and International Trade Center, the building is a monument to the 40th president of the U.S.

Ronald Reagan was born in Tampico, IL, in 1911. He graduated from Eureka College, was a sports caster, and in 1937 started a career as a movie actor with Warner Brothers. He appeared in 53 films. In 1940 he married actress Jane Wyman but divorced in 1948; in 1952 he wed Nancy Davis. He moved into television, hosted "Death Valley Days," and became spokesman for General Electric Company.

Reagan shifted his views from New Deal Democrat to conservative Republican and by the 1960s was a favorite conservative speaker. He was viewed as an ex-movie star with simple views and no constituency but stunned critics when he defeated California Gov. "Pat" Brown in 1966. He was governor for two four-year terms, proved conservative on spending and taxes, was practical when growth required more social services, and left office leaving the state a $550-million surplus. By 1980 he was considered by rivals too old, yet won the nomination for president, then defeated President Carter, carrying 44 states to Carter's 6. Four years later he was re-elected by an even larger margin.

Reagan's administrations were marked by sharp budget reductions, tax cuts, and cutbacks in regulations. Unemployment surged to the highest rate in 40 years and deficits mounted equally high, yet interest rates fell and Americans enjoyed six years of economic prosperity. Defense spending went up dramatically, and Reagan took strong anti-communist and anti-terrorist stands, bombing Libyan military installations, supporting El Salvador, eradicating an anti-American government in Granada, and supporting Nicaraguan contras. He held four meetings with Soviet leader Mikhail Gorbachev, effectively aiding him to change Soviet society, claiming final victory in the Cold War, even visiting Moscow. However, it was made public that the U.S. had sold weapons to Iran in exchange for hostages and that some of the money had been diverted to the Nicaraguan contras (Congress had voted to forbid aid to the contras), so leading White House aides had to resign.

In 1994, in a letter to the American people, Reagan revealed that he suffers from Alzheimer's disease. He lives with his wife in seclusion in California.

The building in Washington that honors him has just been completed, indeed completes the entire Federal Triangle (that area between Pennsylvania and Constitution Avenues and 15th Street). Major organizations it houses are the Agency for International Development and the headquarters of the Environmental Protection Agency.

RUSSELL BUILDING

Just Northeast of the Capitol, on Constitution Avenue, between Delaware Avenue and 1st Street, N.E., and next to the Dirksen Building

In 1972 Congress changed the name of the Old Senate Office Building to the Richard B. Russell Senate Office Building and that of the New Senate Office Building to the Everett M. Dirksen Senate Office Building.

Russell, from Georgia, was elected to the Senate in 1932 and held office until his death in 1971. He was a supporter of Franklin D. Roosevelt's policies, yet also led the Senate's Southern bloc, opposing federal intervention in racial matters. One of the most influential people in the Senate, he served as chairman of the Senate Armed Services and Senate Appropriations committees, and eventually as *president pro tempore* of the Senate. In 1948 and 1952 he was a major contender for the presidential nomination.

MARY E. SWITZER BUILDING, DEPARTMENT OF HEALTH AND HUMAN SERVICES

Between C and D, and 3rd and 4th Streets, S.W.

Mary Switzer was born in Newton, MA, in 1900. She graduated from Radcliffe College in 1921. Only then did she make her first trip outside Massachusetts. The following year she came to Washington "with the Harding gang," she'd later state. She stayed through eight presidents and ended up serving the government for 48 years.

Switzer's first job was as a clerk in Treasury. She had no knack for research and got fired. She was hired back as a mimeograph operator. By the 1930s she was assistant to the assistant secretary in charge of the Public Health Service. In 1939 federal health and welfare programs were consolidated, and she became chief assistant to the administrator. In 1950 she was named commissioner of the Vocational Rehabilitation Administration. In 1953 it was incorporated into what is now Health and Human Services. In 1960 her organization was made part of a larger Social and Rehabilitation Service, and Switzer became its commissioner. When she retired in 1969, her Service had a budget of $8 billion and controlled almost all of the nation's internal assistance programs.

Switzer was involved in almost every aspect of American charitable endeavor from education to disease research to programs for disabled veterans. In 1960 she received the Albert Lasker Award in medicine for work with the physically handicapped, one of over 40 major awards she was given. She received 16 honorary degrees. She was a trustee of Radcliffe, on the board of Brandeis University, and was the first woman on the board of Georgetown University. She died in 1971.

WINDER BUILDING

600 17th Street, N.W., across from the Executive Office Building

This was the first high-rise office building in the District - all five stories - and it pioneered the use of steel beams and central heating. It was built in 1848 and named for Gen. William Winder. He had commanded the losing U.S. forces against the British at the Battle of Bladensburg in 1814, as the British approached Washington. During the Civil War, the building provided offices for Union generals, and afterwards housed the Judge Advocate General and Bureau of Military Justice. Today it continues to lease space to government agencies and is currently the Office of the United States Trade Representative.

FOUNTAINS

Some of Washington's most interesting memorials are fountains - bubbling, cascading, providing a respite from the busy city, especially on a summer day. A separate section for these wonderful places seemed in order. Here are seven named fountains.

FREDERIC BARTHOLDI

Independence Avenue at 1st Street, S.W.

The Bartholdi fountain is 30 feet high, has a 90-foot-wide base, and - it's solid cast iron - weighs 15,000 pounds. It was cast in Paris in 1875 and entered in the Philadelphia Centennial Exhibition of 1876, after which the U.S. government bought it. In the late 1800s it was a major Washington attraction, because it was lighted by twelve bulbs, one of the earliest displays of electric lights in the city.

Frederic Bartholdi was born in Alsace, France, in 1834. Originally a painter, he turned to sculpture. His monumental sculptures include *Lafayette Arriving in America* (1873) in Union Square, New York City, and *Liberty Enlightening the World* (1886) also in New York - the latter one more popularly known as the Statue of Liberty.

BUTT-MILLET

Just southwest of the White House grounds, on E Street, N.W.

This 8-foot memorial fountain, sculpted by Daniel Chester French who did the statue of Lincoln in the Lincoln Memorial, was built by friends of Maj. Archibald Wallingham Butt (1865-1912) and Francis Davis Millet (1846-1912). It stands just to the side of the southern edge of White House grounds, and since it doesn't always bubble, it is virtually ignored by the thousands of people who walk past it to view the White House.

Archibald Butt was born in Augusta, GA. He graduated from the University of the South, started a career in journalism, then while working in Washington became secretary of the Mexican Embassy. Butt was a lieutenant during the Spanish-American War, served in the Philippines and in Cuba, then became military aide to President Theodore Roosevelt. During the political battles between Roosevelt and Taft, he fell into ill health and vacationed in Europe.

Francis Millet was drummer boy to a Massachusetts regiment, Harvard student, a newspaperman, finally an artist. At the Royal Academy of Fine Arts in Belgium he was a medal winner in his first year. During the Russian-Turkish War he represented several papers and was decorated for bravery under fire. He published his travel notes, wrote short stories, translated Tolstoy. His art decorates the

Baltimore Customs House, Boston's Trinity Church, and the Wisconsin and Minnesota capitol buildings. He became head of decoration for the Columbia Exhibition in Chicago in 1893, and his paintings are in world museums.

Both were returning from travels in Europe on the *Titanic* when it struck an iceberg in the Atlantic and sank. The luxurious ship had been considered unsinkable, yet sank on its maiden voyage. Over 1,500 people died. Both men were last seen giving their life preservers to women just before the ship sank.

There is a *Titanic* Memorial to all the men who died in the wreck, at 4th and P Streets, S.W., across the water from East Potomac Park. The Butt-Millet memorial is the only *Titanic* memorial in Washington bearing specific names.

CHRISTOPHER COLUMBUS
In front of Union Station on Massachusetts Avenue, N.E.

One of the District's biggest memorials is this circular fountain with statue of Christopher Columbus. The memorial contains, among other things, an elderly figure representing the Old World, an Indian representing the New World, pictures of Spanish King Ferdinand and Queen Isabella who paid for Columbus' travels, and three flag poles that represent the three ships from his initial voyage.

Columbus was born between 1446 and 1451. He was a sailor by age 14, and made voyages to England, Scotland, and West Africa. He studied astronomy and geometry at the University of Pavia. Current thinking was that the earth was flat; some scholars, Columbus included, believed it was round. For several years he worked for his father weaving. Finished cloth was shipped to the Orient and exchanged for spices, silks, and rare woods, all of which were carried overland. Columbus yearned to find a shorter sea route, and if the world was really round, believed it could be found by sailing westward.

In 1478, Columbus traveled to Portugal, where he married the daughter of a Portuguese captain. He then went to King John of Portugal requesting funds for a voyage west, but was refused. He spent seven years pursuing the Spanish court, and eventually succeeded.

Columbus sailed from Palos August 3, 1492, on the *Santa Maria*, accompanied by the *Pinta* and the *Nina* and 88 crew members. There was a long stop at the Canary Islands off the coast of Africa, and then a final sailing from there on September 6. It was on October 12 that he first sighted land in the New World. He went on to discover what is now Cuba and Haiti, then returned to Spain March 15, 1493, with Indians, gold, cotton, and parrots, and received acclaim.

A second voyage was outfitted, this time with 17 ships and 1,500 people. He landed colonists on Haiti, and went on to discover the Virgin Islands, Puerto

Rico, and Jamaica. In two more voyages he discovered Trinidad, even touched South America. During his absence enemies spread false rumors about him, and he was sent home in chains, but proved his innocence. He died in Spain in 1506, convinced he had found Asia, not realizing what lands he had really found.

SAMUEL DUPONT. (See also **Dupont Circle.**)
In the center of Dupont Circle, which is where Massachusetts, Connecticut, and New Hampshire Avenues and 19th Street, N.W., meet.

Around the base of this fountain is inscribed "Samuel Francis Dupont, Rear Admiral, United States Navy, 1803-1865." There's a large bowl atop a pedestal, and three navigational figures aside the pedestal representing sea, wind, and stars.

ANDREW MELLON
At the intersection of Constitution and Pennsylvania Avenues, N.W.

This big circular fountain is a memorial, donated by friends and erected in 1952, to Andrew W. Mellon.

Mellon was born in Pittsburgh, son of Thomas Mellon, successful lawyer, judge, and banker. He attended what is now the University of Pittsburgh, then joined the family bank, T. Mellon & Sons, taking over the bank from his father in 1882. For 35 years Mellon was immensely successful in identifying potential businesses and supplying their needed capital, becoming enormously wealthy in the process. As examples, he helped found Alcoa, established the construction company that built the Panama Canal locks, started Gulf Oil, and created United States Steel. Mellon was named secretary of the Treasury by President Harding in 1921 and continued as such under Presidents Coolidge and Hoover. In 1937, he gave his extensive and valuable art collection to the federal government along with the funds to house and maintain it. The resulting "house" is the National Gallery of Art, which opened in 1941, and is across the street from the fountain.

FRANCIS DAVIS MILLET. (See **Butt-Millet.**)

FRANCIS NEWLANDS. (See also **Chevy Chase.**)
In Chevy Chase Circle, Connecticut Avenue at the Maryland State Line

In 1890 Col. G. A. Ames had the idea of extending Connecticut Avenue all the way to Maryland and turned to a friend, Sen. Stewart of Nevada for funds. Sen. Stewart went to Nevada Rep. Francis Newlands, whose wife held investments in the Comstock Lode. Newlands said he would invest. The result was the Chevy Chase Land Company. The company was responsible for building the bridges over Rock Creek and Klingle Gap, for laying the trolley line tracks from downtown Washington to Chevy Chase Lake a couple miles into Maryland, and thus indirectly for all the later development along Connecticut Avenue.

Fountains

Francis Griffith Newlands was born near Natchez, MS, in 1848. He studied at Yale and George Washington universities, became a lawyer, and eventually located in Nevada. An advocate of free silver, he was elected to Congress in 1892, and advanced to the Senate in 1902. He oversaw legislation on irrigation projects, rail rates, rivers and harbors, trust and tariffs. He was author of the Federal Trade Commission Act, prepared the way for the Federal Reserve, and established a federal bureau of fine arts. He died in Washington in 1917.

Newlands not only backed the Chevy Chase Land Company but organized the Chevy Chase Country Club and was its first president. It was to be a hunt and riding club (golf came later). Its master of hounds was sent to England, but unfortunately returned with 24 trained dogs on the *Titanic*.

Chevy Chase Circle was built in 1891. In 1932, the Garden Club of America got Congress to authorize a memorial fountain for it, Newlands' widow helped pay for it, and the fountain was dedicated in 1933. It bears Newlands' name and the words, "His statesmanship held true regard for the interests of all men." In the 65 years since then, the circle and fountain have changed very little.

OSCAR STRAUS

14th Street between Pennsylvania and Constitution Avenues at the 14th Street entrance to the Ronald Reagan Building

Oscar Solomon Straus was one of the first career diplomats, assisting several presidents, both Democratic and Republican. His memorial fountain presents him as author, diplomat, and statesman.

Straus emigrated from Bavaria in 1854 and settled in New York City, where he graduated from Columbia College and its law school. One of his first actions was, as part of a committee, to recommend to President Benjamin Harrison how to better the condition of Russian Jews in the Middle East. He was always an active guardian of Jewish minorities in Europe, was a patron of many Jewish organizations, and founded and served as first president of the American Jewish Historical Society. A progressive Democrat, Straus was named minister to Turkey in 1887 by President Cleveland. After obtaining concessions for the U.S. and at the same time pleasing the sultan, he was reappointed by President McKinley. In 1906, President Theodore Roosevelt made him secretary of commerce and labor. Under President Taft, he returned to Turkey as the first American ambassador to the Ottoman Empire. When the Taft-Roosevelt split happened in the Republican Party, he headed the Progressive Party ticket in New York, losing but still garnering more votes than Roosevelt. In 1915 he was appointed chairman of the New York Public Service commission. He provided help to Jewish refugees after World War I and assisted President Wilson in incorporating the League of Nations into the Versailles treaty. He died in 1926.

METRO STATIONS

Metro is Washington's mass transit and subway system. There are over 20 peculiarly named Metro stations covered in this book. So why only six in this section? Because nine stations have the names of neighborhoods (Anacostia, Brookland, Cleveland Park, Deanwood, Foggy Bottom, Shaw, Takoma Park, Tenleytown, Woodley Park). Four have names of circles or squares (Dupont Circle, Farragut Square, McPherson Square, Mt. Vernon Square). One has the same name as the nearby school (Cardozo), one the name of the street (Benning), and one the name of the museum (Smithsonian). They are all discussed in those sections of the book. So here are the six that don't fit those or other book categories yet need a little explanation of their names.

EASTERN MARKET

7th and C Streets, S.E.

Once Washington boasted of several huge market places for fresh meat, fish, eggs, cream, bread, vegetables, and fruit. Eastern Market, built in 1873, is one that remains.

There was a Western Market at 20th and I Streets, N.W., from 1802 until fire destroyed it in 1852. It arose again in 1873 at 21st and K Streets, but has since been torn down. Center Market stood for more than 125 years at 7th and 9th Streets, N.W., and because of the lowland, was sometimes called Marsh Market. It held not only food, but before 1850 also held regular slave auctions. It was demolished in 1931, and the National Archives now stand on the site.

FRIENDSHIP HEIGHTS

Just north of Tenleytown on Wisconsin Avenue, N.W., at the Maryland State Line

In 1711 or 1713, Thomas Addison and James Stoddert (sometimes written Stoddard) received a patent of over 3,000 acres from Charles Calvert, Lord Baltimore. The lands extended from present-day American University to what is now Bethesda, MD. They named this large estate Friendship. In 1760, Addison's grandson, John Murdock, built the first home on the estate; the home existed until 1918. In 1898, John R. McLean, founder of the *Washington Post*, purchased the property and gave his new home the original name, Friendship. About 1900, farmer-prohibitionist Albert Shoemaker and developer-banker Henry Wootton Offutt platted two subdivisions near the District Line and called one of them Friendship Heights. The name has applied to the area ever since.

Metro Stations

FORT TOTTEN

About Gallatin and Galloway Streets, between North Capitol Street and South Dakota Avenue, N.E.

Fort Totten was one of several Civil War forts defending the northern reaches of Washington. It was originally Fort Towson, but its name was changed to honor Brig. Gen. Joseph G. Totten. Totten was born in 1788. He became a military engineer. He was involved in the early studies for the Chesapeake & Ohio Canal. By 1838 he was Chief of Engineers. In 1855, he supervised construction of the Jones Point Lighthouse. By the time the Civil War started, Totten had been a captain of engineers before most other Civil War generals were born. In 1862 he was on the commission called by secretary of war Stanton to study Washington defenses and was in charge of supervising their construction. Totten died in 1864, of pneumonia.

L'ENFANT PLAZA

Adjoining 10th Street, S.W., between Independence and Maine Avenues.

Pierre Charles L'Enfant was born in Paris in 1754. He was trained in architecture and engineering. He volunteered during the Revolution, spent the winter at Valley Forge in 1777, and was later wounded. He also served as an engineer and planned forts that the British couldn't overcome. He became a major.

After the war, Washington had L'Enfant execute designs for the emblems of the Society of the Cincinnati. In New York, L'Enfant converted the old city hall into Federal Hall, the seat of Congress in 1787. Once the site of Federal City was chosen, Washington appointed him to lay out the city.

L'Enfant created for Washington a grand plan reminiscent of Versailles, "magnificent enough to grace a great nation." He placed "Federal House" (the Capitol) and "President's House" (the White House) on high ground where they could command views to the river. He created an avenue (Pennsylvania Avenue) 160 feet wide between them. He laid out the city into a grid, with the numbered and lettered streets that survive today, crossed by broad avenues intersecting at wide squares. He laid down a grand avenue 400 feet wide and a mile long (the Mall), to be filled with trees and fountains.

But landowners felt "the crazy Frenchman" was throwing away land that should become marketable city lots. L'Enfant may have been a genius, but he disregarded orders, overspent his budget, and ignored the landowners. When Daniel Carroll's new manor house (Carroll was lord of Duddington) obstructed one of his vistas, he tore it down. That was "the last straw." L'Enfant was dismissed. Congress offered $2,500 and a lot near the White House, but L'Enfant turned it down, instead submitting fantastic claims for his services. Once he was 40 years old, he did little. He lived on the charity of friends. He died at Green

Hill, Prince Georges County, MD, in 1825. In 1909 his body was moved and he was given the belated honor of a military burial in Arlington Cemetery.

In 1966, architect I.M. Pei was commissioned to develop a mixed-use urban environment in Southwest Washington. He mixed a hotel, underground mall, office buildings, pedestrian main street, fountain, and Metro stop, now all given the name of Washington's first planner.

UNION STATION. (See also **McMillan Reservoir.**)
On Massachusetts Avenue between North Capitol and 2nd Streets, N.E.

The name is not a leftover from the Civil War. In 1900 the Mall was the scene of horses, wagons, stables, shops, hotels, residences, trees, streetcars, and noisy dirty trains. The main railroads in the city were the competing Pennsylvania and Baltimore & Ohio. In 1901 the McMillan Plan called for reviving and extending L'Enfant's plan for the Mall, which meant moving the trains. Master architect Daniel Burnham was a member of the commission. He ran into Pennsylvania Railroad's president Alexander Cassatt in London and urged they build a single "union station" that would not only make the Pennsylvania look good but set the tone for the whole Washington plan. All railroads would use the same terminal. For a federal payment of $3 million to build a tunnel under Capitol Hill to connect with southern lines, Cassatt agreed. And in 1903, President Theodore Roosevelt signed the act "to provide for a union station."

The station design was Burnham's, based on Rome's Arch of Constantine and the Baths of Diocletian, with heroic figures sculpted by Louis Saint-Gaudens and inscriptions selected by Charles Eliot, president of Harvard. The station was the first building built under the McMillan Plan and opened in 1907. It reached its heyday between World Wars I and II, when every president used it, and kings, queens, prime ministers, and celebrities arrived in Washington by going through it. As railroad passenger service declined, so did the station. By 1958, the railroads talked about giving it away. In the 1970s it failed as a Visitor Center. But in the 1980s, spurred partly by Amtrak success, a marvelous redevelopment/ restoration was done, and in 1988, the current version of the terminal opened.

VAN NESS
On Connecticut Avenue at Van Ness Street, N.W.

John Peter Van Ness arrived in Washington from Kinderhook, NY, in 1801 to serve in the House of Representatives. The next year he married Marcia Burnes, heir to more than 600 acres in central Washington. President Jefferson appointed Van Ness a major in the District militia. By 1813 he was a major general, in 1814 president of a bank, in 1816 warden of St. John's Church on Lafayette Square, and by 1830, mayor of the city. He died in 1846. Van Ness Street was named for him, and the Metro stop took its name from the street.

MILITARY RESERVATIONS

The military understandably has a large presence in the nation's capital. Its biggest facility, the Pentagon, is across the Potomac in Virginia, and the airfield that serves the president's long-distance flights, Andrews Air Force Base, is in Maryland. But Washington is home to Bolling Air Force Base, the U.S. Navy Bureau of Medicine and Surgery (on the hill north of the Lincoln Memorial), Washington Navy Yard (at 8th and M Streets, S.E.), Anacostia Naval Station with its helicopter facility (just south of the Frederick Douglass Bridge), Coast Guard Headquarters (at Buzzard Point), Fort Leslie J. McNair and the National War College, and the Walter Reed Army Medical Center. Here are the three whose names serve as memorials.

BOLLING AIR FORCE BASE
Between I-295 and the Potomac River, in Anacostia

Raynal Cawthorne Bolling was born in Arkansas in 1877. He studied law at Harvard, became general counsel for U.S. Steel.

Billy Mitchell, who was much later to become recognized as the father of the American air force, had been urging importance of military aviation since 1912. In 1917 he successfully persuaded the secretary of war to buy the land where the base is now located for a Washington-area airfield. The air force was then the Army Air Service, part of the Signal Corps. Its rapid growth is credited to three young officers, each operating somewhat on his own in this new untried military field: Mitchell, Benjamin Foulois, and Reynal Bolling.

In 1917 Bolling was head of the Aeroplane Board. He soon became a major and commanded the Aviation Section. As a colonel, he joined Mitchell and the AEF. He died the following year. That year, the new Washington airfield was named in his honor.

FORT LESLIE J. MCNAIR. (See also **Greenleaf's Point.**)
At the point of land formed by the Anacostia River and the Washington Channel, entered at 4th and P Streets, S.W.

The fort - never really a fort, but more of a reservation - became an official military reservation in 1797, and an arsenal was constructed there in 1803. It was known only as Greenleaf's Point. In 1826, it was used as a federal prison (actually the first U.S. penitentiary), which in the Civil War was turned over to military authorities. During the war it was called The Arsenal. The trial of the conspirators who killed Lincoln was held, Mary Surratt was hanged, and John Wilkes Booth was initially buried there. By 1881 it was called Washington Barracks. In 1903 the Army War College (today known as National Defense

University) made the fort its home. In 1935 it was called Fort Humphreys in honor of A. A. Humphreys, a general in the Army Engineers who was decorated for bravery in the Civil War. After World War II, the name was changed again, to Fort Leslie J. McNair.

McNair graduated from West Point and served with Gen. Pershing's expeditions into Mexico in 1916 and France in World War I, attaining rank of brigadier general by war's end. In 1940 he was made lieutenant general and given responsibility for the combat training of U.S. troops. His rigorous training programs included exercises with live ammunition and simulated combat maneuvers. In 1944 he entered Normandy to observe aerial bombardments near St. Lo, and was killed by American bombs when they missed their intended targets.

WALTER REED ARMY MEDICAL CENTER
16th Street and Alaska Avenue, N.W.

Walter Reed was born in Belroi, VA, in 1851. He studied medicine at the University of Virginia and at Bellevue Hospital Medical College in New York. In 1875 he entered the Army as a surgeon, and by 1893 reached the rank of major. He was named curator of the Army Medical Museum and served as professor of bacteriology at the Army Medical School in Washington.

Every year yellow fever killed thousands of people in Latin America and the Southeastern U.S. In the late 1800s, it caused work on the canal across Panama to be stopped. Popular theory was that yellow fever was caused by bacteria and was contagious or that it was transmitted by mosquitoes, but it was unclear which.

In 1900, Reed headed an Army commission to study the fever in Cuba. In a classic series of experiments, Reed determined that mosquitoes indeed transmitted the disease and, further, that the disease agent itself was a virus. Yellow fever was the first human disease attributed to a virus. Following Reed's work, mosquito-breeding sites were eliminated in Cuba, and Army surgeon William Gorgas cleaned out mosquito sites in Panama, making possible the completion of the Panama Canal.

Reed resumed his professorship in Washington, but in 1902 died of appendicitis. Congress authorized construction of a Walter Reed United States General Hospital. More buildings were added in the decades that followed, eventually many of the Army's medical organizations were consolidated, and in 1951, on what would have been Reed's 100th birthday, the name was officially changed to the Walter Reed Army Medical Center. Today it has over 300 buildings. The main hospital stands ten stories high, has 5,500 rooms, admits 22,000 patients a year, and cares for thousands more on an outpatient basis.

MUSEUMS AND GALLERIES

There are reportedly 97 museums and galleries in Washington. Some were built as major museums, over a dozen are part of the Smithsonian Institution, others are converted homes, many are commercial art galleries. Most have clear names like the Museum of Natural History. Here are 20 that have intriguing names. One was a synagogue, one a school, another the only home of a U.S. president in the city that is open as a museum. All of these are open to the public.

ANDERSON HOUSE
2118 Massachusetts Avenue, N.W.

Anderson House is headquarters for the Society of the Cincinnati and a museum of Revolutionary War materials. It is named for former owner Larz Anderson III, who willed it to the Society when he died in 1937.

After the Revolutionary War, Gen. Henry Knox, chief of artillery, proposed that officers - regulars in the Continental Army or those with French forces - form a patriotic/fraternal society. By 1783, there were 2,150 such officers enrolled in 13 state societies; France became the fourteenth. The Society's name was taken from Lucius Cincinnatus, Roman leader who twice was called from his farm to lead military forces, saved Rome, refused reward, and twice returned to private life. George Washington was the Society's first president, Alexander Hamilton the second. Pierre L'Enfant designed its membership badge. Membership passes via the eldest son of descendants, and there are 3,500 members today.

Larz Anderson was born in Paris in 1866, grandson of Col. Richard Anderson, aide-de-camp to Gen. Lafayette. He was educated at Harvard, and studied law abroad before entering the American diplomatic corps. He was second secretary of the Embassy in London, first secretary and charge d'affaires in Rome, then enlisted in the Army during the Spanish American War, becoming a captain. Afterwards he was minister to Belgium and ambassador to Japan. He was a member of the Society of Cincinnati for over 40 years and designed his house in Washington with the Society in mind.

BETHUNE MUSEUM-ARCHIVES. (See **Mary McLeod Bethune.**)
1318 Vermont Avenue, N.W.

Mary McLeod Bethune founded Bethune-Cookman College. She was the first president of the National Council of Negro Women and served as advisor to President Franklin Roosevelt on black affairs and youth. This building was bought by the Council of Negro Women in 1943, and was Bethune's home from 1943 to 1950. The museum part has exhibitions on black women's history. The carriage house includes Bethune's papers from her years in Washington.

CEDAR HILL

1411 W Street, at 14th and W Streets, S.E., in Anacostia

Cedar Hill was the home of Frederick Douglass. The cedar trees for which it was named are long gone. The home is now a museum operated by the National Park Service and formally called the Frederick Douglass National Historic Site.

Douglass was born near Easton, MD, in 1817. He was originally Frederick Augustus Washington Bailey, but like many black slaves, he assumed a name - his chosen from Sir Walter Scott's novel *Lady of the Lake*. When 21 Douglass escaped and lectured to antislavery groups throughout the Northeast. He was a tall handsome man and effective speaker. In 1845 he published *The Narrative of the Life of Frederick Douglass* and named his master's identity, which put his life in jeopardy. He had to flee to England, where friends purchased his freedom.

Back in the U.S. he published his own paper in Rochester, NY, and ran the underground railroad station there. During the Civil War he recruited blacks for the Union Army. After the war he campaigned for Republican candidates and supported Reconstruction. He was rewarded with federal appointments, e.g., U.S. Marshall for the District of Columbia. At that time, 1877, he bought Cedar Hill breaking a no-blacks racial ban on ownership in the area. He angered neighbors further in 1884 when he brought his second wife, Helen Pitts, to Cedar Hill; she was white. (His first wife, Anna, died in 1882.) At Cedar Hill he completed his autobiography, *The Life and Times of Frederick Douglass*. He died in 1895.

CORCORAN GALLERY OF ART. (See also **Renwick Gallery**.)

500 17th Street at New York Avenue, N.W.

William Wilson Corcoran was Washington's first philanthropist and patron of American art. He was born in 1798, son of a mayor of Georgetown, and attended Georgetown College. He opened a store on M Street, lost it in the Depression of 1823, worked for a bank, formed his own brokerage firm, and with G. W. Riggs, formed the Corcoran & Riggs Bank. Corcoran was appointed exclusive agent for the sale of Mexican War bonds in Europe. He was a super salesman, sold the entire issue, and made over a million dollars. He put much of the money into his art collection. In 1854, he retired from the bank to devote full time to managing his real estate, art collections, and philanthropic activities. He lived until 1888.

The first Corcoran Gallery (17th Street and Pennsylvania) is now called the Renwick Gallery. It opened in 1869 and was Washington's first art gallery. It became too small for Corcoran's growing collection, and in 1897 the larger current gallery was opened. Today the American collection of over 3,000 paintings illuminates American history and the nation's artistic development. There are also collections of sculpture, photography, prints, drawings, and European art, and there is the renowned Corcoran School of Art.

DECATUR HOUSE
748 Jackson Place, N.W., facing Lafayette Park.

Stephen Decatur was born at Sinepuxent, MD, in 1779. At 19 he became a midshipman. In 1804 the Tripoli pirates captured the American frigate *Philadelphia*. Lt. Decatur, commanding a small ship, entered the harbor, recaptured and burned the *Philadelphia*, and despite guns firing, escaped. During the War of 1812 he captured a British frigate and had it sailed into New York harbor. Later, again on the Barbary Coast, he fought, then negotiated treaties with Algiers, Tripoli, and Tunis forbidding payment of pirates' tribute and providing for release of captive American sailors.

With prize money from his exploits, Decatur had architect Benjamin Latrobe design this house. But Decatur was killed in a duel in 1820 by Commodore James Barron after they disagreed over Barron's court-martial. His wife immediately moved out. The Decaturs lived in the house only 14 months.

The house has since been occupied by the French and Russian legations, the British minister, three secretaries of state (Henry Clay, Martin Van Buren, and Edward Livingston), John Gadsby (the tavern proprietor), George Dallas (vice president under James Polk), and at least five U.S. congressmen, before being bequeathed to the National Trust for Historic Preservation in 1956.

DUMBARTON OAKS. (See also **Georgetown.**)
The house and Byzantine art at 3101 R Street. The Pre-Columbia Museum at 1703 32nd Street, N.W.

This is one of the largest Georgian estates left in Georgetown. The original house was built in 1800 and has had various owners, expansions, and names. In 1891, then-owner Henry Blount, a farm tool manufacturer from Evansville, IN, named the estate "The Oaks." Owner Robert Bliss, a career foreign service office and later ambassador to Sweden and Argentina, added Dumbarton - based on Ninian Beall's original tract, the "Rock of Dunbarton" - to the name. In 1941, the Blisses gave the estate to Harvard University to preserve their gardens and collections of furnishings and Pre-Columbian and Byzantine art.

What brought the estate to national attention, however, weren't the collections. In 1944, President Roosevelt arranged meetings with the four major world powers (United Kingdom, Soviet Union, China, and the U.S.). Representatives met at this estate in what became known as the Dumbarton Oaks Conference. Its outgrowth was the creation of the United Nations a year later.

FREER GALLERY OF ART

On the South side of the Mall, Jefferson Drive, at 12th Street, S.W.

Charles Lang Freer was born in Kingston, NY, in 1856. He was educated in public school but left in the seventh grade to go to work. He became an accomplished accountant. At 24 he moved to Detroit and started a company to manufacture then-new steel railroad cars. Within a dozen years he had merged 13 such companies into American Car and Foundry. He never married. In 1904 at 46 he retired and devoted himself to study, travel, and purchase of art, especially Oriental works. In 1905, Freer started negotiations to give his collection - then over 2,000 art objects - to the Smithsonian, including paying for the gallery building that would house it and bear his name. Freer himself sketched, then commissioned Charles Platt to complete design of the sky-lit Italian Renaissance building. Freer died in 1919. The Freer Gallery opened in 1921.

At Freer's insistence, the collection is to remain as is, i.e., the gallery can not lend, borrow, sell, or add art. Its most famous item is likely the Peacock Room, the London dining room of Frederick Leyland, decorated by James McNeill Whistler. The room was moved into the Freer in its entirety.

HEURICH MANSION

1307 New Hampshire Avenue, N.W.

This home with its large turret was built in the 1890s, still contains some of the original furniture, and is one of the most authentic buildings of its kind. It was built for Christian Heurich and his family. It now serves as headquarters of the Historical Society of Washington.

Christian Heurich was born in Sachsen-Meiningen, Germany, in 1842. As a boy he served as apprentice in his father's inn. His father died when he was 14, and he walked through Europe working in taverns. He arrived in Washington in 1872. He bought an interest in an existing brewery, the Schnell Brewery, but within a year, he owned it all. And he did it all - from brewmeister to accountant. By the 1880s, his was the most successful of 22 Washington breweries. After three fires, he moved his brewery to Foggy Bottom and the site where the Kennedy Center now stands. In 1899, Heurich married for the third time, this time the young niece of his first wife. He had seven children. Germans weren't popular during World War I, and his beer couldn't sell during Prohibition. He once tried making cider; it accidentally fermented, and he had to dump 60,000 gallons into the Potomac. He went into real estate and there proved quite successful, becoming one of the city's leading philanthropists. After Prohibition, Heurich reopened his brewery and continued making beer - until nine days before he died, in 1945 at age 102. Recently, grandson Gary went back into the business and Heurich Beer, though made elsewhere, can still be found occasionally on the market.

Museums and Galleries

HIRSHHORN MUSEUM & SCULPTURE GARDEN

Independence Avenue and 7th Street, S.W.

Joseph H. Hirshhorn was born in 1899 in Latvia. When he was six, he immigrated to the United States with his impoverished family. He made his first $1 million in the stock market in the 1920s - selling out only a few weeks before the 1929 crash. He then made more millions in Canada by gaining control of the biggest uranium deposits ever found. Along the way, Hirshhorn bought art in enormous quantity. In 1966, after encouragement from secretary Dillon Ripley, President Lyndon Johnson, the U.S. Congress, and others, he agreed to give to the Smithsonian his collection - and $1 million toward the building to house it and bear his name. At that time, there were 4,000 paintings and 2,000 sculptures; the final total turned out to be about 12,000. The paintings, in particular, comprise a half century of contemporary (modern) American art.

The gift was controversial. Some thought Hirshhorn got too much for it, especially getting the museum named for him. The museum building was even more controversial. It was designed by modernist Gordon Bunshaft, who also gave New York its first office building with a sloping front, first building on stilts, and first glass-walled skyscraper. It has been called the doughnut on the Mall for its shape - a concrete cylinder hollowed out on the inside. It opened in 1974. Hirshhorn died in 1981.

KLUTZNICK JEWISH MUSEUM

1640 Rhode Island Avenue, N.W.

Officially the B'nai B'rith Klutznick National Jewish Museum, it is named for Philip and Ethel Klutznick. He was president of the B'nai B'rith. The B'nai B'rith International, started in 1843, is the world's largest and oldest Jewish service organization. The building houses its headquarters. The museum displays Jewish art and presents an entire range of Jewish culture and history. There's also the Jewish American Sports Hall of Fame honoring Mel Allen, "Red" Auerbach, Sandy Koufax, Abe Pollin, Shirley Povich, Mark Spitz, and others.

Philip Klutznick was born in Kansas City in 1907. He earned a law degree from Creighton University in 1929. He became a respected Chicago attorney and real estate developer. Klutznick served as federal housing commissioner under President Franklin Roosevelt, ambassador to the United Nations Economic and Social Council under President Kennedy, and as secretary of commerce under President Carter. In 1953, he was elected president of B'nai B'rith and re-elected in 1956. It was at that time that the cornerstone was laid for the building; headquarters staff moved in the following year. And as its name indicates, he was also largely responsible for much of the present museum. Mr. Klutznick is retired and living in the Chicago area.

DOLLEY MADISON HOUSE. (See also **Madison Building.**)
At Madison Place and H Street, N.W., on the east side of Lafayette Park

The house was built in 1818 by Richard Cutts, Dolley's brother-in-law, and inherited by James Madison. Dolly occupied it after the president's death in 1836, until her own in 1849.

Dolley was born in North Carolina. She did not spell her name "Dolly" as is done today, nor was it derived from Dorothea as some state. She married the future president in 1794 when he was a Congressman. Charming and tactful, she was the "unofficial first lady" during the presidency of Thomas Jefferson, a widower, then the unquestioned center of Washington society during her husband's presidency. She is best known for her flight from Washington in 1814 when the British invaded the city during the War of 1812. During the flight she saved many state papers and Gilbert Stuart's "official" portrait of George Washington.

PETERSEN HOUSE
516 Tenth Street, N.W. across from Ford's Theater

The house was built by William Petersen in 1849. He was a Swedish tailor. Because the house had more rooms than needed, the family kept roomers. Following Lincoln's assassination at Ford's Theater, Surgeon General Barnes advised against the rough ride over cobblestones back to the White House, so Lincoln was carried across the street to the Petersen house. William Clark, who worked for the quartermaster general, occupied the room into which Lincoln was taken. Lincoln died there the following morning - only six days after the end of Civil War military action - and the Petersen house ever since has been more commonly known as "The House Where Lincoln Died."

PHILLIPS COLLECTION
1600 21st Street, N.W.

Duncan Phillips was 11 when his family moved to Washington from Pittsburgh and built a brownstone home at 21st and Q Streets. He went on to major in literature at Yale and once act as managing editor of *Vanity Fair*. But his interest was mainly art. His family had been wealthy - his grandfather was the Laughlin of the Jones and Laughlin Steel Company - so money was not a problem as Phillips began his collecting. His emphasis was on living painters. The house had to be expanded a couple times. In 1921 Duncan and his artist wife, Marjorie, opened their home to the public. By 1930, the gallery was so popular that the couple had to move elsewhere. Duncan Phillips lived until 1966. The Phillips is recognized as the first museum of modern art in America and has been called "one of the world's great one-person museums."

RENWICK GALLERY. (See also **Corcoran Gallery of Art** and **The Smithsonian Building.**)
17th Street and Pennsylvania Avenue, N.W.

This gallery bears the name of the building designer, not the collector of the art within. James Renwick received his degree in engineering from Columbia when he was 17 and became successful at designing mansions and churches throughout New York and New England. In 1852 he was commissioned by W. W. Corcoran to design a building to hold Corcoran's art collection, and designed this building in French Renaissance/Second Empire style. Before it could be used as an art gallery, in 1862 the building was seized by the Union Army and used as quartermaster headquarters during the Civil War. In 1869 it was reclaimed by Corcoran as his gallery. After the Corcoran moved in 1897, the building was sold to the government, and from 1899 to 1964, it housed the U.S. Court of Claims. In the late 1960s, it was restored and is now operated as part of the Smithsonian Institution. It emphasizes American design and crafts.

In Washington James Renwick also designed the chapel in Oak Hill Cemetery, Trinity and St. Mary's Episcopal churches, and "The Castle," the main Smithsonian building. However, he's probably best known for designing St. Patrick's Cathedral in New York City. He died in 1895.

ARTHUR M. SACKLER GALLERY. (See also **Freer Gallery.**)
Independence Avenue at 10th Street, S.W.

Arthur M. Sackler was born in Brooklyn, NY, in 1913. He attended NYU and became a doctor. Dr. Sackler was a pioneer in biological psychiatry and with his collaborators issued over 140 research papers in the field. He was also the first to use ultrasound for medical diagnosis. While he practiced medicine, he bought stocks in pharmaceutical companies, and these formed the basis for his eventual fortune. In the 1940s he joined a medical advertising agency and after World War II he bought it, going into the medical publishing field. His publications were printed in 10 languages, and his organization had offices in 11 countries.

During the 1940s, Dr. Sackler began collecting a wide variety of art from many cultures. His holdings eventually numbered in the tens of thousands. He gave much of it away, including buildings to house it. There is a museum at Harvard, a gallery at Princeton, a wing of New York's Metropolitan Museum of Art, and museum in Beijing that bear his name. (There are also a Sackler science center at Clark University in Worcester, MA, and a Sackler School of Medicine in Tel Aviv.) The Smithsonian's Sackler Gallery contains 1,000 items from his Asian and Near Eastern art collection. When donated, it had a value of $75 million.

In the 1970s, with space at the Mall disappearing, Smithsonian secretary Dillon Ripley envisioned a museum underground where a shed and parking lot had been.

By 1980 the project was underway for a three-level underground development with entrance and garden off Independence Avenue. It was then that Ripley persuaded Dr. Sackler to make his donation. The collection nicely supplements the Freer collection next door. The two are even connected by a tunnel. The gallery opened in 1988. Dr. Sackler did not live to see it. He died in 1987.

LILLIAN AND ALBERT SMALL JEWISH MUSEUM
701 3rd Street, N.W.

The Adas Israel synagogue was established in 1869, and its building was completed at 6th and I Streets, N. W., in 1876. The congregation moved out in 1908, and the building saw other uses. By 1968, it was scheduled to be torn down for Metro subway construction, but got saved, moved to its present site, and renovated through efforts of the U.S. and the Jewish Historical Societies and a significant donation by Albert Small and his wife, Lillian.

Albert Small was born in Washington in 1902. He attended public school (McKinley Tech) as well as Hebrew School at Adas Israel, where his father was president. His father operated a hardware business close to 7th Street, Washington's principal street at the time and the heart of a German-Jewish neighborhood. Small married Lillian Friedlander of New York. He entered the real estate business in 1920, was a partner in the mortgage banking firm of Godden and Small, by the 1950s headed Albert Small Mortgage Co., and became one of the most successful developers in the city. He once said, there's "hardly a street in Washington that I didn't have something to do with." Small was a director of the Washington Board of Trade, Board of Realtors, and the Hebrew Congregation. Albert Small died in 1987. Lillian Small resides in Florida.

THE SMITHSONIAN BUILDING ("THE CASTLE"). (See also **Joseph Henry** and **Renwick Gallery**.)
1000 Jefferson Drive, S.W., on the Mall between 9th and 12th Streets

James Smithson was born James Macie in 1766. His father was Hugh Smithson, a Duke of Northumberland. His mother was a widow, Elizabeth Macie, a cousin of Hugh Smithson's wife and a descendent of Henry VII. When his mother died, he came into her considerable inheritance. Some time later he was permitted to take the name of Smithson. Thwarted by his illegitimacy to careers in politics, church, or military, he turned to science. In 1783 he entered Oxford and in 1786 obtained a master's degree. In 1787 he became a member of the Royal Society. He never married and devoted himself to chemical and mineralogical studies, published 27 papers, had the mineral smithsonite (a zinc silicate) named for him. He died in Genoa in 1829.

Smithson left his fortune to his nephew with the provision that if the nephew did not have a child - and he did not - the estate would come to Washington "to found, under the name of the Smithsonian Institution, an establishment for the increase and diffusion of knowledge." The estate was over $500,000; the entire budget of the U.S. was $34,000,000. There was much anti-British feeling (they had burned Washington 20 years earlier) about accepting the gift, but President Polk signed the Institution into law. Then there were arguments over what it ought to be. It was finally agreed to be a national museum for government collections, laboratory, art gallery, and library. Its director was to have the title of secretary, same as those in the president's cabinet. Joseph Henry was its first, Spencer Fullerton Baird his assistant. The first building erected was this Victorian "castle" designed by James Renwick, opened in 1855.

In 1904, Smithson's remains were moved to Washington (with Smithsonian regent Alexander Graham Bell providing an escort) where they now lie in a chapel in this original building.

SUMNER SCHOOL
17th and M Streets, N.W.

This former school was created in 1872 by architect Adolph Cluss. It has innovative hallways and arrangements, a tower, arched windows, and won a medal for school design at the Vienna World's Exposition of 1873. It was the first black high school in the country, and its offices housed headquarters of the Colored Public Schools of Washington and Georgetown. With desegregation, it fell into disuse. In 1986, the District's Board of Education had it restored, and it is a beautiful historic site, museum, and archive for Washington education history. It is named for abolitionist Charles Sumner.

Charles Sumner was born in Boston in 1811. He graduated from Harvard Law School in 1833, but found politics preferable to legal practice. In 1851 he got elected to the U.S. Senate. There, Sumner was an antislavery extremist, thought Lincoln too slow to act, believed President Andrew Johnson's reconstruction plans too moderate, and opposed all of President Grant's administration. In 1856, he made a speech criticizing South Carolina's Sen. Andrew Butler, and afterwards was beaten unconscious on the Senate floor by Rep. Preston Brooks, also of South Carolina. It took him almost three years to resume his seat regularly. He went on to serve as chairman of the Committee on Foreign Relations for over ten years and to hold his seat until his death in 1874.

WOODROW WILSON HOUSE (See **Woodrow Wilson Bridge**.)
2340 S Street, N.W.

This is where the Wilsons moved in 1921, after Woodrow Wilson's presidency. He died here in 1924. His widow continued to live in the house until her death in 1962. The house was then left to the National Trust for Historic Preservation, and is today a public museum.

NEIGHBORHOODS

Probably nothing reflects the history of Washington better than its neighborhoods. They are named for early settlers, estates, a couple of presidents, developers, even nearby schools. One is an Indian name, and another comes from a Masonic temple never built. And Georgetown - a name familiar to visitors as well as residents - comes not as one might guess from English King George or George Washington but from a totally different source. Here are the stories behind 25 neighborhood names.

ADAMS MORGAN. (See also **Temple Heights.**)
North of Florida Avenue, between Connecticut and 16th Street, N.W., and centered at 18th Street and Columbia Road

In the 1890s, the area was one of the first middle-class suburbs. By the 1950s, two elementary schools were in place, John Quincy Adams, attended by whites, and Thomas P. Morgan, attended by blacks. In 1955, Washington integrated its schools. In 1958, the two school principals, Florence Cornell and Bernice Brown, met to talk about making a better neighborhood. They organized a group to foster appreciation and respect of racial and cultural differences, and it was called the Adams Morgan Community Council. The council drew a boundary through four neighborhoods, forming the new one named after the two schools.

John Quincy Adams was born in what is now Quincy, MA, in 1767, the son of John and Abigail Adams. His father was the 2nd U. S. president. John Quincy Adams studied abroad, graduated from Harvard. In 1803, he was elected to the U. S. Senate. In 1817, President Monroe named him secretary of state, and he negotiated cession of Florida from Spain and helped formulate the Monroe Doctrine. In 1824, Adams was elected president. A Federalist, he tried to expand the executive, which proved unpopular, and he lost the following election to Andrew Jackson. Adams then entered the House of Representatives where he spent 17 years, serving with distinction. He opposed slavery and the Mexican War. He helped establish the Smithsonian Institution. He had a stroke in the House and died in the Speaker's Room in 1848.

Thomas P. Morgan was a member of the Washington city council, alderman, chief of the fire board, the city's first police chief, and from 1878 to 1883, a District commissioner.

Neighborhoods

ANACOSTIA. (See also **Cedar Hill, Randle Highlands,** and **St. Elizabeths Hospital.**)

The area of the District east of the Anacostia River

The area was originally inhabited by Nacostine Indians. The area was visited by a Jesuit priest, Father Andrew White, traveling with Leonard Calvert in 1634, who wrote to Rome of the natives whom he called *Anacostines*. The Latin *ia* ending is believed to have been added later by other traveling Jesuits.

Anacostia was incorporated into the City of Washington in 1854 as its first suburb. It was then called Uniontown and housed middle-class workers many of whom worked at the Navy Yard just across the river. It was a white-only community until 1877 when Frederick Douglass took up residence at Cedar Hill. So many other communities were named Uniontown after the Civil War that this Uniontown's name was formally changed to Anacostia in 1886. After World War II came school desegregation and suburban expansion. Whites began leaving Anacostia. In 1940, 20% of its population was black; by 1970, 96% was black.

BRENTWOOD. (See also **Gallaudet University.**)

The area north of Gallaudet University, across the Ivy City railroad yards and New York Avenue, to Rhode Island Avenue

Gallaudet University is situated on the original Kendall Green estate. It also covers part of a second estate, Brentwood, which was named for Washington's first mayor, Robert Brent, who gave the estate to his daughter as a wedding present. Robert Brent was born in Woodstock, VA, in 1764. He was appointed mayor - the only appointed mayor in District history - by President Jefferson and served ten consecutive terms. He helped finance the War of 1812, and resigned as mayor only to serve as paymaster-general of the army. Brent was also a District justice of the peace and judge of the orphan's court. He died in 1819.

BROOKLAND

East of Catholic University and north of Rhode Island Avenue, N.E.

In 1830, Col. Jehiel Brooks, a War of 1812 veteran, settled in the city as a gentleman farmer on an old country estate. The estate had been inherited by his wife, Anne Queen Brooks. In 1840 they built a mansion, which they called Bellair, on the estate. By 1873, the Baltimore & Ohio Railroad touched the area with a stop near the mansion called Brooks Station. In 1885, Catholic University of America formed its suburban campus just west of the estate. Col. Brooks died in 1886, and his heirs sold the property. A year later the new developers laid out streets, sold lots, and for the first time used the term Brookland. The old Brooks mansion still stands on Monroe Street, between 9th and 10th Streets, N.E. The Brookland Metro station is virtually in its back yard.

BURLEITH

Just north of Georgetown University, bounded by Reservoir Road and Whitehaven Park, and 35th and 39th Streets

The city L'Enfant planned took a while to fill in. Construction of homes in this area began only in 1923. The name comes from an estate of 1,000 acres bought by Henry Threlkeld in the 1700s. It ran from the Potomac River to what is now Georgetown University. Threlkeld's son John was mayor of Georgetown, and the newly formed city enveloped the estate. The 1920s development was designed to provide "Moderate Priced Homes up to Larger Home standards." The resulting little area has been called a village in the city, the Cinderella of Old Georgetown, and the poor man's Georgetown.

CHEVY CHASE. (See also **Francis Newlands.**)

Surrounding the north ends of Wisconsin and Connecticut Avenues, N.W.

Col. Joseph Belt was born in Anne Arundel County, MD, in 1680. He was a member of the Maryland House and led the Prince George's militia during the French and Indian War. About 1721 he patented over 500 acres under the name Cheivy Chase. One source says the name is a pun on the name of the prominent Chase family. Another says it refers to the Cheviot Hills bordering England and Scotland and Chevaux Chase, its restricted hunt area. There's an old ballad in which an English Percy decides to hunt inside Scottish Douglas lands. "Of fifteen hundred Englishmen, went home but fifty-three; the rest were slain in Chevie Chase, under the greenwood tree." As early as 1751, Belt's land was advertised as Chevy Chase. In the 1890s, the Chevy Chase Land Development Company was formed, and by 1909, sixteen houses had been built.

CLEVELAND PARK

Bordered approximately by Wisconsin Avenue on the west, Rock Creek Park east, Woodley Park south, and Van Ness north

In the late 1800s, wealthy Washingtonians preferred a townhouse in the city for business and week-night stays, and a home (or at least a cottage) in the country for weekends and family. President Glover Cleveland was such a person, and in 1886 bought a farm house on upper Wisconsin Avenue. It was originally called Oak View, but renamed Red Top after it was remodeled with Victorian towers and a painted red roof. It served as Cleveland's "summer White House." Neighbors named the area Cleveland Park to welcome the president. In the 1890s, when a bridge was built over Rock Creek Park and trolley cars arrived, other home builders followed. The house no longer stands.

Stephen Grover Cleveland was born in Caldwell, NJ, in 1837. The family moved to western New York where he grew up. After being admitted to the bar, Cleveland began political activity as a Democratic ward worker, became assistant district attorney, sheriff of Erie county, finally in 1881 mayor of Buffalo. He campaigned on a platform of honesty and reform and actually carried out his promises once in office. That led to his becoming governor, where he was vigorous in the belief that government should not interfere in the economic and social lives of people except to maintain law and order. That view impressed sufficient business interests so that the Democrats nominated him for president in 1884. Republican "Mugwumps" bolted their party for reformist Cleveland, and he won the election over James Blaine. Cleveland's election ended 24 straight years of Republican rule.

In 1886, Cleveland married Frances Folsom in the first White House wedding. As president, he enlarged civil service, vetoed Civil War pension raids on the Treasury, fought against tariffs. In 1888 he won the popular vote but lost the Electoral College and was defeated for re-election by Benjamin Harrison. Four years after that, he was re-elected over Harrison. He faced a depression brought about by low gold reserves and silver speculation, still refused to interfere in business matters. But Cleveland's presidency isn't measured so much on his actions as on his steadfast character: He restored honesty to government, planted in American minds the evil of protective tariffs, preserved the gold standard, and taught that conscience should always be the dominant force in the handling of foreign affairs. Nevertheless, in 1896 Democrats chose silverite William Jennings Bryan instead of renominating Cleveland. Cleveland retired in Princeton, NJ. He died there in 1908.

DEANWOOD. (See also **Benning Road.**)

East of Minnesota Avenue and just below the Northeast District Line

In 1833, one of the Benning heirs sold the Benning farm to Levi Sheriff, a Maryland merchant. Sheriff died in 1853 and left the farm to his three daughters. After the Civil War, they further divided the land and made it for sale. Sales went poorly. By 1880 only a handful of nonfarmers lived on what had been the Sheriff farm. One was Dr. Julian Dean, a physician. In 1888 he added an "e" to his name and initiated the name of Deanewood. The "e" was later dropped. But for Deanewood he built 20 houses. In 1895, Deane's real estate was sold at public auction. He moved away, only to return in 1904. He died in 1905 and is buried there in the family cemetery.

ECKINGTON

Just East of North Capitol Street, between New York Avenue on the south and Rhode Island Avenue on its north

Another large estate that was bought, subdivided, and made into a residential neighborhood after the Civil War was Eckington. It had been owned by Joseph Gales, Jr. Joseph Gales, Sr., had arrived in Philadelphia in 1792 and been the first reporter of the proceedings of Congress and official publisher for the general government. Young Gales became editor of the *National Intelligencer*, Washington's leading newspaper. The Gales hailed from Eckington, England.

The key to success of such neighborhoods was reliable streetcar service. The first electric streetcar was introduced in Washington in 1888 by the Eckington & Soldiers Home Railway Company, which ran through Eckington and essentially connected the Brookland area with downtown.

FOGGY BOTTOM

Between 17th and 25th Streets, south of K Street, N.W.

Much of the Mall was once creek, lowlands, and swamp. The western area near the Potomac was perhaps the worst - soupy, steamy bottom land that some sources say gave Foggy Bottom its name. The original neighborhood was started in 1756 by a German, Jacob Funk, and was known as Funkstown. He divided the land into lots and attracted other German immigrants, who called the area Hamburgh. As Washington was being planned, the area was called Camp Hill for a fort that was to stand on the area's lone hill. Later, the area was home to Washington's brewery and glass industries and to a giant gas plant. The smoke and fumes provided for what others consider source of the name.

GEORGETOWN

North from the Potomac past Reservoir Road, roughly bounded on the west by Foxhall Road and on the east by Rock Creek Park

Georgetown is not named for King George or for George Washington. In 1703, Ninian Beall obtained a patent to over 700 acres he called "Rock of Dumbarton" after a castle on the River Clyde near where he was born in Scotland. Soon thereafter George Gordon bought a patent in the area, calling it "Rock Creek Plantation." The area became a port with extensive shipping. At the same time, wars in Scotland caused many Scots to move to America, some of whom settled in the area and formed a community. In 1751, the Maryland Assembly authorized the Scotch community to form a town with the name of George. The commissioners of the new town were authorized to buy or condemn 60 acres of land belonging to George Gordon and to George Beall, Ninian's son. The two refused to sell, and the land was seized, but eventually the two apparently became reconciled, for the town was going to bear their names. The town was officially incorporated as George Town in 1789. The separate governments of George Town and Washington existed until 1871, when Congress abolished them, referring to the area as "Georgetown," its name ever since.

Neighborhoods

GLOVER PARK. (See **Glover-Archbold Park.**)
Centered about Calvert Street, west of Wisconsin Avenue, N.W.

This small residential area is named for Washington banker, Charles Glover.

KALORAMA HEIGHTS
Between Massachusetts and Connecticut Avenues, N.W., with Sheridan Circle on the south and Rock Creek Park on the north

In 1805, Joe Barlow purchased about 30 acres of land approximately one mile from the District boundary at the time, built a magnificent home on it, and gave it the Greek name of Kalorama, for "beautiful view." Barlow was a poet and political writer, friend of Thomas Jefferson and James Madison, a diplomat and consul, and a backer of steamboat inventor Robert Fulton. Barlow died in a snow storm in Poland while trying to negotiate a trade agreement with Napoleon Bonaparte while Napoleon was retreating from Moscow. The house continued under various owners until the government made definite plans to cut Massachusetts Avenue through the property. Then in 1889 the estate was sold to a development company that planned to build the neighborhood, Kalorama Heights, on the site. Many of the resulting mansions are now embassies and consulates and include "Embassy Row."

LAMOND-RIGGS
An area South of Riggs Road, along South Dakota Avenue, N.E.

An 1887 Hopkins map shows the Metropolitan Branch of the Baltimore & Ohio Railroad. Just before the Takoma Park Station is Lamonds Station, at the home plotted by Angus Lamond in 1847. According to his grandson, Angus Lamond hailed from Dunfermline, Scotland, same as Andrew Carnegie. He spent time in Ohio, then settled here, became known for his clay pots. The business later expanded into a brick factory. As residential growth spread to the suburbs, the area became Lamond Heights. In 1954, the Lamond Heights Citizens Association merged with the Riggs Citizens Association that represented the growing Riggs residential area to the east - hence the current combined name.

LANGDON. (See **LeDroit Park.**)
South of Rhode Island Avenue, between Montana and South Dakota Avenues, N.E. - just east of Brentwood

Andrew Langdon was a local land speculator and among those who helped develop LeDroit Park.

LEDROIT PARK

Just east of Howard University, immediately north of Florida and Rhode Island Avenues and between 2nd and 6th Streets, N.W.

In 1873 Howard University sold 40 acres of its land to Amzi L. Barber, a white faculty member at the school. He and his partners, including Andrew Langdon, developed the area as a landscaped park with 60 beautiful mini-chateau homes, complete with servant call bells and security watchmen. Many of the houses still exist today. The area was named after Andrew's father and Barber's father-in-law, LeDroit Langdon.

MOUNT PLEASANT

North of Columbia Road and Harvard Street, between Rock Creek Park on the west and 16th Street on the east

In 1861, a Civil War army contractor from Maine, Samuel Brown, bought the land and began to develop it. He named the area Mount Pleasant after William James Stone's original 1840 estate nearby. Stone was a Londoner with a successful Washington engraving business.

PETWORTH

East of 16th Street and north of Rock Creek Church Road, and centered around Grant and Sherman Circles, N.W.

In the 1600s Lord Holmeade received a grant from the king for a tract of land in the area. It was called Holmeade Manor. The land was later owned by a Capt. Balch. In 1803 it was purchased by Col. John Tayloe and was the first estate east of Georgia Avenue and north of Rock Creek Church Road. Tayloe named it Petworth for the English town of that name. In 1890 B. H. Warner purchased the area for a syndicate that subdivided it to fit the new city plan. Grant Circle was built in the early 1900s to be the center of Petworth. Most of its original homes were constructed between 1910 and 1920. The area was linked to downtown by a streetcar line and soon became one of the city's largest residential neighborhoods.

RANDLE HIGHLANDS. (See also **Randle Circle.**)

East of the Anacostia River, between Pennsylvania Avenue and Naylor Road, S.E.

Colonel Arthur E. Randle founded five towns and communities in the District and in Maryland, including Congress Heights and Randle Highlands.

Col. Randle was born in Artesia, MS, in 1859. He attended University of Pennsylvania and came to Washington in 1885 to start his rail and real estate businesses. In 1890 he bought John Jay Knox's farm and founded Congress

Heights. He formed the U.S. Realty Company, became its president, and started development of the area according to L'Enfant's original plan. He built a school, had streets paved, established a post office, built churches. He got rail rights across the Pennsylvania Avenue bridge and built an electric rail line into the area north of Congress Heights. He made his own home in what is now Randle Highlands. He was a benefactor for the reclamation of the Anacostia River and its flats, which were contaminated breeding places for disease. During World War I he offered his property to the government for use as a camp site. He bought Liberty bonds, then gave them back to the government or donated them to local churches. He funded a celebration at the Belasco Theatre on Christmas Day, 1919, in observance of the capture of Jerusalem from the Turks; the event brought a letter of praise from President Wilson. He continued his development activities well into the 1930s.

Col. Randle was a member of the New York Chamber of Commerce (the first Washingtonian to be elected to it) and the Washington Chamber of Commerce and Board of Trade. He was often asked to return to Mississippi to run for governor, but refused. The governor there appointed him colonel of cavalry, and he regularly used the title.

SHAW. (See also **Logan Circle.**)
Between North Capitol Street and 15th Street, and north of M Street, N.W.

Shaw Junior High School, built in 1977, is at R and 9th Street, N.W. It used to be - in 1902 - a few blocks away at Rhode Island Avenue and 7th Street. The neighborhood took its name from the junior high school.

The school was named for Colonel Robert G. Shaw, white commander of the first black unit to serve in the Civil War. The unit was the 54th Massachusetts Volunteers, a regiment. The regiment distinguished itself in the battle for Fort Wagner, during which Shaw was killed. There is a statue of Shaw, not in Washington, but in downtown Boston.

Shaw and the 54th are the subject of the 1989 motion picture, *Glory.*

In 1862, black soldiers received pay of $7 a month plus $3 for clothing; white soldiers received $13 a month plus $3.50. The Massachusetts 54th refused any pay at all for a year as a protest against this inequity. In 1863, Corporal John Gooding of the 54th wrote President Lincoln asking for equal pay. It took until mid-1864 for the attorney general to so rule, and members of the 54th then received all their back pay.

SHEPHERD PARK. (See also **Alexander Shepherd.**)
Around 16th Street and Georgia Avenue north of the Walter Reed Army Medical Center

Alexander Robey Shepherd was born in Washington in 1835. He worked as a clerk, carpenter, and plumber. After the Civil War, President Grant named Shepherd to the Board of Public Works. Shepherd was tall, powerful, and exuded confidence, so that Territorial Governor Henry Cooke and other officials soon referred to him as "Boss." Beginning in 1871, Shepherd began modernizing the District. It was certainly in disrepair: Population had doubled in less than ten years, the war had left it physically shabby, there were no trees (they had been used by Civil War troops for firewood), streets were dusty or muddy depending on the weather, canals were open and mosquito-infested. Shepherd ordered old buildings torn down, railroad tracks taken up, hills leveled, curbs laid, streets paved, street lamps erected and sidewalks lit, sewer and gas lines installed, the canals filled in, parks laid out, and 60,000 trees planted. There were some problems: Improvements seemed to favor wealthier neighborhoods, record-keeping was lax, and a lot of the money seemed to disappear into the pockets of Shepherd and his friends. By 1872, Shepherd had spent over $2 million and had incurred a debt over $9 million. By 1873, the District was broke, local banks failed, and the Panic of 1873 was precipitated, followed by a long depression. Embarrassed Governor Cooke resigned, and Grant made Shepherd governor. Shepherd continued his construction program, but also started levying taxes which angered even his supporters, and a congressional investigation followed. Congress heard all sorts of tales of wrongdoing so fired Shepherd, dissolved the territorial government, and named three commissioners instead.

In the Depression of 1873, Shepherd lost most of his money, sold his downtown home, and moved to Bleak House, his estate near the present Walter Reed Hospital. The house name came from the novel by Charles Dickens, which Shepherd was reading when construction on the house began. The middle-class residential area around the house took its name from its famous resident.

Whatever his faults, Washington owed Boss Shepherd its gratitude, for he changed the city from a squalid town into a beautiful city. By the 1876 celebration, Washington was hailed as a city reborn.

In 1880, Shepherd fled to Mexico. There he took over a defunct mine, discovered new veins of silver and gold, and became a millionaire. In 1887 he returned to Washington and was honored with a great celebration and a parade down Pennsylvania Avenue. He died in Mexico in 1902, but he is buried in Rock Creek Cemetery.

Neighborhoods

TAKOMA PARK

East of Georgia Avenue and north of Van Buren Street, N.W.

Benjamin Gilbert arrived in Washington in 1862 and began his career as a real estate developer in 1867. He thought the city would grow toward the north, especially along the planned Baltimore & Ohio Railroad's branch into Washington. The branch was completed in 1873, and in 1883, Gilbert bought 90 acres near the railroad, part in Maryland, part in the District. The acres were 300 to 400 cool feet above the Potomac and hot still-swampy Washington, and he named it Takoma, after an Indian word meaning "high up, near heaven." He specifically changed the "c" to a "k" to avoid confusion with Tacoma, WA, and later added the word "park" for promotion purposes. He continued to buy land, and by 1888, had over 1,000 acres. In 1892 he built the North Takoma Hotel, but in the Panic of 1893 and its subsequent depression, found himself over-extended, forced to manage the hotel himself, and his role as developer and promoter over.

TEMPLE HEIGHTS

Between Connecticut Avenue and 18th Street, north of Florida Avenue, N.W.

Where Connecticut Avenue rises up the hill beyond Florida Avenue was originally a prominence with a commanding view of the city. It was at this location that Thomas P. Morgan built his elaborate French Second Empire house in 1873. Nearby was an ancient oak said to have been site of a treaty between early whites and native Indians, and Morgan's home became known as Oak Lawn. In 1922, the Grand Lodge of Masons purchased the 10-acre parcel for a national Masonic memorial. The site then took the designation Temple Heights. The Masons' plan never materialized because of the Great Depression, but the name stuck. Today the Washington Hilton Hotel occupies most of the site, and what view is left is limited to hotel guests who have rooms on the highest floors.

TENLEYTOWN

Centered on Wisconsin Avenue and its intersections with River Road just north of Nebraska Avenue, N.W.

What is now Wisconsin Avenue originally followed an Indian trail up from the Potomac River at Georgetown northwest toward Frederick, MD, about 50 miles away. In 1755 the route was used by Gen. Edward Braddock trying to attack the French at Fort Duquesne. About 1779, Jacob Funk, who created Hamburg(h) in Georgetown, started River Road, pointing away from the Wisconsin Avenue route toward Great Falls and eventually Harper's Ferry, WV. In 1790 John Tennally opened a tavern at the intersection. He apparently died before 1800, but a sister lived in the area for many years. Right after 1800, the area became known as Tennallytown and the nearby portion of Wisconsin Avenue as

Tennallytown Road. In the 1850s a large Tennallytown Inn was an overnight stop for travelers. By 1890, streetcars came through, running all the way to Rockville, and by 1900, several families had made homes in the area. There have been various confused spellings of the original name, and in 1920 the post office for some reason decreed the spelling to be Tenleytown, which has been used ever since.

WOODLEY PARK. (See also **Francis Scott Key Bridge** and **Georgetown.**)
Just north of Rock Creek Park along Connecticut Avenue, N.W.

Woodley Park takes its name from the mansion, Woodley, originally built in the area and named by the uncle of Francis Scott Key, Philip Barton Key. The older Key was a Marylander, was in the English Service as a captain, and left when he refused to bear arms against the colonies. He became a lawyer in Georgetown, once served in the House of Representatives. It was his law business that he turned over to his young nephew in 1806. His mansion was built about 1803 on part of the original Rock of Dumbarton grant. In later years, it served as a summer residence for Presidents Van Buren, Tyler, and Buchanan. President Cleveland's Red Top was next door, so after he sold Red Top but was later elected to a second term, he too used Woodley. The building still stands, and is now part of the Maret School.

OTHER PLACES AND NAMES

There are, of course, places that don't fit nicely into the preceding categories and sections of this book yet have fascinating names. Many serve as memorials too. Here are over 35 frequently used Washington names - ranging from those of the best hotels to the sewage plant - and the stories behind their names.

BLAIR HOUSE

Pennsylvania Avenue between 17th Street, N.W., and Lafayette Park

Not all houses retain the name of the original owner - in this case Surgeon General Joseph Lovell, in 1810. Francis Preston Blair purchased the home in 1830 and added its third story. He had come to Washington at President Jackson's request to establish the Washington *Globe*. He willed the house to his son, Montgomery Blair, who was postmaster general under President Lincoln. Montgomery added the fourth floor attic parapet to the house. The house is used as temporary residence for the president (the Trumans lived in it from 1948 to 1952 while the White House was repaired) and for visiting dignitaries.

Among many historic events at Blair house was, at the start of the Civil War, a meeting in which Robert E. Lee was asked to take command of the Union forces. He said no.

BLUE PLAINS SEWAGE TREATMENT PLANT

At the tip of Southeast Washington between the Anacostia Freeway (I-295) and the Potomac River

No, this isn't a tourist attraction. However, the name is interesting. In 1663 a land patent was issued in the name of Beau Plaine (i.e., beautiful plain). In neighboring Prince George's County in 1714, there was a plantation called Bew or Beau Playnes. Those words were convoluted over time, so that the area has become known as Blue Plains instead.

CONGRESSIONAL CEMETERY

Main entrance at 18th and E Streets, S.E.

The cemetery was established in 1807 by Capitol Hill residents. About 1812 it was turned over to Christ Episcopal Church. In 1816 a committee selected part of the area for members of Congress, and the grounds have been known ever since as Congressional Cemetery. It is the oldest national cemetery. For years it was known as "the American Westminster Abbey." Before Arlington National Cemetery was established as the nation's leading burial ground, it was the most desirable interment place for Washington's major figures.

The cemetery features cenotaphs, tomb markers for people buried elsewhere. Still 80 of these square and pointed memorials do mark real graves. From 1839 to 1870, one was created for every member, but Congress finally ended the program. During the debate about it, Sen. Hoar of Massachusetts stated that being buried under one of these stubby monuments added a new terror to death.

The cemetery contains more than 150 senators and congressmen, plus military leaders, politicians, artists, and ordinary people:

Matthew Brady, the famous Civil War photographer
Elbridge Gerry, signer of the Declaration of Independence, vice president, and inspiration for the term *gerrymander*
J. Edgar Hoover, head of the FBI
Marion Kahlert, aged ten, in 1904 Washington's first motor vehicle victim
Benjamin Latrobe, architect of the Capitol, White House terraces, churches, and designer of the cemetery's cenotaphs
Robert Mills, designer of the Washington monument
Push-Ma-Ha-Ta, Choctaw chief who fought under Jackson, then died in Washington of diphtheria while negotiating a treaty between his people and the United States
John Philip Sousa, the march king
George Waterston, first librarian of Congress
21 Women killed in an explosion at Washington Arsenal, now Fort McNair

DEMONET BUILDING

Southeast Corner of Connecticut Avenue and M Street, N.W.

Built in 1880, this red brick building with its Florentine tower was once a fine Victorian townhouse. As the area changed from residential to commercial, it was home to a dentist. But from 1901 until 1928, it was the home of Jules Demonet Catering and Confectionery, and it has since carried the Demonet name. Today the building houses Burberry's.

Demonet's catering and confectionery business was founded in 1848 by John Charles Demonet. By 1884, it was one of the city's leaders. John's son Jules, who was said to have trained at Delmonico's in New York, moved the business to this building in 1901. He added the show windows. By 1911, he also added a factory to manufacture his confections - things like cakes, cookies, ladyfingers, tarts, and their special ingredients. The White House was included among Demonet's customers. In 1926, Jules died. In 1928, the business moved farther uptown. It continued through World War II despite sugar rationing, but soon afterwards the business ended.

Other Places and Names

EMANCIPATION MONUMENT. (See also **Abraham Lincoln.**)
In the midst of Lincoln Park, at East Capitol and 11th Streets, S.E.

The monument depicts Lincoln holding the Emancipation Proclamation, bidding a slave to rise to freedom. The sculpture was erected by the Western Sanitary Commission of St. Louis with funds collected from former slaves. It was dedicated in 1876, on the 11th anniversary of Lincoln's assassination. The slave depicted is Archer Alexander, last to be recaptured under the Fugitive Slave Act.

FLETCHER'S BOATHOUSE
Canal Road just north of its intersection with Reservoir Road, N.W.

Fletcher's Boathouse rents rowboats and canoes, furnishes fishing craft and tackle, and sells snacks at a beautiful spot next to the C&O Canal and along the Potomac River. It's been doing that for generations. The boathouse was founded by Capt. Joseph Fletcher when the canal was busy with barges carrying goods between Georgetown and Cumberland, MD. That was about 1850. It's been in the Fletcher family ever since and is currently run by fifth-generation Joe Fletcher.

FOLGER SHAKESPEARE LIBRARY
201 E. Capitol Street, behind the Library of Congress main building and between 2nd and 3rd Streets, S.E.

Henry Clay Folger became interested in the works of Shakespeare in 1879 while a student at Amherst College and Columbia University Law School. He became president of the Standard Oil Company of New York in 1911 and board chairman in 1923, but retired in 1928 to devote all his time to his library of Shakespeareana, which he then bequeathed to the American people, endowing it with his entire estate.

The Library houses the greatest collection of Shakespeare in the Western Hemisphere. Folger hoped to have a building of Elizabethan design, but zoning requirements didn't permit it. Paul Cret, the architect, produced a modern exterior that agreed with other Capitol Hill buildings, yet created an interior in Elizabethan style. The building includes an exhibition gallery, library, reading room, theater, and the crypt in which Folger is buried. Folger died in 1930, two weeks after the cornerstone was laid. The building was dedicated on April 23, 1932, on the 368th anniversary of Shakespeare's birth.

HAUPT GARDEN

Independence Avenue at 10th Street, S.W., at the entrance to the Smithsonian Castle, Sackler Gallery and Museum of African Art

This garden was a $3 million gift to the Smithsonian Institution from Enid Annenberg Haupt, journalist, horticulturist, and philanthropist. Mrs. Haupt was born in Chicago, grew up in Milwaukee, and educated at Mount Ida Seminary in Newton, MA. In 1936, she married stockbroker Ira Haupt. At an early age, she became interested in flowers, especially orchids, won prizes for them, even made a name for herself (as in Cymbidium Enid Haupt), and became well known for her indoor arrangements.

During World War II she worked briefly for the *Philadelphia Inquirer*. In 1954, her brother, publisher Walter Annenberg, asked her to take over his teen-age magazine, *Seventeen*. A year later, she became editor-in-chief, and for the next 15 years was responsible for turning the magazine into one for American youth - and a huge success. She published several books about and received numerous awards, many from other countries, for her work with youth.

In 1970, her brother had become ambassador in London, and she returned full time to horticulture. She made a major donation to the American Horticultural Society. She saved the conservatory that now bears her name at the New York Botanical Garden. She created a greenhouse playground complete with pool and birds for sick children at the New York University Medical Center. And her gift to the Smithsonian has brought about the Victorian garden that forms the entrance to the Sackler Gallery and Museum of African Art. This garden that carries her name is over four acres and includes trees, plants, flowers, all in 19th century landscaping, and with places to stop and rest.

HAY-ADAMS HOTEL

On 16th Street, N.W., across from Lafayette Park

This elegant hotel was built in 1927 by master Washington developer Harry Wardman. From 1885 until 1927, the site held twin homes of two longtime friends, quite separate facilities but with a single facade. One belonged to John Hay. A Brown graduate, Hay came to Washington as a secretary to President Lincoln, had a career as a diplomat, was ambassador to Great Britain, and served as secretary of state under Presidents William McKinley and Theodore Roosevelt. The other belonged to Henry Adams, grandson of President John Quincy Adams. A Harvard graduate, Adams moved to Washington in 1877 where he wrote many books including biographies of Albert Gallatin, John Randolph, and Henry Cabot Lodge. He is best known for his autobiography, *The Education of Henry Adams*. The hotel retained the names of these well-known and powerful former residents.

Other Places and Names

GARDINER GREEN HUBBARD MEMORIAL

M and 16th Streets, N.W.

This building used to house the Hubbard Memorial Library. It is now part of National Geographic Society offices and is no longer open to the public. However, it remains a memorial to the man whose name is engraved on it and who was the Society's founder and first president.

Gardiner Greene Hubbard was born in 1822 in Boston. He graduated from Dartmouth, then studied law at Harvard, and for 30 years practiced law in Boston and Washington. But he had many other interests: In 1857 he introduced gas lighting to Cambridge. In 1862, his daughter lost her hearing from scarlet fever, and he became interested in education of the deaf, leading the creation of Clarke School for the Deaf in Northampton. He served on the Massachusetts Board of Education for a dozen years. In 1871, Hubbard met Alexander Graham Bell who was introducing visible speech for the deaf in Boston, and became interested in his electrical work. When Bell invented the telephone in 1875, Hubbard directed its early business development and rented telephones instead of selling them, leading to the structure of the Bell System. In 1877, Hubbard's daughter and Bell were married.

In 1879 Hubbard moved to Washington. He became a trustee of George Washington University, joined Bell in founding *Science* magazine, and with Bell formed the American Association to Promote the Teaching of Speech to the Deaf, serving as vice-president. He became a regent of the Smithsonian Institution, and was president of what became the Washington Academy of Sciences. He founded the National Geographic Society in 1888 and became its president. Hubbard died in 1897. This building, built in 1902, served as the Society's first home.

KENILWORTH AQUATIC GARDENS

North of Benning Road, west of Kenilworth Avenue, N.E.

The gardens consist of acres of ponds planted with waterlilies and lotuses, as well as hundreds of other swamp and marsh plants and trees. There are lots of turtles, frogs, and fish. The gardens started in 1882 when a Civil War veteran and government clerk named W. B. Shaw brought some white waterlilies to his property from his native Maine. He acquired other species, his hobby changed into his vocation, and Kenilworth became a large commercial enterprise, supplying flowers to florists and tubers to other growers. In 1938, the gardens were purchased by and are maintained by the National Park Service.

ROBERT F. KENNEDY STADIUM. (See **Robert F. Kennedy.**)
East Capitol and 22nd Streets, N.E.

Robert Francis Kennedy was born in Brookline, MA, in 1925, the seventh of nine children. As a child and throughout his life he excelled at football and similar competitive sports. He attended Harvard, left in 1944 to serve in the Navy, and returned and graduated in 1948. He then obtained a law degree from the University of Virginia. He became an attorney in the department of justice, prosecuting graft and income-tax cases. He served as assistant counsel to the Senate subcommittee chaired by Sen. Joseph McCarthy, but soon resigned in protest against McCarthy's methods. Later he was chief counsel for the Senate Select Committee on Improper Activities in the Labor or Management Field where he brought to light the underworld connections of David Beck and James Hoffa, Teamsters presidents.

In 1960, Robert managed his brother John's presidential campaign. Successful, he was appointed attorney general. He vigorously promoted civil rights and was a chief advisor on domestic policy and political management. When Lyndon Johnson became president, Robert continued as attorney general, but in 1964 decided to run for the Senate from New York. He was easily elected.

In 1968, Kennedy entered Democratic presidential primaries. President Johnson announced that he would not run for re-election, and Kennedy faced Sen. Eugene McCarthy and the favored Vice President Hubert Humphrey. But Kennedy won five of the six primaries that he entered, including one in California. Celebrating with his supporters at the Ambassador Hotel in Los Angeles, Kennedy was shot by Sirhan Sirhan, an Arab immigrant, and died the following day.

The stadium was built in 1961 and was home to the Washington Senators baseball team until the team moved, to become first the Minnesota Twins and finally the Texas Rangers. It was also the home of the Washington Redskins football team until that team moved to Maryland in 1997. It is now home to Washington's professional soccer team, D.C. United. The stadium was originally called D.C. Stadium. It was renamed Robert F. Kennedy Stadium by Secretary of Interior Stewart Udall on the last day of Johnson's presidency.

KENNEDY-WARREN APARTMENTS
3133 Connecticut Avenue, N.W.

This example of 1920s grandeur and Art Deco architecture is not named for President Kennedy or Chief Justice Warren. The original owners were Edgar Kennedy and Monroe Warren, Sr., no relation to the better-known figures with the same last names. Edgar Kennedy, from Westmoreland County, VA, together with his brother William were major Washington apartment builders. So was Monroe, from Clayton, AL, and his brother R. Bates Warren. In 1930 they formed a partnership to build this great apartment complex, but in the Great Depression they lost it to the holder of the mortgage before construction was completed. Large as it is today, it is only a portion of the original design.

MARTIN LUTHER KING, JR., MEMORIAL LIBRARY

901 G Street, NW

The library opened in 1972, replacing the Carnegie one at Mt. Vernon Square as the main library of the District of Columbia.

Martin Luther King, Jr., was born in Atlanta in 1929. He graduated from Morehouse College at 19, obtained a B.D. from Crozer Theological Seminary, and was awarded his Ph.D. in 1955 at Boston University. It was at Crozer that he discovered Mahatma Gandhi, whose teachings influenced his life as a leader of passive resistance.

At BU he met and married Coretta Scott. In 1954 he became pastor of the Dexter Avenue Baptist Church in Montgomery, AL. They hadn't been there a year when Rosa Parks defied segregated seating on a city bus. With Ralph Abernathy and Edward Nixon, King organized a year-long boycott of city busing that made him known nationally as a civil rights leader. After Montgomery, he toured and lectured. In 1960 he became co-pastor with his father of Atlanta's Ebenezer Baptist Church and president of the Southern Christian Leadership Conference (SCLC). In 1963 King organized a march on Washington where he delivered his "I Have a Dream" speech at the Lincoln Memorial. In 1964, *Time* chose King as Man of the Year, the first black American so chosen. Also that year, he became the youngest recipient of the Nobel Peace Prize. Following a 1965 voter registration campaign in Selma, AL, King lead an anti segregation march from Selma to Montgomery.

King then shifted SCLC strategy to focus more on economic issues, to "bring the Negro into the mainstream of American life." He called for "reconstruction of the entire society, a revolution." In 1967 he assailed The Great Society, President Johnson's antipoverty program. The next year he planned another march on Washington, this time to demand a $12 billion "economic bill of rights." He stopped during the planning to assist striking sanitation workers in Memphis, and there he was assassinated. His death brought violent riots in black areas of cities throughout the country. James Earl Ray was convicted of his murder, but whether Ray acted alone or not has not been conclusively decided.

The library contains a mural in its lobby that depicts events in King's life, including the church in Atlanta, Gandhi, Rosa Parks, SCLC leaders, King receiving the Nobel Peace Prize, his delivering the address at the Lincoln Memorial, etc. The mural is by artist Don Miller.

LANGSTON GOLF COURSE
26th Street and Benning Road, N.E.

The District of Columbia has three golf courses: East Potomac, Rock Creek, and this one named for John Mercer Langston.

Langston was born in Louisa County, VA, in 1829. When his father died, he moved to Ohio, where he graduated from Oberlin College and studied law. When he was elected clerk of Brownhelm Township, he became the first black elected to public office in the United States. During the Civil War, Langston helped recruit the 54th and 55th Massachusetts and 5th Ohio regiments. He was appointed inspector-general of the Freeman's Bureau and so came to Washington. President Garfield recommended him so that he could practice law before the Supreme Court. In 1869, Langston became professor of law, then dean, and in 1872, vice president and acting president of Howard University. In 1877, President Hayes appointed him minister to Haiti. Langston returned to practice law in Petersburg, VA, and in 1890, was elected to Congress - the first (and only) black elected to Congress from Virginia. Langston died in 1897.

J. W. MARRIOTT HOTEL
14th Street and Pennsylvania Avenue, N.W.

J. Willard Marriott was born in 1900 in the Mormon settlement of Marriott, UT, named for his grandfather. The young Marriott grew up farming and tending flocks. He spent two obligatory years of Mormon missionary service, then attended Weber State College and the University of Utah, graduating in 1926. He obtained the Washington area franchise for A&W root beer (newly developed by two westerners named Allen and Wright) and opened Washington's first root beer stand, a nine-stool affair at 3128 14th Street. He went back to Utah to marry his college sweetheart, then returned to Washington. The business prospered, but something besides a cold soft drink was needed for the winter months. It was decided to add Southwestern/Mexican food. A friend inquired when they were going to open this "hot shop" with its hot spicy food, and the name Hot Shoppe was born. It was the first time anyone had sold Tex-Mex food this far north.

Marriott expanded: He hired carhops for his stands, creating the first drive-in restaurants in the Northeast. He sold lunch boxes to Eastern Air Lines, the first food served on many flights. His Hot Shoppes sold a double-decker hamburger called the Mighty Mo long before the Big Mac was invented. He opened a motor hotel, the Twin Bridges, on the Virginia side of the 14th Street Bridge, the first to combine drive-in lodging and drive-in dining into one business. Eventually the Hot Shoppes gave way to Roy Rogers Family Restaurants, Bob's Big Boy Coffee Shops, Farrell's Ice Cream Parlours, and others. When Marriott died, there were 143 Marriott hotels, 1,400 restaurants, airline kitchens, a catering service, theme parks, 140,000 employees, and $4 billion in annual sales.

J. W. Marriott was also president of the Washington Stake of the Church of Jesus Christ of Latter-day Saints. He served as a director of the Riggs National Bank, the Washington Board of Trade, and a host of other organizations. He was a lifelong Republican and was chairman of President Nixon's inaugural committees in 1969 and 1973. In 1970, he was a principal organizer of the Honor America Day celebration near the Washington Monument where Bob Hope was master of ceremonies, Rev. Billy Graham conducted a service, and 450,000 people attended. Marriott died in 1984. The hotel that bears his name had just opened that same year.

MAYFLOWER HOTEL
1127 Connecticut Avenue, N.W.

On the site of the Academy of the Visitation, real estate developer Allen E. Walker began in 1922 to build what he hoped would be the luxurious Hotel Walker. It began the largest private construction project in the city. Before it was completed in 1925, Walker had to sell out - partly because excavation bogged down in water, quicksand, and tree stumps - some eight feet across and later found to be 38,000 years old!

The new owners wanted an American symbol for the hotel and chose *The Mayflower*. It was just after the 300th anniversary celebration of landing of the pilgrims, and *The Mayflower* had been the ship that carried them from England. Guests for the 1925 opening were sent invitations mailed with pilgrim tercentenary postage stamps and given specially minted pilgrim half dollars. The ship was pictured in the hotel's first ads. The ship's crest was used on the china. Even today, there's a model and ship paintings in the lobby. The hotel has passed through many owners. Current owner is Renaissance Hotels International.

MCMILLAN RESERVOIR. (See also **Union Station.**)
Between Georgia Avenue and North Capitol Street, just south of Michigan Avenue, along 4th Street, N.W.

James McMillan was the U.S. senator from Michigan at the start of the 20th century. He was born in Hamilton, Ontario, Canada, in 1838, moved to nearby Detroit in 1855, and was active there in manufacturing, commercial ventures, transportation, and banking. He served in the Senate from 1889 to his death in 1902.

In 1901 McMillan chaired the Senate Committee on the District of Columbia. He commissioned a grand scheme for the further development of Washington based on the principles of Pierre L'Enfant's plan of 1791, which had in recent years been ignored. A plan was drawn by leading architects and artists covering the entire District of Columbia, to secure a harmonious building up of the city to replace the haphazard way it had grown previously. The plan had three unique features: It adhered pretty much to L'Enfant's original, it asked for no immediate appropriations, and it admitted it would take a time frame of 100 years to accomplish. The plan was not immediately popular - it was too grandiose - but, given modifications for changing technologies and implementation of one little piece at a time, it has proven surprisingly successful.

One immediate and specific part of the plan was to move the railways off the Mall into a single great terminal half a mile away. The Mall was to have trees and terraces. The plan created the axis to which the then-future Lincoln and Jefferson Memorials would be placed, and off of that, Memorial Bridge leading to the Lee Mansion in Arlington. It also called for construction of memorial parkways, reclamation in Anacostia, a system of parks, creation of the National Arboretum, and improvement of the city's sewer and water-supply systems.

It was this last that caused McMillan's name to be attached to the reservoir and filtration plant that supplies water to most of downtown Washington. Some of its facilities are underground, with seldom-seen beautiful vaulted ceilings.

OCTAGON HOUSE

New York Avenue and 18th Street, N.W.

If this house had eight sides, its name would be self-explanatory, and it wouldn't be included in this book. However, the house has six sides and a round entrance.

Octagon House was built between 1798 and 1800 for Col. John Tayloe. He had a 3,000-acre plantation at Mount Airy, VA, but wanted a city home. His friend, George Washington, convinced him to build in the new capital. Dr. William Thornton, architect for the Capitol building, designed the house. Once opened, it was a center of social activity.

In the War of 1812, when the British reached the city, the Tayloes had left for the summer, and the house was occupied by the French minister, flying the French flag. Although the British burned the White House, they weren't at war with the French, so spared Octagon House. After the war, when the Madisons returned to Washington, Octagon House served as the temporary White House. Thus the Treaty of Ghent that ended the war was signed in the house.

The Tayloe family continued to occupy the house until 1855. In 1902, the American Institute of Architects (AIA) purchased the house for its headquarters, then in 1972 constructed its new headquarters building behind Octagon House. Octagon House was then restored as close as possible to its original condition.

The origin of its name is unknown. It is known that the Tayloe's always called it Octagon House. One explanation is that the house has six sides yet eight angles. A more recent theory, discovered during the latest restoration, is that the base of the round entry hall may have been eight-sided. Indeed inside it one can clearly see eight doors, windows, and recesses evenly spaced.

OLD EBBITT GRILL. (See also the **Willard Hotel.**)
675 15th Street, N.W.

In 1856, a boardinghouse was built at 14th and F Streets by William E. Ebbitt and was known as the Ebbitt House. In 1864, one of the Willard brothers, who were operating the Willard Hotel across the street, purchased the property and converted it into a hotel. In 1872, Willard razed the original hotel and built a better one, retaining the Ebbitt House name. It lasted until 1926. One of its features was a popular and elaborate bar. The bar was saved and moved to a saloon-restaurant on F Street that called itself the Old Ebbitt Grill. In 1983, the bar and restaurant moved again, to this location and still using the Ebbitt name.

PIERCE MILL
In Rock Creek Park near the intersection of Beach Drive and Park Road, N.W.

About 1800, Pennsylvanian millwright Isaac Pierce acquired land from the middle of the District north to the Maryland state line. In 1821 he built a spring house on Rock Creek, and later added mill, house, and barns. In the mid-1800s, the business of grinding corn, wheat, and rye was brisk. In 1890, Congress created Rock Creek Park and condemned the mill, which stopped operating in 1897 when the main shaft broke. It then served as a teahouse. In the 1930s it was restored and opened to visitors as a typical 19th century flour mill.

POTOMAC RIVER
Forming the western border of Washington

The word is first found on a 1608 John Smith map of Virginia as "Patowmeck." It is a Powhatan Indian word, part of the Algonquian language, and means, "Where it is brought in" (i.e., traded). What did the Indians bring in? Reportedly soapstone, antimony, corn, and local furs.

RIGGS NATIONAL BANK. (See also **Corcoran Art Gallery** and **Glover-Archbold Park.**)
Pennsylvania Avenue and 15th Street, N.W.

In 1820, the Second Bank of the United States in Philadelphia bought land in Washington at this site for a Washington bank. It opened in 1824. But the bank was crushed in 1836 when President Andrew Jackson stopped putting federal money in it. The Second Bank ceased its Washington operations in 1838.

George Washington Riggs was born in 1813 to Elisha Riggs, a former Marylander and Georgetown resident who had made a successful career in banking in New York. The young Riggs graduated from Yale. In 1840, he went into partnership with W. W. Corcoran and formed the Corcoran and Riggs Bank in Washington. The Riggs family provided a supply of capital, the Corcorans provided connections with Jacksonian Democrats. In 1845 they bought the old Second Bank property. And by 1848 they had made a lot of money. In 1854, when Corcoran retired, the name became Riggs and Company. Riggs died in 1881, and the name was changed further in 1886 by new president Charles Glover to the Riggs National Bank. In 1898 Glover also demolished the standing bank and built the bank's current building.

RIPLEY CENTER
On the Mall between the Smithsonian's "Castle" and the Freer Gallery

The Ripley Center is part of the Smithsonian Institution. It includes an international gallery, offices, and classrooms, and is adjacent to the underground Sackler Gallery and Museum of African Art. It provides exhibitions, symposia, and performances, most of which grow out of Smithsonian research. It is named for the Institution's eighth secretary, Sidney Dillon Ripley.

Ripley was born in 1913 in Manhattan. When 10, he visited Paris. When 13, he traveled by foot in Tibet. He developed an interest in birds. He graduated from Yale, went on a collecting voyage in the South Pacific. Afterwards, he studied zoology at Harvard and received his Ph.D. World War II found Ripley in the Office of Strategic Services in Ceylon, training spies for Southeast Asia. After the war, he became assistant professor at Yale and assistant curator of the school's Peabody Museum of Natural History; he would later take over as its director. He published his first of several books, *Trail of the Money Bird.* In 1949, he married, and he and his wife traveled to India and Nepal. In 1964, Ripley was named to succeed Leonard Carmichael as secretary of the Smithsonian. He served for 20 years, until retiring at 70.

During Ripley's tenure the Museum of American History and the Air and Space Museum opened, the Hirschhorn was built, both Smithson's and the country's bicentennials were celebrated with major activities, a neighborhood museum was established in Anacostia, the Renwick Gallery was acquired, the Museum of African Art was merged into the Institution, *Smithsonian* magazine was begun and publishing expanded, and Smithsonian collections grew to 100 million items. Too, exhibits were made more friendly - the carousel in front of the Castle and the confectionery at the Museum of American History were Ripley ideas. In an extraordinary concept, Ripley converted the parking lot behind the Castle into a three-level underground complex containing the Sackler Gallery and Museum of African Art. Thus a major part of the complex bears his name.

Other Places and Names

RIPLEY GARDEN

On the Mall between the Smithsonian Arts and Industries Building and Hirshhorn Museum

This attractive garden is named for Mary Livingston Ripley, wife of S. Dillon Ripley, eighth secretary of the Smithsonian Institution. Mrs. Ripley was an accomplished entomologist, photographer, and horticulturist. Like her husband to be, she served with the Office of Strategic Services during World War II. She married Ripley in 1949. They went on many ornithological expeditions together around the world. In 1967 Mrs. Ripley founded the Smithsonian Women's Committee with which she was active for over 20 years. She was also a Smithsonian research associate. In 1984, she received the Joseph Henry medal for her contributions to the Institution. She died in 1996. Her love for horticulture inspired creation of the garden that has her name.

ST. ELIZABETHS HOSPITAL.

2700 Martin Luther King Avenue, S.E., in Anacostia

Until the 1850s, Washington treated its mental patients like criminals, locking them in jails. Stimulated by reformer Dorthea Dix's six-year campaign, the U.S. Government Asylum for the Insane opened in 1855. Patients could finally receive care and treatment. During the Civil War, wounded soldiers were treated at the hospital, and they used the name St. Elizabeth's Hospital so they wouldn't have to put "Insane Asylum" as a return address on their letters. The name came from the original land grant. The name continued to be used informally, and in 1916, Congress changed the name formally - leaving out the apostrophe.

Among its famous residents was poet Ezra Pound, accused of treason for opposing the U.S. entry into World War II and judged incompetent to stand trial. A current patient is John Hinckley, Jr., who shot President Reagan in 1981.

SHOREHAM HOTEL

2500 Calvert Street, N.W.

The original Shoreham Hotel was built at H and 15th Streets, N.W., in 1887 as a personal venture by Congressman Levi P. Morton of New York. He named it after his birthplace, Shoreham, VT. The building was torn down in 1929. Immediately thereafter, the current hotel was built and claimed the name. It is now operated by Omni International.

SIBLEY MEMORIAL HOSPITAL

5255 Loughboro Drive, N.W.

The establishment of deaconess (ministering) work in the Methodist Episcopal Church was authorized by the Church in 1888. In 1890 the Women's Home

Missionary Society of the Church founded a home and nurse training school for deaconesses and missionaries. The school was named in honor of Lucy Webb Hayes, wife of the 19th U.S. president, Rutherford B. Hayes.

William J. Sibley had come to Washington in 1837 and had become successful in the lumber trade. He was a trustee of the Foundry M. E. Church, director of the Bank of the Republic, and director of the Washington City Bible Society. He heard of the deaconess work and their need for additional training. In 1890 he donated funds for the construction of a hospital in memory of his wife, Dorothy Lounde Sibley. The hospital and training school were incorporated, and the hospital opened in 1895. William Sibley died in 1897. In 1925, the original building was replaced by a new one on North Capitol Street at Pierce and M Streets. By the 1960s an even larger facility was required and was opened at the current site in far northwest Washington in 1961. One of the main buildings at the present Sibley Hospital is called the Lucy Webb Hayes Building.

William Sibley is also credited with helping to originate our system of postage stamps. For the Post Office Department, he personally made the first distribution of stamps to Boston, New York, and Philadelphia.

TIDAL BASIN

Between Independence Avenue, S.W., and the front of the Jefferson Memorial

The nearby Washington Channel is where ships are docked. It was once feared that the tidal waters of the Potomac River would recede sufficiently that the ships would be stranded. So in 1897, the Army Corps of Engineers constructed the Tidal Basin as a reservoir from which more water could be put into the Channel if needed. It was apparently never needed for the Tidal Basin soon became a recreation area, at one time complete with a beach of imported sand where the Jefferson Memorial now stands.

TUDOR PLACE

1644 31st Street, N.W.

When Martha Custis married then-Col. George Washington, she was a widow with a son and daughter. The son had four children. One of these, Martha Parke Custis, married Thomas Peter and together they built a classic mansion in Georgetown. They called it Tudor Place. It was built in 1794 by William Thornton, who went on to design the U.S. Capitol. The house was in the Peter family for several generations until 1983, when it was opened as a museum. The house features a unique salon and circular patio with high columns looking out over a large lawn and garden. Otherwise, the design of the house is traditional Georgian. There apparently is no documented reason why it was ever called Tudor Place.

Other Places and Names

VOLTA BUREAU. (See also **Bell Multicultural Senior High School.**)
1537 35th Street, N.W., across from gates to Georgetown University

Alexander Graham Bell provided money made from his patent of the telephone for this building. And it was named after his receipt of France's Volta Award - $10,000 - much of which he used to establish the American Association for the Teaching of Speech to the Deaf. Today that organization has the building as its headquarters. Bell's Washington home and laboratory were behind the Bureau.

WARDMAN-PARK HOTEL
On Woodley Road, N.W., just west of Connecticut Avenue. The Wardman Tower is right at the intersection of the two streets.

Harry Wardman was born in Bradford, England, in 1872. Searching for adventure, he was a stowaway on a ship bound for Australia when he was discovered and put off at the next port - New York. He traveled to Philadelphia where he learned to be a carpenter and excelled at building staircases. He arrived in Washington in 1897 and got into the construction business. For 30 years, he was the city's principal builder. His biggest venture was the Wardman-Park Hotel, inspired by the Homestead resort in Virginia. In the 1920s, he became overextended financially, and the Great Depression bankrupted him. Still he came back to build middle-class housing in the 1930s. When he died in 1938, he had built the Hay-Adams and Ritz-Carlton hotels, 5,000 homes, 400 apartment buildings, and over 80,000 District residents were reportedly living in Wardman buildings.

The Wardman-Park became the Sheraton-Park in 1953. It was torn down and replaced by the Sheraton-Washington in 1980. At this writing, it is undergoing another refurbishment, this time under the Marriott flag. The original annex, which Wardman built in 1928 as a residential annex to the hotel and called the Eastern Wing, remains and is known as the Wardman Tower.

WATERGATE
At Virginia and New Hampshire Avenues, just north of the Kennedy Center

To current visitors, Watergate refers to the complex of condominiums, hotel, shops, and offices at this intersection. To those remembering the 1970s, it refers to the burglary of Democratic Party national headquarters in the office complex that led to the resignation of President Nixon. But the original Watergate concept was that of a ceremonial entrance to Washington from the Potomac by which visiting dignitaries could arrive by barge, much like from England's Royal Barge on the Thames. In 1932 steps were built just aside the Arlington Memorial Bridge. Dignitaries on barges never appeared, but the National Symphony Orchestra did, and outdoor concerts became popular. They continued until World War II and noise from low-flying airplanes brought them to an end.

"Boss" Shepherd made messy Washington into a grand city (and bankrupted it). His statue used to stand prominently, but now it's out by the Blue Plains sewage plant. (pp. 63 and 135)

Robert Latham Owen park is perhaps the smallest, yet features one of the city's largest fountains. (p. 18)

Inventor **John Ericsson's** *Monitor* was only one of his achievements. Here's part of his memorial, one of many overlooked by locals and tourists who notice only the major ones, like the Lincoln memorial in the background. (p. 109)

Jose Artigas, called the father of Uruguay. For years he was ignored by historians. Now he's hidden by tour buses. (p. 101)

This statue of **George Washington** is by Herbert Hazeltine, known for his animal figures. The horse has nothing to do with Washington. It's Man O' War! (p. 162)

Part of **Congressional Cemetery**, showing its cenotaphs. Matthew Brady, J. Edgar Hoover, and John Philip Sousa are among those buried there. (p. 66)

White house viewers in the background pay no attention to this adjacent fountain. It memorializes **Archibald Butt** and **Francis Millet**, victims of the sinking of the *Titanic*. (p. 37)

Probably the most famous theater in Washington - **Ford's Theater** c. 1945. (p. 148)

In 1870 Dunbar High School became the first black public high school in the country. It is named for Ohio poet **Paul Dunbar**. It's one of over a dozen similarly named local high schools that serve as memorials. (p. 95)

The city is home to beautiful parks. Here's one for secretary of war Gen. **John Rawlins**, whose statue is just barely visible at the far end. (p. 19)

Of the 275-plus names described in this book and memorialized in the city, only 26 are names of women. Here's **Frances Perkins**, for whom the Department of Labor building is named. (p. 34)

An experimental streetcar on the **Eckington** & Soldiers Home line about 1890. That railway was among the first to tie suburbs to downtown. (p. 58)

Albert Pike wrote the rituals for the Scottish Rite of Freemasonry, and the Masons donated his statue. Because of time in the military under Jefferson Davis, he's the only Confederate general with a statue in Washington. (p. 129)

President **Franklin Roosevelt** asked that his memorial be no larger than his desk. In 1965 this memorial was placed in front of the National Archives. His new 1997 memorial, however, is as large as three football fields. (p. 131)

Simon Bolivar, the George Washington of South America. Because of the sword, this is the tallest equestrian statue in the country. (p. 103)

Octagon House once served as home for the Madisons. Eight sides? No, it has only six, plus the round front portico. (p. 75)

WILLARD HOTEL

Pennsylvania Avenue at 14th Street, N.W.

In 1816, John Tayloe, one of Washington's first landowners, acquired this corner and built six two-story buildings on it. In 1818, the corner one was leased as a hotel. A hotel has been on the corner ever since. By 1822, the property had been inherited by Benjamin Tayloe, and for years it was managed unprofitably. In 1847, Tayloe learned from his fiancée of an enterprising steamboat steward and hired him to run the hotel. The steward was Henry Willard.

Henry Augustus Willard was born in Westminster, VT, in 1822. He worked as a clerk. A brother, Joseph, clerked at a hotel in Troy, NY. Both were hired by the New York & Troy Hudson River Steamboat Line. Henry was steward and gained a reputation for excellent service. Phoebe Warren of Troy traveled on one of the boats served by Henry, and thus it was she recommended him to her fiancé.

Once in Washington at Tayloe's City Hotel, Henry asked his older brother, Edwin, to help. They worked hard to provide the best food and service. A third brother, Caleb, arrived. Joseph, who'd become second captain on the steamboat (and unsuccessfully tried his luck in the California gold rush) also joined the hotel. By the 1850s, the hotel was a success and the Willard name added.

Edwin left to run other businesses, including the National Theater. Caleb obtained the Ebbitt House across the street and became a highly regarded Washington businessman. Joseph served in the Civil War and became a major. Henry was appointed to the Board of Public Works by President Grant and helped Alexander Shepherd during his city improvement program, served on the boards of local businesses, and built the adjoining Occidental Hotel. Willards eventually purchased the property and adjoining properties. Willard heirs were involved in ownership through World War II. At war's end, the family sold the hotel.

In 1962 the forerunner of the Pennsylvania Avenue Development Corporation (PADC) was formed. It planned a national square to be built by razing the entire block in which the Willard stood. Unsure of its future, the hotel closed in 1968. An argument over whether to destroy the Willard per the plan or renovate it as envisioned by preservationists continued until 1978. That year the government, via the PADC, took over the hotel. A team of Stuart Golding, Oliver T. Carr Company, and Inter-Continental Hotels (the current operator) obtained financing and artisans, and the hotel was painstakingly renovated to what it was in 1901. Included was the adjacent Occidental Hotel and Restaurant. The present hotel opened in 1986.

Tales about this old hotel abound: Franklin Pierce was the first of many presidents to stay there. Henry Clay introduced the mint julep. P. T. Barnum brought Jenny Lind, the Swedish Nightingale. Nathaniel Hawthorne, Walt

Whitman, and Julia Howe wrote there, she penning *The Battle Hymn of the Republic.* So many people crowded the lobby trying to get jobs from President Grant that he coined the term "lobbyist." The city's first soda fountain was in the hotel's drugstore. One time, the National Geographic Society honored Cmd. Robert Perry for discovering the North Pole and Capt. Roald Amundsen for discovering the South Pole at the same dinner. Introduced at dinner that night was the jujube. After her performance at the National Theater, Ruth Gordon walked to the hotel with the cast of *The Three Little Sisters* to marry Garson Kanin. And the night before the hotel reopened in 1986, the National Theater, doing *Legends*, had a bomb scare. Stars Mary Martin and Carol Channing asked for safety and thus got a day-early preview of the renovated Willard.

WILSON BUILDING

Pennsylvania Avenue and 14th Street, N.W.

For years this 1908 building was known as the District Building, and it housed the city council and related offices. In 1994, it was renamed the Wilson Building in honor of John Wilson, long-time District councilman.

Wilson was raised on Maryland's Eastern Shore by adoptive parents. He spent several years as a lobbyist with the National Sharecroppers Fund. He got started in politics as an organizer for the Student Non-Violence Coordinating Committee. In 1974, in the first "home rule" election, Wilson was elected to the District city council, where he would serve for 18 years. From 1991 to 1993, he served as its chairman. He was the council's self-appointed curmudgeon, fiscal conservative, a pessimist about the District's finances. (His financial worries later proved justified.) At the same time, he had major concerns for the dispossessed. He shocked the city when he committed suicide in 1993.

POINTS

Most folks don't think of it this way, but Washington is a river town. As such, it has many small points of land jutting out into either the Potomac or Anacostia rivers. Here are three whose names have interesting origins and are still in common use.

BUZZARD POINT. (See **Greenleaf Point.**)
Where 1st Street ends at the Anacostia River. Also, the area between Fort McNair and South Capitol Street, south of P Street, S.W.

The marshy area where the Potomac and Anacostia rivers meet was part of land owned by James Thompson in 1656. In 1673, famous map maker Augustine Herrman made the first map of the area, and on it the area was called Turkey Buzzard Point.

The Saint James Creek flowed through the middle of Turkey Buzzard Point. A map dated 1792 shows Tiber Creek joined to Saint James Creek by a canal. The canal and creek separated this southwest part of the city into Buzzard and Greenleaf's Points.

The land east of the creek, known as Buzzard Point, belonged to Daniel Carroll, who plotted a town he hoped would develop there. It didn't. Carroll died bankrupt in 1849. The only significant inhabitant of Buzzard Point today is the Buzzard Point Power Plant.

GREENLEAF POINT. (See also **Buzzard Point.**)
Where 2nd and Canal Streets, S.W., meet the Anacostia River. Also the area just north of Fort McNair

James Greenleaf was born in Boston in 1765. He married a wealthy and titled lady from Holland and became a merchant near Allentown, PA. When he heard about the proposed federal city, he obtained backing of Amsterdam bankers and bought 3,000 lots. With a partner, in 1793, he bought 6,000 more. He sold and donated some of the land for L'Enfant's proposed military district that eventually became Fort McNair.

As the city began, Saint James Creek separated its southwest extremity into Buzzard and Greenleaf's Points. Greenleaf's land was west of the creek and, adjacent to a military reservation, not very attractive. Yet some fine homes were built in the area, especially around 4th and N Streets. But the city grew to the north. And Saint James Creek had been joined to Tiber Creek by a canal. Sewage from the city that didn't flow into Tiber Creek and the Potomac ran into the canal and Saint James Creek. The subdivision simply smelled bad. The area was taken over by squatters and became the scene of violence and crime. Greenleaf spent most of his time in Allentown, got appointed U.S. Consul in Amsterdam from 1793 to 1802, and in 1796, sold his Washington lands. In 1831 he built a house at 1st and C Streets, N.E., and lived there while his wife remained in Allentown. He died in 1843 and is buried in Congressional Cemetery.

What's left of the creek is now known as James Creek. Greenleaf succeeded in getting the "Saint" dropped, making the creek appear to bear his first name. Today, still unattractive Greenleaf Point is scene of Coast Guard Headquarters and the James Creek Marina.

HAINS POINT

In East Potomac Park, where the Potomac and Anacostia Rivers meet

Hains Point is named for the man who created it, Maj. Gen. Peter Conover Hains. Hains was born in 1840 in Philadelphia, entered West Point in 1857, graduated in 1861. He commanded a battery of field artillery at Bull Run and fired the first gun as a signal to start the battle. He participated in thirty Civil War engagements. In 1862, he transferred to the Engineers and in two years became chief engineer of the Department of the Gulf. Hains served in the Spanish-American War and during World War I. He is one of only two officers to serve on active duty in all three wars and was the oldest in World War I.

As an Engineer officer, Hains engaged in works of river and harbor fortifications in many parts of the world and served on numerous boards and commissions. One of his most important projects was the betterment of the river channel to Washington. The Potomac had silted so much that large ships could no longer reach the city. About 300 acres - flats - had accumulated. In 1882 Congress appropriated funds for a dredging project. Hains was put in charge. His biggest problem was disposing of the tons of dredged material. He solved the problem by dredging both the Potomac and the Washington Channel, piling the material between the two and building a stone sea wall to retain it, thus building what is now East Potomac Park.

In 1905 Hains was on the Nicaragua Canal Commission, arguing against the sea-level canal project there and paving the way instead for a canal with locks through Panama. Hains died in 1921. He is buried in Arlington National Cemetery.

SCHOOLS AND UNIVERSITIES

Throughout America, school names serve as memorials for presidents, statesmen and politicians, writers and artists, local celebrities and heroes, teachers and school administrators, and still others. The same is true in Washington. Describing names of all the city's schools is beyond the scope of this book, but here's a look at its university and high school names.

Washington is home to seven major universities: American, Catholic, District of Columbia, Gallaudet, Georgetown, George Washington, and Howard. It operates 15 high schools. Included are Anacostia, Banneker, Douglass, Theodore Roosevelt, and Woodrow Wilson, names of which are explained in other sections of this book. In this section, Gallaudet, Howard, and 11 high school names are described. If the numbers don't add up it's because McKinley High School closed during editing of this book. I left it here, however, partly because it was already written and partly because it was that president's lone memorial in the city.

BALLOU SENIOR HIGH SCHOOL
4th and Trenton Streets, S.E.

Frank Washington Ballou was born in Fort Jackson, NY, in 1880. In 1902, he graduated from New York State Normal, went on to get his B.S. degree from Columbia, M.A. from Cincinnati, and Ph.D. from Harvard. He started teaching in a one-room school in New York state, eventually became Boston's assistant superintendent of schools. He arrived in Washington just after World War I, and spent 23 years as superintendent of District schools. He not only increased standards, but saw over 60 schools built during his tenure. He died in 1955.

BELL MULTICULTURAL HIGH SCHOOL. (See also **Volta Bureau.**)
Hiatt Place and Park Road, N.W.

This school is named for Alexander Graham Bell, the Scottish-American scientist who invented the telephone.

Bell was born in Edinburgh in 1847. Educated at home, by 16 he was teaching others. By 1867 he was assisting his father, Alexander Melville Bell, who originated the phonetic "visible speech" system for teaching the deaf. But Bell became ill with tuberculosis - his two brothers both died of it - and his father moved the family to Canada where Bell regained his health. In 1871, he began teaching "visible speech" in Boston and became professor of vocal physiology at Boston University. One of his pupils was Mabel Hubbard, they fell in love, and she inspired his work on several inventions. In 1876 he received the patent for his telephone. A year later they were married.

In 1880, Bell patented a photophone that enabled transmitting speech on a beam of light, the first wireless transmission of speech and a precursor to the photoelectric cell and transistor. France awarded him its Volta Award, and Bell used the money to establish the Volta Laboratory in Washington. There he produced and patented wax recording cylinders, improving Thomas Edison's metal phonograph cylinders.

In 1882, Bell became an American citizen and Washington resident, although in 1885, he established a family home at Cape Breton Island in Nova Scotia. Other inventions followed ranging from new sheep breeds and home air-cooling to ones anticipating flying. At one time future airplane developer Glenn Curtis was a Bell assistant. In 1888 Bell was a founding member of the National Geographic Society. He served as it president from 1898 to 1903. As a regent of the Smithsonian Institution, he accompanied James Smithson's remains when they were moved from Italy to Washington. Bell died in Nova Scotia in 1922.

CARDOZO SENIOR HIGH SCHOOL

13th and Clifton Streets, N.W.

Francis Cardozo was born in 1836. He was educated as a free man in Charleston, SC, and wanted to become a minister. He studied at the universities of Glasgow and Edinburgh in Scotland and at the London Theological Seminary. He became minister in New Haven, CT.

In 1865, Cardozo returned to South Carolina to establish schools for educating former slaves. From 1868 to 1871, he was South Carolina's secretary of state, the first black person to hold an administrative office in that state. Later in the 1870s, he served as the state's secretary of the treasury. In the District, from 1871 to 1872, Cardozo taught at Howard University. From 1891 to 1896, he was principal of Dunbar High School. Cardozo died in 1903. This high school was established in his honor in 1928.

COOLIDGE SENIOR HIGH SCHOOL

5th and Tuckerman Streets, N.W.

This school is named for the 30th president of the United States, John Calvin Coolidge. He was born in Plymouth Notch, VT, in 1872. He dropped John from his name at an early age. He was brought up believing in caution, dependability, thrift, and unpretentiousness - and that man had a God-given duty to public service. Coolidge attended Amherst College in Massachusetts, graduating *cum laude* in 1895. He then became a lawyer and active in politics. In 1905 he married Grace Anna Goodhue, who would become one of the most charming and politically wise of first ladies. By 1918, Coolidge had served as mayor of Northampton, MA, state senator, lieutenant governor, and governor. As state senate president, he showed his simple ways when he advised the senators, "Do the day's work" and "Be brief." When he was governor, the Boston police had grievances over pay and went on strike. Coolidge took command of the national guard to restore order and told union leader Samuel Gompers, "There is no right to strike against the public safety by anybody, anywhere, any time." He received national acclaim, and at the 1920 Republican convention, secured the vice-presidential nomination under Warren Harding.

Vice President Coolidge presided over the Senate without enthusiasm, contributed little at cabinet meetings, and did not develop as a national figure. All that changed when President Harding died in 1923 and Coolidge found himself president, just as the scandals of the Harding administration were coming to light. Thanks to his plain-spoken nature and integrity, he restored confidence in the office and the following year was elected for a full term over Democrat John Davis and Progressive Robert La Follette. It was not a completely happy year, however, as son Calvin, Jr., 16, died from blood poisoning after hurting his toe on a rusty nail while playing his brother on the White House tennis court.

As president, Coolidge substantially reduced the budget, cut taxes, helped the growth of military aviation, regulated broadcasting, developed flood control, and encouraged cooperative solutions to farm problems (rather than proposed dumping of surpluses on the world market). In 1927, Coolidge refused to run for re-election, making his famous curt statement, "I do not choose to run for president in 1928." He retired to Northampton, did not take a further role in politics. He died unexpectedly of a blood clot in 1933. He is buried in Plymouth Notch.

DUNBAR SENIOR HIGH SCHOOL

1st and N Streets, N.W.

When Dunbar High School was established in 1870, it was the first black public high school in the U.S. It drew its students from the black elite of Washington and Georgetown, and it graduated the largest number of black graduates to continue on to college. It was integrated in 1955. It has changed location (and name) several times.

The school is named for Paul Laurence Dunbar, America's first black poet. Dunbar was born in Dayton, OH, in 1872. He had visions of being a lawyer, but unable to afford law school, he took a job as an elevator operator. In 1893 he published his first volume of poetry, *Oak and Ivy*, and sold copies to passengers in the elevator. He gained national prominence when his second work, *Majors and Minors* (1895), was reviewed by *Harper's Weekly*. His third book, *Lyrics of Lowly Life* (1896), took the best parts of the first two, and became quite popular among both blacks and whites. He produced other volumes, and his *Complete Poems* was published in 1913.

Dunbar not only wrote poetry but also short stories and novels. His verses used Southern Negro dialect. Not wanting to be characterized as black only, he wrote his novels with primarily white characters. Dunbar died in Dayton in 1906.

DUKE ELLINGTON SCHOOL OF THE ARTS

35th and R Streets, N.W.

In 1890, Western High School was established as a counterpart to Eastern High School. Following Duke Ellington's death in 1974, the school was given his name to keep his spirit alive. Today it educates the most artistically gifted of the District's young students.

Edward Kennedy Ellington was born in Washington in 1899. As a teenager growing up on respectable T Street, he was known for his impeccable dress, articulate manner, and social elegance - thus his nickname "Duke." He loved baseball (and sold ice cream at Griffith Stadium), won but turned down an art scholarship to Pratt Institute in New York, studied piano instead, played with jazz bands around town. He was married (briefly) at 20 and had one son, Mercer.

By 1920, Ellington's Washingtonians was one of the city's most popular bands. In 1923, he left for New York, where he organized a "big band" (initially 10 pieces) that he would lead for the next fifty years. It revolutionized jazz: complex arrangements required both improvisation and reading of scores, and the scores themselves got more complicated, sometimes as classical compositions. Great musicians (e.g., Billy Strayhorn, Harry Carney, Barney Bigard, Johnny Hodges, Cootie Williams) joined the band, and music was written specially for their talents. As Mercer grew up, he became business manager for the band.

In 1959, Ellington was given the NAACP's Spingarn Medal. He made trips for the State Department and in 1970 during the Cold War toured Russia; he also went to Latin America, Japan, and Australia. He received the Presidential Medal of Freedom. In 1971, he was elected to the Songwriters Hall of Fame. In 1973, he was the first jazz musician to receive an honorary degree from Columbia University.

Among his best known pieces are *Black and Tan Fantasy, Mood Indigo, Sophisticated Lady, Bojangles,* and *Don't Get Around Much Anymore.* With Billy Strayhorn, he wrote *Take the A Train* and *Perdido.* In 1943, he wrote a tone poem on American black history, *Black, Brown and Beige.* In 1947, he wrote *Liberian Suite* for that country's centennial. In 1950, he was commissioned by Arturo Toscanini to write *Harlem* for the NBC Symphony Orchestra. In 1963, he composed *My People* for the 100th anniversary of the Emancipation Proclamation. In 1970 he wrote a ballet, *The River.* Several motion pictures feature his scores, most notably *Anatomy of a Murder.* Most sources credit him with over 1,000 compositions, some with as many as 6,000.

GALLAUDET UNIVERSITY

Florida Avenue and 8th Street, N.E.

Amos Kendall was postmaster general for Andrew Jackson. He became wealthy as business manager for Samuel F. B. Morse. In 1856, he formed a school on his farm, Kendall Green, to tutor five deaf mute children. Next year the school became the Columbia School Institute for the Deaf, Dumb, and Blind.

Thomas Hopkins Gallaudet was born in Philadelphia in 1787, grew up in Hartford, graduated from Yale and the Andover Theological Seminary. Through an acquaintance who was deaf, he became interested in the education of the deaf. In 1815 he studied in Paris at one of the earliest schools for the deaf, and two years later, returned to Hartford. There he set up the first free public school for the deaf in the United States. He died in 1851.

Thomas Gallaudet had two sons. One became an Episcopalian minister who served the deaf in New York City. The other, Edward Miner Gallaudet, graduated from Trinity College in Hartford and taught at his father's school. When he was 20, he joined the school at Kendall Green as its first teacher and became its president, a position he held for 53 years. In 1864 the school was renamed the National Deaf Mute College and authorized to grant college degrees. In 1894, it was renamed Gallaudet College after Thomas Hopkins Gallaudet, the father.

Gallaudet College was awarded university status by Congress in 1986. It is largely supported through appropriations from Congress. The president serves as patron and signs its diplomas.

HOWARD UNIVERSITY

2400 6th Street, N.W., about a block east of 2400 Georgia Avenue.

Howard University was created in 1867 by President Andrew Johnson. During its early years, it was primarily a school for ministers. It is now the nation's most important and diverse school for black Americans. It encompasses over 30 buildings on 75 acres. Its alumni include Thurgood Marshall, associate justice of the Supreme Court; Andrew Young, mayor of Atlanta and U.S. ambassador to the United Nations; and Ralph Bunche, first black American to win the Nobel Peace Prize.

The university is named after Oliver Otis Howard. Howard was born in Leeds, ME, in 1930, educated at Bowdoin and West Point, served as an ordnance officer. In 1861 he became colonel of a Maine militia regiment and, with increasing responsibilities, saw action at Manassas, Fair Oaks, South Mountain, Antietam, Fredericksburg, Chancellorsville, and Gettysburg. At Fair Oaks he lost his right arm. In 1864 he was part of Gen. Sherman's Georgia campaign and won command of the Army of the Tennessee. After the Civil War, he was appointed by President Andrew Johnson as commissioner of the Bureau of Refugees, Freedmen, and Abandoned Lands, known informally as the Freedmen's Bureau. To that job he brought enthusiasm and humanitarianism but poor administration, and corruption was rampant. During this time, though, several schools were established, including Howard University. From 1869 to 1873 he served as president of the university.

Howard was then sent by President Grant to Arizona to talk Cochise and his Chiricahua Apaches into accepting life on a reservation. In 1877 he fought the war with the Nez Perce under Chief Joseph. He became superintendent of West Point. After other appointments, he retired in 1894, having achieved rank of major general. He was awarded the Congressional Medal of Honor for his earlier action at Fair Oaks. He spent his remaining years in Burlington, VT, writing books of military history and his autobiography. He died in 1909.

MCKINLEY SENIOR HIGH SCHOOL

T and 2nd Streets, N.E.

The school was named for the 25th president of the United States, William McKinley. McKinley was born in Niles, OH, in 1843, the seventh of nine children. He enlisted in the Civil War, saw action, became a brevet major. He was admitted to the Ohio bar, practiced in Canton and participated in politics by working for future president Rutherford Hayes, who had been his commanding officer. In 1871, he married Ida Saxton of a wealthy Canton family. They had two daughters. Both died young. Ida never fully recovered, and he never let his subsequent formal duties interfere with his concern for her. His entire political life was marked by skill in handling problems with sympathy and moderation.

Between 1877 and 1891, except for one two-year term, McKinley served in the House of Representatives. He was defeated for re-election because of gerrymandering, but was then twice elected governor of Ohio. In 1896, he sought and won the Republican nomination for president, and defeated Democrat William Jennings Bryan after a campaign that stressed sound money (the gold standard) and protective tariffs.

McKinley's administration was one of prosperity and expansion. Foreign policy dominated. He tried to persuade Spain to withdraw from Cuba, but after the battleship *Maine* was destroyed in Havana harbor, reluctantly intervened. The Spanish-American War was brief and decisive. By 1898, the U.S. had occupied Cuba and Puerto Rico and defeated the Spanish fleet in the Philippines. McKinley secured support for the Treaty of Paris which freed Cuba; the U.S. kept the other possessions plus Guam. He appointed Gen. Leonard Wood and William Howard Taft to guide Cuba and the Philippines toward self-government. No sooner was the Spanish problem over than troops had to be sent toward China to aid Westerners during the Boxer Rebellion led by Chinese who resented

Western influence and killed hundreds. And by peaceful means, the Hawaiian and some Samoan Islands were added to U.S. territory.

Vice president Garret Hobart died in 1899 and in 1900 was replaced on the ticket by Theodore Roosevelt. In that election, McKinley got the largest majority ever, up to that time. McKinley's second term started in March 1901, and in September, he attended the Pan-American Exposition in Buffalo. Anarchist Leon Czolgosz shot him, and McKinley died eight days later. He is buried in Canton.

PHELPS SENIOR HIGH SCHOOL AND CAREER DEVELOPMENT CENTER

24th Street and Benning Road, N.E.

This school is named for soldier, commissioner, and diplomat Seth Ledyard Phelps. Phelps was born in Parkham, OH, in 1824. He was educated at the U.S. Naval Academy and saw naval service in China, Japan, and Mexico. He also served during the Mexican and Civil wars. After the Civil War, he formed his own Pacific Mail Steamship Line. President Grant appointed him a commissioner of the District of Columbia, and he served from 1875 to 1879. In 1883, President Arthur sent him as minister to Peru. He died in Lima in 1885.

SPINGARN SENIOR HIGH SCHOOL

26th Street and Benning Road, N.E.

Jack Elias Spingarn was born in 1875. He received his Ph.D. degree from Columbia, taught there, and was a renowned literary critic. One of his literary efforts was as editor of *The European Library* - all 25 volumes. In 1917, Spingarn helped form Ft. DesMoines for training of black officers. During World War I he volunteered, served in France, and returned as a lieutenant colonel. The major effort of his life, however, was in the National Association for the Advancement of Colored People (NAACP). He was a member for over 25 years, chairman of the board from 1913 to 1919, treasurer from 1919 to 1930, and finally president from 1930 to his death in 1939. In 1941, the Spingarn Medal was established by the NAACP to honor distinguished black persons.

M. M. WASHINGTON SENIOR HIGH SCHOOL AND CAREER DEVELOPMENT CENTER

On O Street, between 1st and North Capitol Streets, N.W.

This school is named for Margaret Murray Washington. She was born in Macon, MS, in 1865, graduated from Fisk University in 1893, and married educator Booker T. Washington in 1895. With him at Tuskegee Institute, she supervised girls' industries, stressed practical living for women, organized women's and mothers' clubs, and helped establish the area's first reform school. She was dean of the women's department from 1889 until her death in 1925.

Schools and Universities

H. D. WOODSON SENIOR HIGH SCHOOL

55th and Eads Streets, N.E.

Howard Dilworth Woodson was born in Pittsburgh in 1876. He graduated from the University of Pittsburgh in 1899 with a degree in civil engineering and worked for Carnegie Steel and American Bridge companies. He arrived in the District of Columbia in 1907 to spend the next 36 years with the Public Buildings Service of the General Services Administration, where he worked on the structural design of many federal buildings, especially Union Station. Even after that, he had his own consulting business until 1959. Woodson was quite active in District affairs, concentrating in the northeast section where he was a leader in efforts to provide schools, water systems, lighting, parks, and bridges. More than anyone, he was instrumental in getting Benning Road widened into a major District artery and the bridge built over the Anacostia River at East Capitol Street.

STATUES

There are hundreds of statues of people in Washington. In the Capitol Statuary Hall alone there are almost a hundred (each state is entitled to two). Busts of the vice presidents surround the Senate chamber. There are statues in the major memorials - those of Lincoln and Jefferson. Statues abound in the city's circles, squares, and parks (in this book, those are discussed in that section). Most stand or rest in various poses, outside, sometimes in strange locales, alone. People walk by, traffic moves by, and most frequently the answer to "Who exactly is that?" is "Gee, I'm not sure." So here are the stories of 57 men and women, from the country's most famous to the relatively obscure - almost all of the "outside" sculpture memorials of Washington.

The definitive book on the city's outside sculpture is *The Outdoor Sculpture of Washington, D.C.*, by James M. Goode, published by Smithsonian Institution Press in 1974. Some of the following statue descriptions are based on that book's information. Biographies that follow are from other sources.

JOSE GERVASIO ARTIGAS

On the triangle formed by Constitution Avenue, 18th Street, and Virginia Avenue, N.W.

Jose Artigas, "Father of Uruguay," was born in 1764. He was an officer in the militia when Uruguay and Argentina were part of the Spanish viceroyalty Rio de la Plata. He commanded in the Banda Oriental, or East Bank - today's Uruguay.

In 1811 Artigas raised an army to help liberate the area from Spain and obtain autonomy for Uruguay. But the Portuguese invaded from Brazil, and Artigas and his army fled into Argentina. They were followed by over 15,000 people. Nowhere else in the South American struggles for independence was there such popular support. For the next decade Artigas defended the East Bank territory against military invasions by the Spanish, Portuguese, and British. He issued several far-sighted decrees modeled after legal principles of the United States, including the basis for a federal constitution to unite Uruguayan provinces. In 1820, a trusted lieutenant, Fructuoso Rivera, deserted Artigas' army and signed an armistice with the Portuguese. (He later became president of Uruguay too.) Several other lieutenants independently negotiated ends to conflicts. Artigas had to flee to Paraguay. Paraguayan dictators gave him a small farm and pension, and Artigas lived there in obscurity for 30 years until his death in 1850.

The statue of Artigas shows him in uniform standing with hat in hand. It is known as the "Gaucho Statue." A tourist bus parking lot has been created aside the statue so that it is frequently impossible to see it except from Constitution Avenue. It might be said that Artigas is again sometimes in obscurity.

Statues

FRANCIS ASBURY. (See also **John Wesley.**)
3000 16th Street, at Mt. Pleasant Street, N.W.

Francis Asbury, one of the first American Methodist bishops, was born at Handsworth, England, in 1745. He had only a limited education, but became a Wesleyan preacher at 16. In 1771, he was sent to America as a volunteer missionary. When the Revolutionary War broke out, all the other Methodist preachers returned to England. Only Asbury remained active in America.

In 1784, John Wesley joined other Anglican churchmen to ordain Methodist elders for America. He made Thomas Coke and Asbury superintendents. Asbury insisted they be elected by their American preachers. So in Baltimore, in 1784, the American Methodist Episcopal Church was established, independent of the Church of England. Coke and Asbury were soon called bishops. Because of his strong personality, Asbury emerged dominant - a strict disciplinarian and fine organizer. He traveled 270,000 miles, mostly on horseback, preached 16,000 sermons, ordained 4,000 clergymen, and formed hundreds of church districts - despite years of failing health. He died at Spotsylvania, VA, in 1816.

Asbury, like John Wesley, is shown atop his horse, relaxed, bible in hand.

JOHN BARRY. (See also **Franklin** and **Stanton Squares.**)
In Franklin Square on 14th between I and K Streets, N.W.

Commodore John Barry, called "Father of the U.S. Navy," was born in Ireland in 1745. By 1775, he was a successful merchant captain operating out of Philadelphia. He was given command of the brig *Lexington* by the Continental Congress and executed the first capture of a British ship in the war. He went on to numerous engagements, even fought the last naval engagement of the Revolution. He had the honor of taking Lafayette home after Yorktown. In 1794, he was called out of retirement as senior captain of the U.S. Navy, supervised construction of the *USS United States*, became its commander. After 1801 he was too ill for active duty and had to turn down command of a squadron intended for the Mediterranean to deal with the Barbary pirates. (But among the officers he had trained was one Stephen Decatur.)

Barry's statue was authorized by Congress in 1906, and when it was unveiled in 1914, thousands of Irish-Americans attended the dedication. Today, Barry stands in Franklin Square - one of two statues in squares named for other people.

MARY MCLEOD BETHUNE. (See also **Bethune Museum-Archives.**)
In Lincoln Park, East Capitol and 12th Streets, N.E.

Mrs. Bethune was born in 1875, the 15th child of freed slaves from a South Carolina plantation. After education in North Carolina and Chicago, she taught for several years, then founded the Daytona Literary and Industrial School for Training Negro Girls. In 1923, the school merged with Cookman Institute to become Bethune-Cookman, and the Methodist Church assumed financial support. For more than 30 years, Mrs. Bethune served as its president. More importantly, she was recognized by educational groups and government agencies, invited to a child welfare conference at the White House by President Coolidge, was President Roosevelt's lone black woman adviser in the 1930s, and became Director of the Division of Negro Affairs of the National Youth Administration. Her dedication to young people won her worldwide acclaim. She died in 1955.

The memorial in Lincoln Park was erected in 1974. It represents two firsts: First memorial in Washington to a black leader and the first to an American woman.

SIMON BOLIVAR

In the triangle formed by Virginia Avenue, C Street, and 18th Street, N.W., behind the Organization of American States Building

Simon Bolivar, the "George Washington of South America," was born in 1783 in Caracas, Venezuela. His father and mother died when he was a boy, so he was sent to Madrid to be educated - and influenced by the revolutionary ideas. At 18, he married, but upon return to the colonies, his young wife died of yellow fever. Heartbroken and with no home, Bolivar returned to Europe. In 1804, he attended Napoleon's coronation in Paris, which he saw as a betrayal of the French revolution. The next year, in a romantic moment in Rome, he promised to dedicate his life to freedom - a promise he certainly kept.

In 1810, Bolivar led revolutionists to drive out the Spanish leader of Venezuela and set up the first local government on the continent. In 1819, he held a congress to lay the political foundations for the future of northern South America. His opening address is considered one of his greatest discussions of the politics of independence. He then marched his force of 2,500 west through swamps and over the snow-clad Andes and defeated his enemy so New Granada, Venezuela, and Quito (now Ecuador) could be united. The march was one of the most terrible forced marches in history.

It took until 1822 to beat the Spanish completely in Venezuela. Bolivar was named president. In 1824, his forces again went west to defeat Spanish troops in Peru, and there Bolivar was named dictator. Upper Peru declared its independence of Lima in 1825, and the new country was named Bolivia in his honor.

But Bolivar's grand scheme for one united country was not achieved. An attempt was made on his life, and by 1830, he was disillusioned, nearly friendless, and exhausted. He wanted to return to Europe, but didn't have the money. He retired in Columbia where he died of tuberculosis. He was only 47. He's buried in the national Pantheon in Caracas.

Statues

Bolivar's statue shows him on his horse. Because he has his sword pointing upward, it is the tallest such statue in the country. It was designed by Felix de Weldon, who also designed the Marine Memorial (i.e., the Iwo Jima statue). It's base reads, "Simon Bolivar, The Liberator," a title officially given to him by the congresses of Venezuela, Columbia, Ecuador, Peru, Chile, and Panama.

WILLIAM BLACKSTONE

Constitution Avenue and 3rd Street, N.W.

Sir William Blackstone's statue stands nine feet tall. He's dressed in his judicial robes and wig, and holds a copy of his book, *Commentaries*. The statue was to be a gift from the American Bar Association to the English Bar Association, but it turned out to be too big to stand with other statues in the London Hall of Courts, so it was donated to the United States instead.

Blackstone was born in 1723. By 1750 he received his doctor of laws from Oxford and was publishing legal tracts. He undertook a series of lectures at Oxford, their importance was recognized right away, and he was made an Oxford professor, a post he held until 1766. He was made king's counsel, solicitor to the queen, and in 1761, was elected to Parliament. Early in 1770 he was appointed to the Court of Common Pleas and was knighted. He was on the court when he died in 1780.

Blackstone's *Commentaries* were written in a clear, readable style and designed as a comprehensive introduction to the laws of England. The *Commentaries* influenced the writers of the Constitution, as well as subsequent American law. Indeed, it was Blackstone's theory that judges find but do not make law. The *Commentaries* are required reading for lawyers and have been the authority for thousands of U.S. judicial decisions.

JAMES BUCHANAN

In the Southeast corner of Meridian Hill Park, 16th Street and Florida Avenue, N.W.

James Buchanan spent over 40 years in public service - *before* he became the 15th president of the United States. Born at a frontier trading post near Mercersburg, PA, in 1791, he graduated from Dickinson College, served in the War of 1812, and was admitted to the bar in 1813.

In 1819 Buchanan became engaged to Ann Caroline Coleman, daughter of a wealthy iron maker. Her family disapproved and gossiped that Buchanan was fortune hunting. Ann was forced to break the engagement. A week later, she died, a possible suicide. Some held Buchanan responsible, others the Colemans. In any case, Buchanan never married. He remains the country's only bachelor president. His niece Harriet Lane served as official hostess of the White House.

Buchanan served five terms in the House of Representatives. President Jackson made him minister to Russia, where he negotiated the first commercial treaty between the two countries. Upon his return he was elected to the Senate and chaired the Foreign Relations Committee. He also chaired the committee to abolish slave trade in the District. In 1845, President Polk made him secretary of state. Buchanan settled the Oregon boundary dispute, but couldn't stop the war with Mexico. President Pierce named Buchanan minister to Great Britain, where he was involved in an unsuccessful move to "buy" Cuba from Spain. In the election of 1856, Democrat Buchanan topped Republican John Fremont and Whig Millard Fillmore.

As president, Buchanan did his best to solve slavery and secession problems, but the opposition dominated Congress so that his compromises could not be carried out. He did not run for re-election in 1860. When Lincoln won in November, "lame duck" Buchanan still had to serve until Lincoln took office in March. It was then that the seven Southern states formed the Confederacy and that the Civil War began. For years, Buchanan was vilified for starting the war, but more recently it's recognized that he had devoted all his efforts to averting it. Buchanan retired to his Wheatland farm in Pennsylvania. He died there in 1868.

When the president's niece died she left a bequest for a monument to her uncle. Congress finally acted in 1918. It was 1930 when the statue was put in place. Buchanan is seated. Figures on each side represent Law and Diplomacy.

EDMUND BURKE

Massachusetts Avenue and 11th Street, N.W.

Edmund Burke was born in Dublin in 1729. He graduated from Trinity College, practiced law, became a writer, entered Parliament in 1765. He was a spokesman for religious tolerance, public liberty, and financial reform. He also spoke on behalf of the American colonies - an unpopular thing to do then in Britain - and favored repeal of the Stamp Act and offered plans for conciliation with the colonies. He became agent to the British government - the same then as ambassador today - for the New York assembly.

His statue shows him as he might have appeared in Parliament. It was presented to America in 1922 by the mayor of London on behalf of the Sulgrave Institution, which promotes Anglo-American understanding. Sulgrave Manor was the English estate of George Washington's family.

JOHN CARROLL

37th and O Streets, N.W., at the entrance to Georgetown University

John Carroll was born in Upper Marlboro, MD, in 1735. He attended school in Flanders and entered the Jesuit order in France in 1753. He was ordained in 1769.

In 1773, Carroll returned to America. In 1776 he joined Benjamin Franklin, Samuel Chase, and his cousin Charles in their unsuccessful effort to obtain support for the Revolution from French Canada. (Charles Carroll of Carrollton, MD, was a signer of the Declaration of Independence.) In 1784 John Carroll was appointed superior of Maryland, and in 1789 Pius VI confirmed his election as bishop of Baltimore. He was consecrated in England in 1790. Thus he became the first American Catholic bishop. Carroll died in Baltimore in 1815.

Carroll established several Catholic colleges. One became Georgetown University. His statue was erected by the Georgetown Alumni Association in 1912. Carroll, dressed in Jesuit robes, is seated. The statue has been the scene of college pranks, a favorite of which was placing a commode in the space under his chair. In 1934 the space was filled with bronzed books.

WINSTON CHURCHILL

3100 Massachusetts Avenue, N.W., in front of the British Embassy

Winston Churchill was born in 1874. His father was a son of the Duke of Marlborough, his mother an American from Brooklyn. As a boy, he was unhappy, stuttered, and last in his class. At 20 he began a military career that saw him in Cuba, India, Egypt, the Sudan, and South Africa. He fought, wrote for newspapers. It was during his visit to Cuba that he discovered the Havana cigars that became his trademark.

In 1900 he was elected to Parliament. He served as undersecretary of state, president of the board of trade, and home secretary. In 1908 he married Clementine Hozier. They had five children. Churchill was a devoted father.

During World War I Churchill was named first lord of the admiralty and modernized the navy, developed antisubmarine tactics, created the first naval air service. But his attack at Gallipoli in Turkey to open a route to ally Russia failed, and Churchill resigned. He joined the army in France and was ultimately a lieutenant colonel.

In 1922 he tried to run for Parliament again, but just before the campaign had his appendix removed, couldn't campaign, and lost. In a typically humorous remark, he said he was "without office, without a seat, without a party, and without an appendix." But in 1924 Churchill was returned to Parliament. He served as chancellor of the exchequer. He discovered painting and displayed significant talent, and he wrote a four-volume history of World War I and a six-volume study of Marlborough. He foresaw the danger of Nazi Germany and tried to arouse the country, but was labeled a warmonger.

In 1939 Germany invaded Poland. Great Britain and France declared war. Churchill was again made first lord of the admiralty. The British fleet happily received the simple message, "Winston is back." In 1940, British troops were defeated in Norway. Belgium, Luxembourg, and the Netherlands were overrun. That same day, at 66, Churchill was named prime minister. Britain was desperate. Churchill said, "I have nothing to offer but blood, toil, tears, and sweat." Soon France asked Germany for an armistice. Britain stood alone. The Germans had to defeat the British royal air force before they could invade, so the Luftwaffe began bombing English ports and made nightly raids on London. Churchill was everywhere, defying air-raids, touring headquarters, inspecting defenses, visiting victims. Everywhere he held up two fingers in a "V for Victory," which became an Allied symbol.

As the war wound down in 1945, Churchill met with President Truman and the USSR's Stalin at Potsdam. On his mind was preventing the Soviets from taking over the eastern European countries their armies occupied. His role in the meeting was cut short when his party suffered a major election defeat and he was suddenly no longer prime minister. In 1946, at Fulton, MO, he warned, "Beware...time may be short.... An iron curtain has descended across the continent." He was again called a warmonger, his warning ignored.

Churchill painted and wrote, raised cattle and race horses. He wrote a six-volume history of World War II. In 1951, Conservatives retook the government, and at 77, Churchill again became prime minister. He was knighted. He won the Nobel Prize for literature. In 1955 he retired. He completed a four-volume history of the English-speaking peoples. And he still took his seat in Commons. In 1963, the U.S. made him an honorary citizen. His career ended in 1964 when he decided not to run for re-election. He started to serve his country in 1895 as an army lieutenant under Queen Victoria and ended his career under Queen Elizabeth II, Queen Victoria's great great granddaughter. He died in 1965. He was 90.

Churchill's statue in Washington shows him standing, giving his V for Victory sign with one hand while holding his cane and cigar with the other. One foot stands on British embassy soil, the other on U.S. soil.

DANTE

In the Southeast portion of Meridian Hill Park, 16th Street and Florida Avenue, N.W.

The great Italian poet stands holding a copy of *Commedia* (*The Divine Comedy*). The statue was a gift on behalf of Italian-Americans by Carlo Barsotti, editor of a New York Italian-American newspaper. Dedication was in 1921, the 600th anniversary of Dante's death.

Dante Aligheri was born in Florence in 1265. When he was nine, he fell in love with Beatrice, a girl also nine. They later married other persons, but Beatrice served as a major inspiration throughout his life. Dante fought for Florence against Pisa, then took part in politics. In 1301, opposition forces exiled him from the city, and he wandered from place to place. During this time he wrote his poem masterpiece. He died at Ravenna in 1321.

In *The Divine Comedy* Dante is led through hell by Virgil where they see tortured souls (many popes, kings, warriors, and Florentine citizens). He is then taken to purgatory, where there is hope. Dante finally meets Beatrice who leads him to paradise in heaven. The poem was written in Tuscan, and Dante is credited with making the dialect the language of the people, forerunner of Italian.

ALBERT EINSTEIN

Constitution Avenue and 22nd Street, on the grounds of the National Academy of Sciences

Albert Einstein was one of the greatest theoretical physicists, creator of theories of relativity, contributor to the kinetic theory of matter, and pioneer of the quantum theory.

Einstein was born of Jewish parents in 1879 in Ulm, Germany. He did not do well in school, but taught himself calculus by the time he was 14. He graduated from school in Zurich and became a Swiss citizen. He worked in the patent office in Bern. In 1905 he received his doctorate from the University of Zurich. That same year, he published three scientific papers: The first described light as energy particles or quanta. The second described the electrodynamics of moving bodies and related mass to energy ($E=mc^2$). The third explained Brownian motion, the movement of particles suspended in a gas or liquid. These papers earned for him a series of professorships in Switzerland, Prague, and Berlin.

In 1914 Einstein became director of the Kaiser Wilhelm Physical Institute in Berlin. In 1921 he received the Nobel Prize in physics. Throughout his life, he received honorary degrees, medals, and decorations. In 1933, when Hitler came to power, Einstein came to the U.S. and became professor for life at the Institute for Advanced Study at Princeton University. He became a U.S. citizen in 1941.

In 1942, Einstein was elected to the National Academy of Sciences. After World War II he played a lead role toward world peace. In 1952, on the death of Dr. Chaim Weizmann, Einstein was offered but refused the presidency of Israel. He died at Princeton in 1955.

Einstein's memorial is hidden in a small grove of trees. It consists of his statue - a surprising 21 feet high and weighing 7,000 pounds - where he sits contemplating 2,700 stars (shown by studs in the floor of black granite) laid out exactly as the universe existed on April 22, 1979, when the memorial was dedicated. He holds a paper containing his major formulas. His expression is so friendly that visitors have a tendency to pat his leg and sit in his lap.

ROBERT EMMET

Massachusetts Avenue and 24th Street, N.W.

Robert Emmet was born in Dublin in 1778, distinguished himself at Trinity College, got immersed in politics, and became a member of the revolutionary United Irishmen's Party. In 1802 Emmet met Napoleon and got him to promise aid for the next Irish rebellion. In 1803, with a small force, he tried to capture Dublin Castle and hold the English viceroy hostage but failed. Emmet was arrested, tried, and condemned to death by hanging. He was 25 years old.

On the dock before the hanging, Emmet made an impassioned speech. His statue shows him as he is doing so. The statue was commissioned by Irish Americans to commemorate the independence of Ireland and presented in 1917 to the Smithsonian Institution. It is officially "on loan" from the Smithsonian and was moved to its present location about two blocks from the Irish Embassy in 1966 on the 50th anniversary of Irish independence.

JOHN ERICSSON

Independence Avenue and Ohio Drive, S.W., in West Potomac Park

John Ericsson was born in Varmland, Sweden, in 1803. At 13 he joined the Swedish navy. Ericsson made the first practicable screw propeller, first used in ships he built in England. In 1839 he moved to New York, and in 1848 became a U.S. citizen. He built the *Princeton*, first warship with a metal hull, screw propeller, and engines below the waterline for protection. He built the *Monitor* with the first armored revolving gun turret. That was the ship that defeated the *Merrimack* at Hampton Roads, VA, in the most famous sea battle of the Civil War. Similar turrets were used on all subsequent ships, and brought him fame. Although much of Ericsson's fame rests on the *Monitor* and its gun turret, he was an inventor far ahead of his time, laying down the principle of the gas turbine, and inventing apparatus to extract salt from sea water, fans for forced ventilation, a shipboard depth finder, the first practical steam fire engine, and use of solar energy.

Ericsson died in New York City in 1889. In 1890, the *USS Baltimore* carried his body back to Sweden. At his monument, he sits in front of the Norse tree of life and three appropriate allegorical figures - Vision, Adventure, and Labor.

BENJAMIN FRANKLIN. (See also **Franklin Park.**)

Pennsylvania Avenue at 10th Street, N.W.

Benjamin Franklin was born in Boston in 1706. Without funds for education, he became at 12 an apprentice to his older brother who was printing one of Boston's first newspapers. By 20, he owned his own press in Philadelphia, published the *Pennsylvania Gazette* (later The *Saturday Evening Post*), and began writing *Poor*

Richard's Almanack (published in 1732). He also served as clerk of the Pennsylvania Assembly and ran a book store. By 1748, at 42, Franklin was able to retire and live off the income of his business. He proved his view that by hard work, thrift, and honesty, a poor man might rise above poverty.

Franklin undertook numerous scientific experiments, inventing the Franklin stove (more efficient than a fireplace), proving (through his now famous kite experiment) that lightning is electricity, and subsequently inventing the lightning rod.

Franklin was 46 when he was elected to the Pennsylvania Assembly and began an almost-40-year political career. In 1757 he went to England as an agent of the Assembly, and by the important decade between 1765 to 1776 he was agent for Georgia, New Jersey, and Massachusetts. By then he knew more about America than anyone in England, and more about England than any American. Back in America he served in the 2nd Continental Congress and helped draft the Declaration of Independence. In 1776, he became commissioner to France. Through his efforts almost all outside aid for the American rebels came from France. By 1783, he, John Adams, and John Jay had obtained the peace treaty that guaranteed national independence. In 1787, he attended the Constitutional Convention, and urged ratification of the Constitution and inauguration of the new government under his friend George Washington. Franklin died in 1790.

Franklin's statue portrays him in his dress as minister to the French court. Despite all his achievements, the front of his statue is labeled "Printer." And it doesn't stand in Franklin Park, but is instead on Pennsylvania Avenue. There's a reason: The statue was donated by Stilson Hutchins, who founded *The Washington Post*. In 1889, when the statue was unveiled by Franklin's great granddaughter, the *Post* offices were right across the street.

ALBERT GALLATIN (See also **Alexander Hamilton.**)
On the north side of the Treasury Building, Pennsylvania Avenue and 15th Street, N.W.

Abraham Alfonse Albert Gallatin was born in 1761 in Geneva, Switzerland. Well educated, he came to America and taught French at Harvard College. After the Revolutionary War, he opened a general store and farmed in Fayette County, PA. He was elected to the U.S. Senate in 1793, but was expelled - he hadn't been a citizen for the required nine years. His Pennsylvania district then sent him to the U.S. House of Representatives, where he served from 1795 to 1801. He criticized Federalist fiscal policies and was responsible for creating the House Ways and Means Committee with which the House initiates revenue measures.

In 1801, President Jefferson named Gallatin secretary of the treasury, a position he held through the first year of the War of 1812. He left the position to join the

U.S. peace commission and was the major contributor to the Treaty of Ghent. From 1816 to 1823 he was minister to France. By 1831, he retired from public service and became president of the National Bank of New York. He also became an expert on American Indian languages, founded the American Ethnological Society, and became president of the New York Historical Society. He died at Astoria, NY, in 1849.

In 1923, the Alexander Hamilton statue was placed on the south side of the Treasury Department building. Hamilton had been the arch rival of Thomas Jefferson, founder of the Democratic Party. Democrats felt Albert Gallatin, Jefferson's secretary of the treasury, was more deserving than Hamilton. (Hamilton had left a national debt of $14 million. In six years, Gallatin had gotten the debt paid off.) So in 1926, they moved to get Gallatin's statue placed on this opposite side of the building. It took 20 years to obtain funds, get approval of the U.S. Fine Arts Commission, wait out World War II bronze shortages, and put the statue in place, but the determined Democrats got it done.

EDWARD MINER GALLAUDET. (See **Gallaudet University**.)
On the Gallaudet University grounds, Florida Avenue and 8th Street

Edward Gallaudet was president of what is now Gallaudet University for 53 years. The 1969 sculpture shows him standing, in his academic robe, conferring a degree.

THOMAS HOPKINS GALLAUDET. (See **Gallaudet University** .)
Near the entrance to the chapel on the Gallaudet University grounds.

This memorial shows the pioneer educator of the deaf seated and holding his first student, Alice Cogswell. Their right hands show the sign for the letter A. The sculpture is by Daniel Chester French.

BERNARDO DE GALVEZ
Virginia Avenue and E Street, N.W.

Bernardo de Galvez was born in Spain in 1746 to a family that held important government posts under the Spanish Bourbons. In 1769 he went with his uncle, Jose de Galvez, to New Spain, which covered not only Mexico but Central America, half of what is now the United States, and more. He gained experience against the Apaches on New Spain's northern frontier. Five years later he served with the French against Algeria. In 1776 King Charles III made him commander of the Louisiana regiment.

Galvez became governor of Louisiana just as the American Revolution began. He increased strength of the colony, supplied arms to revolutionaries operating in the Mississippi valley, aided George Rogers Clark. When Spain declared war on England, he won major military victories at Baton Rouge, Mobile, and Pensacola, helping the American cause. Galvez' victories also enabled Spain to recover Florida under the 1783 Treaty of Paris that ended the Revolutionary War. Galvez was promoted to governor of Cuba, after which he succeeded his father, Matias de Galvez, as viceroy of New Spain. He died in Mexico City in 1786.

The base of his statue contains a statement by King Don Juan Carlos I of Spain when the statue was dedicated in 1976. It explains why the statue is in Washington - "to serve as a reminder that Spain offered the blood of her soldiers for the cause of American Independence."

JAMES GARFIELD. (See also **Garfield Park.**)
First Street and Maryland Avenue, at the base of the Capitol

James Abram Garfield, 20th president of the U.S., is recognized mainly because he was fatally shot after being in office only three months. That's unfortunate, because Garfield's is a real American success story.

Garfield was born in a log cabin outside Cleveland, OH, in 1831. His father died when he was two, and his mother raised her five children in poverty with no chance to attend school. When 17, Garfield decided to get an education himself. He attended a seminary, taught in local schools, taught and studied at what is now Hiram College, became quite religious, and finally graduated from Williams College with honors in 1856. By 1858, he took over as principal at Hiram.

Garfield became interested in politics and in 1859 was elected to the Ohio Senate. He was also admitted to the bar. And he married Lucretia Rudolph, a former classmate. They had six children.

In the Civil War, Garfield proved an excellent military man. He headed a brigade that turned back Confederates in Kentucky, led another at Shiloh and Corinth, became chief of staff of the Army of the Cumberland. He rose to major general. In 1862 he was elected to the U.S. House of Representatives, ending his military service.

Garfield served in the House from 1863 to 1880 in a long, distinguished career. He saw that the great hope for democracy was education. He established a department of education, supported the education of the deaf, served as regent of the Smithsonian Institution. He helped create the U.S. Geological Survey.

In 1880 he was elected to the Senate - but never became a senator. He was a delegate to the Republican National Convention and placed John Sherman's name in nomination. After 34 ballots in which contenders Sherman, Ulysses S. Grant, and James Blaine failed to win nomination, Sherman and Blaine supporters united on Garfield, who won on the 36th ballot. The new president took office in March. But on July 2, Garfield was shot by Charles Guiteau, a mentally disturbed man who had sought a federal appointment but had been turned down. The president never recovered and died in September.

His memorial was erected in 1887 by veterans of the Army of the Cumberland. Garfield stands atop, holding in his hand his inaugural address on which is written, "Law, Justice, Equality." Three allegorical figures sit at the base, representing his careers as scholar, soldier, and statesman.

JAMES CARDINAL GIBBONS

About 3200 16th Street, at Park Road, N.W., in front of the Shrine of the Sacred Heart

James Gibbons was born in Baltimore in 1834. When he was three, his family moved to Ireland, returning after his father's death, when he was 19. Gibbons studied for the priesthood in Baltimore, was ordained there in 1861, and became pastor of Baltimore's St. Bridget's Church. During the Civil War, he served as chaplain at Fort McHenry. In 1868 he was made vicar of North Carolina. He was promoted to bishop of Richmond and later to archbishop of Baltimore.

In 1883 Gibbons led the delegation of U.S. bishops in Rome planning for the Third Plenary Council of Baltimore, which he then presided over the following year. In 1885, Pope Leo XIII named him cardinal.

Gibbons was able to explain to Rome's officials attitudes of American Catholics during a difficult period in Church-American relations. He led his Church in the U.S. as it grew to become one of the leading U.S. churches. He also was friend and advisor to presidents from Andrew Johnson to Warren Harding. Gibbons died in Baltimore in 1921.

The statue of James Cardinal Gibbons is the Knights of Columbus memorial in Washington. Gibbons, seated and wearing his robes, has his arm extended as though giving a blessing to all those who pass by.

SAMUEL GOMPERS. (See also **Gompers Square.**)

Massachusetts Avenue and 10th Street, N.W.

Samuel Gompers was born in London in 1850. He moved to New York City when he was 13, got a job making cigars, and within a year formed the Cigar-Makers' International Union. In 1896 he founded the American Federation of Labor (AFL) and served as its president until his death in 1924. Gompers believed that unions should rely on bargaining, ties with government and political parties should be avoided, dues should be collected to offset union expenses, and there should be one union to one trade. He worked hard for labor and antitrust laws, and was influential in establishing the Department of Labor.

The AFL donated funds for the statue. It was erected in 1933, with President Roosevelt present. Gompers is seated. Behind him are figures representing home, industrial exploitation, justice, and unity of the unions. Some of his writings appear on the base.

In the 1940s, thieves discovered that the inside of the memorial's base was hollow and had a trap door - and used it as a hideout.

ULYSSES S. GRANT

First Street, N.W., at the foot of the Capitol's west side

The 18th president of the U.S. was born at Point Pleasant, OH, in 1822. He was named Hiram Ulysses Grant and called himself H. Ulysses Grant. A congressman secured his appointment to West Point but assumed his first name was Ulysses and his middle name the same as his mother's, so listed him as Ulysses Simpson Grant. At school the initials U.S. attracted a lot of attention, and so the Ulysses S. stuck for the rest of his life.

Grant graduated in 1843, served with Zachary Taylor at Monterey and Winfield Scott at Mexico City. He married in 1848 and was stationed near the Great Lakes. In 1852 he was sent to the Pacific Northwest and had to leave his family. He drank so much there that he had to resign. For six years, mostly in Missouri, he worked as farmer, salesman, and customs agent, and finally in Galena, IL, as a store clerk.

When the Civil War started, he recruited and trained volunteers in Galena and offered his services to the U.S. He got no reply, so he joined an Illinois regiment. He demonstrated superior strategy, was made brigadier general of volunteers. He seized strategic points in Kentucky, captured Fort Henry on the Tennessee, and laid siege to Fort Donelson on the Cumberland. When the Confederate commander asked commissioners be appointed to decide terms of surrender, Grant replied, "No terms other than an unconditional and immediate surrender can be accepted. I propose to move immediately upon your works." This was the biggest Union victory at that point in the war. Everyone was impressed. Grant was given the nickname of "Unconditional Surrender," again making use of his initials. He also was made major general in the regular army.

Grant followed with other victories - a major one the capture of Vicksburg. At Chattanooga he destroyed the Confederacy in the West. Congress gave him a gold medal. He became a lieutenant general and was given command of all Union armies. His Virginia campaign led to the conclusive struggle of the war, the siege of Petersburg, and the surrender of Gen. Robert E. Lee's army at Appomattox Court House. Grant's surrender terms were memorable: he refused to accept Lee's sword, gave Confederate soldiers Union rations and supplies, and let them return home with their horses "for spring plowing."

In 1866 Grant became general, the highest rank. In the North he was regarded as the nation's savior. Republicans nominated him for president, and he defeated Horatio Seymour. During his first term, the 15th Amendment (race no ban to voting) was adopted, there was a friendly policy with South America, acts were passed to tone down reconstruction in the South, and civil rights were restored for nearly everyone. The second term, though, saw financial scandals and fraudulent practices. Grant was so trusting, he wouldn't condemn his friends even when they were caught.

After leaving office, Grant toured the world. He was exploited in business and failed. To get his family out of debt, he wrote his memoirs - while dying of throat cancer. The memoirs made $450,000 for his family and have become an American classic. Grant died in 1885 and is buried in the imposing tomb that bears his name on Riverside Drive in New York City.

His memorial in Washington is one of the largest. Grant is shown on his horse *Cincinnatus* and wearing a typical old hat, sitting as though watching a battle. The statue and flags are guarded by lions. On each side are dramatic sculptures: a cavalry group - seven charging horsemen - and an artillery group - three soldiers and horse-drawn cannon. On his statue's base is only one word: GRANT.

NATHANIEL GREENE

In Stanton Square, Massachusetts and Maryland Avenues, N.E.

Maj. Gen. Nathaniel Greene sits atop his horse leading his troops into battle, not in a Greene circle or Greene park or Greene anything, but inexplicably in the middle of Stanton Square.

Nathaniel Greene was born in Warwick, RI, in 1742. He had little schooling, but read a lot, and obtained a good education partly through the guidance of clergyman Ezra Stiles, later president of Yale. In 1774 Greene helped organize a local military company, but because of a bad knee, felt he shouldn't be an officer. Instead he served as a private. But the next year, as the Revolution was underway, Rhode Island created a force of 1,500 soldiers and suddenly Greene was appointed brigadier general. The brigade joined Washington's army defending Boston, and from that time, Greene was active in all army operations until 1778. Washington came to depend upon him, and he became virtually second in command. From 1778 to 1780, Greene served as quartermaster general. In 1780, he presided over the trial of Maj. John Andre, the British spy. In command again in 1781, he outmaneuvered Cornwallis to win the Southern campaign. After the war, he was given land by the state of Georgia, and he made his home in Savannah. He died there in 1786, only 44 years of age.

SAMUEL HAHNEMANN

In Scott Circle on Massachusetts Avenue and 16th Street, N.W.

Dr. Christian Friedrich Samuel Hahnemann (1755-1843) was a German physician who originated therapy that treats disease symptoms with drugs that cause the same symptoms to appear in healthy people. The belief is that "like cures like." Hahnemann popularized the practice and named it "homeopathy." It reached its height in the mid-1800s. It has been opposed by the American Medical Association. Only a small percentage of physicians practice it today.

The memorial has Hahnemann sitting, thinking. Four panels display him as student, chemist, teacher, and physician. "Likes are cured by likes" is inscribed in Latin on the base. The memorial was erected by the American Institute of Homeopathy in 1900.

NATHAN HALE

Constitution Avenue between 9th and 10th Streets, N.W.

Nathan Hale was born in Coventry, CT, in 1755. He graduated from Yale in 1773, then taught school. In July 1775 he was commissioned as a lieutenant by the Connecticut assembly and aided in the siege of Boston. He became a captain. Against the British in New York he captured a supply ship and won a membership in the Rangers. About that time Gen. George Washington asked the Ranger commander to select a man to go through British lines to get information about British positions. The commander asked for a volunteer. Hale disguised himself as a Dutch schoolmaster, crossed through the lines, and obtained the needed information. As he returned to his own lines, he was betrayed by his Tory cousin and captured. Because he was in civilian clothes, Gen. William Howe, British commander, saw him as a spy and had him hanged the very next day. Before the hanging, Hale made a speech. There is no record of what he actually said, but it supposedly ended with the now famous sentence, "I only regret that I have but one life to lose for my country." He was only 21.

His statue shows him at the time of his speech. It previously stood at his birthplace, but was purchased by George Seymour, a biographer of Hale. Upon Seymour's death, he left the statue to the United States.

ALEXANDER HAMILTON

At the south end of the Treasury Building between 15th Street, N.W., and the White House grounds

Alexander Hamilton was born on Nevis in the West Indies about 1755. A clergyman raised the funds needed to send him to the mainland, and he was educated at King's College, now Columbia University. When 21, he was commissioned captain of an artillery company. During the Revolutionary War, he distinguished himself at the battles of White Plains, Princeton, and Monmouth, and became a lieutenant colonel and aide-de-camp to George Washington. By 28, he was admitted to the bar, opened a law office on Wall Street, and was a New York delegate to the Continental Congress. A year later, concerned over the need for a sound banking system, he founded the Bank of New York.

At 34, he was appointed by President Washington as the nation's first secretary of the treasury. Hamilton's administration was marked by masterful planning, clear reporting, creation of a national currency, and establishment of the mint. He repeatedly urged for a system of federal taxation and a national bank, with the new federal government assuming the debts of the states. Thomas Jefferson and James Madison opposed, but settled the matter by a compromise: Jefferson would support assumption of a national debt, and Hamilton would agree to locate the new national capital on the Potomac instead of in New York.

In 1804, Hamilton rightfully spoke against Aaron Burr, who sought the New York governorship. When he lost, Burr challenged Hamilton to a duel. Opposed to dueling - his son Philip had been killed in a duel only a couple of years before - Hamilton fired into the air. Burr did not. Hamilton died from the gunshot wound the next day. His statue wasn't created until 1923. At its dedication, President Harding mentioned a donor, but not by name. It is said it was a veiled woman who had supplied the funds. The donor's identity remains a mystery.

WINFIELD SCOTT HANCOCK

Pennsylvania Avenue and 7th Street, N.W.

Winfield Scott Hancock was born in 1824 at Montgomery Square, PA. He graduated from West Point, saw action in the Mexican War, and served in Florida, Kansas, Utah, and California. When the Civil War began, he was commissioned a brigadier general. He took command of a division at Antietam, as a major general led the division at Fredericksburg, again at Chancellorsville. In 1863 he was made a corps commander and, under Maj. Gen. George Meade, took command of troops at Gettysburg. On the third day he drove back the famous Pickett's charge by the Confederates. He led his corps further at Spotsylvania and Petersburg. When the war ended, he had been a corps commander longer than any officer in the U.S. Army. He was known as "Hancock the Superb."

In 1880, Hancock was nominated as Democratic candidate for president, but was defeated by James Garfield, who won with a plurality of only 10,000 votes. Hancock died at Governor's Island, NY, in 1886.

His equestrian statue on Pennsylvania Avenue was dedicated in 1896. Every major official in Washington, including President Cleveland and Vice President Adlai Stevenson, attended.

Statues

JOSEPH HENRY. (See also **The Smithsonian Building, "The Castle"**.)

On The Mall in front of the main Smithsonian Institution Building

Joseph Henry was born in Albany, NY, in 1797. He attended Albany Academy, taught science there. By winding wire around the iron core of a magnet in a certain way, Henry made electromagnets powerful and practical. In 1832, Henry became professor at Princeton University. He found that a current interrupted in a wire induced an opposite current in the same wire, and in 1835, published a paper explaining self-induction. In his honor, the standard unit of inductive resistance is named the *henry*. Later research led him to devise an electric motor, invent and demonstrate the first telegraph, and invent the electric relay.

In 1846 Henry became the secretary of the newly formed Smithsonian Institution. He worked there for 29 years, and his family lived in "The Castle" building. He is credited with supporting original research and publishing of related papers, establishing the first system of weather reports, devising inventions for lighthouses along the Atlantic Coast, and organizing the Association for the Advancement of Science. For his final ten years, he served as president of the National Academy of Science. He died in Washington in 1878.

His nine-foot statue stands in front of the main Smithsonian building and shows him leaning on a pedestal that pictures his electromagnet.

ANDREW JACKSON

In the center of Lafayette Park

After formation of the United States, a wealthy class formed the Federalist party. City workers, small farmers, and frontiersmen saw their equal rights vanishing. They found their champion in a hotheaded fighter from Tennessee and elected him seventh president of the United States.

Andrew Jackson was born in North Carolina in 1767. His father died before he was born, his mother and two brothers of sickness during the Revolution. In the war, when 13, Jackson served as a courier. He was captured, refused to shine an officer's shoes, and was cut in the face by the officer's saber. He grew up hating the British. He studied law. In 1788 he moved to the frontier town of Nashville as a public prosecutor. He helped draft the Tennessee constitution and became the state's first representative in Congress. In 1797 he was elected to the U.S. Senate. After 1798 he served as a judge. He had one quarrel after another and fought three duels. He expanded his land holdings, developed a home (The Hermitage), and became major general of the Tennessee militia. In the War of 1812, with 6,000 backwoods fighters, Jackson won a sweeping victory over 12,000 British troops at New Orleans. In 1818 he defeated the Seminole Indians in Florida. In 1821, when the United States purchased Florida, Jackson was made military governor. The city of Jacksonville bears his name.

In 1824, Jackson ran for president and received the most electoral votes but not a majority. The election was thrown to the House of Representatives which gave John Quincy Adams the office. In 1828 Jackson ran again and swept into victory. He is considered founder of the Democratic party and the first president elected by "common people." The people demonstrated their support in a near riot at his inauguration and left the White House in a shambles.

As president, Jackson tried to further democracy by firing nearly all officeholders and appointing Democrats to their posts, innovating the "spoils system." The qualifications of many were only that they voted for him. In December his wife died, and Jackson surrounded himself with friends, ignoring his formally appointed cabinet. The friends were known as the "kitchen cabinet." In his most controversial action, he insisted that federal funds be deposited, not in the Bank of the U.S., but in banks run by his Democratic friends.

The Treasury building had been burned by the British in 1814. In 1833, the second Treasury burned down. There was a lot of haggling about where to rebuild it - until Jackson got fed up with the talk, walked out of the White House, stuck his walking stick into the ground next door, and said to build it there. Congress objected to the location - it blocks Pennsylvania Avenue between the Capitol and the White House - but after a six-month argument voted to proceed. After two terms, Jackson retired to The Hermitage. He died there in 1845.

Jackson's statue shows him on his horse as a major general. It was commissioned by the Democratic Party. Clark Mills was the sculptor, it was the first equestrian statue cast in the U.S. by an American, and Mills earned immense recognition for that and for balancing the statue on the hind legs of the horse. It was dedicated in 1853 with President Pierce and 15,000 looking on.

THOMAS JEFFERSON. (See **Jefferson Building, Library of Congress.**)
At the Tidal Basin in East Potomac Park, adjacent to 14th Street, S.W.

Thomas Jefferson was born at Shadwell, VA, in 1743. His father was a landowner, his mother a Randolph, one of the first families of Virginia. He attended William and Mary College, was grounded in the classics, studied law, and excelled in class and as a violinist and athlete. He decided on politics and served as a burgess. In 1772, he married Martha Skelton. They had six children, two of whom survived into adulthood.

In 1774 Jefferson wrote resolutions blaming England for its treatment of the colonies, and he was suddenly prominent as a leader of opposition to the king. He was asked to (and did) draft the Declaration of Independence. He summarized the revolutionary philosophy - that all men are equal in rights regardless of birth, wealth, or status, and that government is their servant not master - in a single paragraph that has been regarded ever since as the charter of American liberty.

Statues

Jefferson returned to Virginia where he reformed several laws: providing for religious freedom, abolishing the tax that supported the state church, abolishing right of the oldest son to inherit all property, and limiting the death penalty to murder and treason. He succeeded Patrick Henry as governor of Virginia.

In 1784 Jefferson went to France with John Adams and Benjamin Franklin to make commercial treaties and became minister to France. In 1789 he became President Washington's secretary of state. In 1796 he ran for president, finished second to Adams, thus became vice president. In 1800 he defeated Adams, but in the electoral college tied with Aaron Burr. Congress broke the tie in Jefferson's favor, and he became the third president of the U.S. Washington and Adams had belonged to one party, Jefferson the opposing party, so his taking office was a major shift in government, made procedurally and peacefully for the first time.

Jefferson was frugal in office and balanced the budget. When Tripoli's Barbary Coast pirates attacked shipping, he sent the fleet to bomb its ports and forced it to ask for peace. In 1803, he took his most important action when he purchased the Louisiana Territory from Napoleon, doubling the country's size. In his second term, the first national highway was created (it went to Ohio), and West Point was established.

Jefferson retired to Monticello, where there are many examples of his inventiveness: basements replacing outbuildings, a weathervane that can be read inside, a clock with faces inside and out, dumbwaiters from the wine cellar, his bed that can be raised when not in use. He devised a copy machine, invented a revolving music stand, kept charts of temperature, improved agriculture. He read classics in their original French, Spanish, Italian, or Greek. He conceived the University of Virginia, got it located in his own county, designed its buildings, supervised its construction, hired the faculty, and even served as its first regent.

Jefferson died in 1823. In one of the great coincidences of history, Jefferson and Adams both died on the same day - July 4 - exactly 50 years after signing of the Declaration of Independence.

The Jefferson Memorial is the third of the three great monuments to U.S. presidents in Washington, after the Washington Monument and the Lincoln Memorial. It has a prime location on the Tidal Basin and is aligned with the White House and Washington Monument. It was dedicated by President Franklin Roosevelt in 1943 on the 200th anniversary of Jefferson's birth. At its center is a 19-foot statue of Jefferson, who stands with the Declaration of Independence in one hand. Around the walls are four panels inscribed with Jefferson's words. The quotes from the Declaration of Independence have been paraphrased, a couple words misspelled or omitted, and punctuation changed. The Department of Interior says it was intentional, to save space.

ST. JEROME

2343 Massachusetts Avenue, N.W.

St. Jerome was born as Eusebius Hieronymus in Dalmatia about 342. He studied in Rome, learning Latin and Greek. He traveled widely, moved to Syria, lived near Antioch, was for a time a hermit, learned Hebrew. At Antioch he was ordained priest. From 382 to 385 he was secretary to Pope Damasus in Rome, who directed him to revise the Latin version of the New Testament. At Damasus' death, St. Jerome moved to Bethlehem. Practically the whole of the Bible, known since as "the Vulgate," was either translated from Hebrew and Greek or worked over by St. Jerome. (Vulgate means common, and his version is the basis for the common one used today by the Roman Catholic Church.) The task was finished in 404. He died in 420. St. Jerome is considered the greatest of the Latin doctors. (Doctor of the Church is a title given by the Pope to Christian theologians noted for their great learning and sanctity.)

St. Jerome sits, head in hand, legs crossed, reading his Bible. Sculptor was Ivan Mestrovic (1883-1962), a Croatian protégé of Rodin. The statue was commissioned by the Croatian Franciscan Fathers and originally stood outside their residence. It now sits in front of the Embassy of the Republic of Croatia.

JOAN OF ARC

In the center of Meridian Hill Park, 16th Street and Florida Avenue, N.W.

Joan, dressed in armor, sits atop her horse, with sword raised. The statue was a gift from the women of France to the women of the United States in 1922.

Joan was born in 1412. She was a simple and kind peasant girl. At the time, English king Henry V claimed the throne of France. When 16, Joan heard voices of St. Michael, St. Catherine, and St. Margaret telling her to fight for France - that the English had no claim on her country. She convinced dauphin Charles, son of French king Charles VI, and was given command of troops, with whom she drove the English from Orleans. Other victories followed, and Charles was crowned Charles VII. Joan rode against the English ally, the duke of Burgundy. She was captured, and Charles was unable to rescue her. She was found guilty of heresy because she insisted her visions and missions came from God, and she was burned at the stake. She was only 19.

Twenty-five years later, the Pope revoked her sentence, and in 1919 (488 years later!), she was canonized as a saint. She remains a major symbol of patriotism to the French.

JOHN PAUL JONES

Independence Avenue and 17th Street, S.W.

This statue to Revolutionary naval hero John Paul Jones (like John Barry, often called "Father of the U.S. Navy") was authorized by Congress in 1906 and erected in 1912.

John Paul (Paul was his last name) was born in Kirkbean, Scotland, in 1747. When 12 he sailed to Virginia to join his brother. He served in merchant vessels, and by the time he was 21, he was master of a merchant ship, the *John*. In 1770, at Tobago, he punished with cat-o'-nine-tails a crew member who later died, but proved his innocence of the death. In 1773, when a mutineer swung at him, John Paul shot him. The admiralty court was not in session, and he was able to leave the island. He spent 20 months in Fredericksburg, VA, under the assumed name of Jones.

In 1775 he was commissioned first lieutenant on the frigate *Alfred* and hoisted the Continental flag on a vessel for the first time. He soon was captain of both the sloop of war *Providence* and the *Alfred*, and captured valuable British merchantmen and vessels. In 1777 the Marine Committee under Robert Morris almost gave him the entire Continental fleet, but jealousy of others defeated the plan. John Hancock, president of Congress, gave him command of the new sloop *Ranger*, and Jones sailed it to England, tried to burn ships and to capture an earl for the exchange of prisoners. In 1778, he captured the *Drake*, the first victory of a Continental vessel over a British warship.

Political intrigues conspired against him, and he received command of an old, slow merchant ship, the *Bonhomme Richard*, named in honor of Benjamin Franklin. In 1779 he challenged two British ships, and completely outmanned and outgunned, outwitted the British captain and boarded his ship, just as his own was sinking. It was during this four-hour battle that a gunner, thinking Jones had been killed, called to surrender. The British captain responded with "Do you ask for quarter?" at which time Jones reappeared, threw his two pistols at the gunner, and yelled, "I have not yet begun to fight!"

Jones proceeded to Paris where he was a popular hero, had romances, even wrote poetry. In 1781, he returned to America where Congress gave him a gold medal and command of the ship *America* with the rank of rear admiral. Because there was "nothing doing" at home, Jones went to Russia, commanded a squadron in the Black Sea and saved the Crimea for the Russians. More intrigues followed, so Jones returned to Paris. He died there in 1792.

After a hundred years in an unmarked Paris grave, his remains were moved in 1905 to the chapel of the U.S. Naval Academy in Annapolis, MD. It is said that his remains had been preserved - in a barrel of rum.

BENITO JUAREZ

In the circle at Virginia and New Hampshire Avenues, N.W.

In 1966 President Lyndon Johnson presented Mexico with a statue of Abraham Lincoln. In return in 1969 Mexico made a gift to the United States of the statue of one of its greatest leaders, Benito Juarez. The Lincoln statue stands in the city of Juarez, across the border from El Paso. The Juarez statue stands here.

Benito Juarez was born in 1806 in southern Mexico. He was a full-blooded Zapotec Indian. His parents were illiterate, and he was orphaned when only three. A priest encouraged him to study, and in 1832, he received a Bachelor of Law degree. He served as state legislator, judge, district attorney, representative in Congress, governor. His desire to give more democracy to common folks scared conservatives, and when Santa Anna seized the government in 1853, Juarez was arrested. He escaped to New Orleans. When Santa Anna was overthrown, Juarez returned. When a reformed constitution was put into effect, he became minister of justice, second only to the president. When a coup took over the capital and the president fled, Juarez declared himself president and set up government in Vera Cruz. He was later able to reclaim Mexico City and be elected president.

As if that success story isn't enough, there's more: Juarez inherited a huge national debt and had to suspend payment of foreign debts. Napoleon III used the debt to France as an excuse to send troops to Mexico, declared the country a monarchy, and crowned Archduke Maximilian emperor. Juarez withdrew to El Paso del Norte (now the city of Juarez). After the U.S. Civil War, Napoleon, afraid the U.S. might intervene under the Monroe Doctrine, withdrew his troops, and Maximilian was captured and executed. Juarez returned to Mexico City and was again elected president, an office he held until his death in 1872.

ROBERT F. KENNEDY. (See **Robert F. Kennedy Stadium.**)

In the Department of Justice courtyard between Pennsylvania and Constitution Avenues on 10th Street

A sculpted head of the former attorney general is atop a pedestal in this courtyard. Kennedy was assassinated in 1968. The top corner of the pedestal is intentionally broken off, representing his incomplete life.

TADEUSZ KOSCIUSZKO

In the Northeast corner of Lafayette Park

Tadeusz (or Thaddeus) Kosciuszko was born in Lithuania in 1746 and sent for military training at Warsaw and Versailles, later in Italy, France, and Germany. Soon after becoming a captain in the Polish army, he sailed to America and in 1776, as a military engineer, offered his services. He built the valuable fortifications along the Delaware River and at Saratoga and West Point in New

York. He became a brigadier general and adjutant to Gen. George Washington. In 1783 a grateful Congress granted him $15,000 and 500 acres in Ohio.

In 1784 he returned to Poland and by 1789 became a major general in that army. He fought against the Russians and, with only peasants and few weapons, successfully defended Warsaw. Later he was wounded and captured. When Czar Paul I took over, he was freed and offered an estate, which he refused. He lived for a time in Philadelphia, refused a command offered him by Napoleon, worked the rest of his life in behalf of Polish freedom. He died in 1817.

His statue shows him as a general, holding a map. At the four sides of the base an eagle guards a globe that shows America, another fights a snake above a globe that shows Poland, there's a wounded Kosciuszko, and another Kosciuszko freeing a soldier who represents America.

GILBERT LAFAYETTE

In the Southeast corner of Lafayette Park

He came from French nobility, and his full name was Marie Joseph Paul Yves Roch Gilbert Motier Lafayette. His formal title became Major General, the Marquis de Lafayette. He was called Gilbert by close friends.

At 16, Lafayette entered the French army. At 19, enthused over the Declaration of Independence, he set out to aid the Americans. He was capable and courageous and soon became a major general and Gen. George Washington's aide-de-camp at Valley Forge. He fought at Brandywine, Barren Hill, and Monmouth. He secured financial aid and volunteers from France. He fought further in Virginia against Benedict Arnold and made Cornwallis retreat to Yorktown and surrender.

In 1781 he returned to France. As a nobleman, he desired to uphold the law; as a freedom fighter, he wanted to help common people fight oppression. He was the first who suggested the tricolor flag for France. But because of his middle-of-the-road positions, radicals on both sides distrusted him. He was betrayed, then captured during the war between France and Austria and held captive by the Austrians for five years. Napoleon secured his release. After Napoleon's fall, he served in the Chamber of Deputies and commanded the National Guard.

Lafayette made two more visits to America and was enthusiastically greeted. He had spent $200,000 of his own money in the American cause. Congress granted him $200,000 and land. Several states made him an honorary citizen. He died in France in 1834, and his grave was covered with earth from Bunker Hill.

His statue shows him petitioning the French National Assembly for American aid. Other figures are d'Estaing and Grasse, who headed French naval forces, Rochambeau and Portail, army commanders, a symbolic America, even cherubs.

ABRAHAM LINCOLN. (See also **Lincoln Square,** the **Emancipation Monument, Ford's Theater,** and **Petersen House.**)
Lincoln Statue is on D Street, N.W., between 4th and 5th Streets. Lincoln Memorial is at the west end of the Mall.

Abraham Lincoln was born in 1809 in a log cabin in Larue County, KY. Little is known about his mother, Nancy Hanks Lincoln; his father, Thomas, was a carpenter. In 1816 the Lincolns moved to Spencer County, IN, because as Baptists they disapproved of Kentucky's tolerance for slavery. Lincoln attended school for less than a year. In 1830 they moved again, to New Salem, IL. Abraham left for nearby Springfield where he held various jobs and served briefly in the Black Hawk War, being voted captain of his volunteer company.

In 1834 Lincoln was elected to the state legislature, serving about four terms. He became a lawyer. In 1842, he married Mary Todd, of a prestigious Kentucky family. They had four sons. From 1847 to 1848 he served in the U.S. House of Representatives. He did not run for re-election. He opposed the Mexican War and felt President Polk violated the Constitution to conduct it.

By 1854 the Kansas-Nebraska Act OK'd slavery in lands previously free. Lincoln was not an abolitionist and thought slavery was protected by the Constitution in states where it already existed, but he was alarmed that the new act encouraged it. Sen. Douglas had sponsored the act. In 1856 Lincoln joined the new Republican Party, and in 1858 he campaigned for the Senate against Douglas. Like in recent elections, the underdog wanted to share the leading candidate's fame by debating with him. Seven debates were held. Lincoln "took the high road" that slavery was a moral wrong. He was eloquent and achieved national fame. But he lost.

In 1860 the Republican presidential convention was held in Chicago. William Seward was the leading candidate, but Lincoln was nominated instead. Democrats split votes between Douglas, John Breckenridge, and third-party candidate John Bell, so Lincoln won the election. By the time Lincoln was inaugurated in 1861, seven states had seceded. Against the advice of his cabinet, Lincoln sent supplies to Fort Sumter at Charleston. The fort symbolized federal power in the very state that had led secession. South Carolina fired on the fort, and the Civil War began.

Lincoln left military details to his commanders, first Gen. George McClellan, later Ulysses S. Grant. McClellan favored slavery and turned out to be Lincoln's Democratic opponent in 1864. The Constitution protected slavery, but Lincoln believed the commander in chief could abolish it during war, so he issued the Emancipation Proclamation. Lincoln "stretched" the Constitution as he criticized President Polk for doing years before. In 1863, while dedicating the cemetery at Gettysburg, Lincoln said the North was fighting as a rededication to the ideals of the Declaration of Independence, not just against slavery. But in the 1864 election, it was Republican Lincoln endorsing the 13th Amendment that would abolish it versus Democrat McClellan pledging states rights. Lincoln's win changed the country's racial future. It also angered Southern sympathizer John Wilkes Booth enough to kill Lincoln while the Lincolns attended Ford's Theater.

In 1867 Lincoln Square was named. In 1868 a Lincoln statue was dedicated with President Johnson present. It was by Lot Flannery, a local sculptor who knew Lincoln. Lincoln stands with one hand on the Roman symbol of union. The statue was put in front of City Hall, now the U.S. Courthouse, where it stands today. In 1876 the Emancipation Monument was dedicated.

In 1922 the Lincoln Memorial was dedicated. It was designed by architect Henry Bacon. It is like the Parthenon in Athens. There are 56 steps because Lincoln was 56 years old. There are 36 columns because there were 36 states when he died. The names of 48 states appear because there were 48 when the memorial was built. Inside are murals by Jules Guerin. On one wall is Lincoln's Gettysburg address, on the other his second inaugural address. In the center is Daniel Chester French's giant statue of Lincoln seated. French had a deaf son and had just completed the statue of deaf school founder Thomas Gallaudet. He positioned Lincoln's left hand for A and his right hand for L in sign language.

HENRY WADSWORTH LONGFELLOW

Connecticut Avenue at M Street, N.W.

One of America's most popular poets, Longfellow was born in Portland, ME, in 1807. His father was a Congressman, his mother daughter of a Revolutionary War hero. Brought up with many books, he entered Bowdoin College at 15, a classmate of Nathaniel Hawthorne. His goal was a literary career, but as a practical measure, he settled on teaching. In preparation, he spent 1826 to 1829 traveling in Europe. He mastered ten languages. Returning to Bowdoin, he held a professorship. During this time he married, then returned to Europe, only to have his young wife die there of fever. In 1836 he became professor of modern languages at Harvard. He remarried and had six children and a happy life until 1861, when his second wife died of burns after her dress caught fire. His later years were filled with many writings, public appearances, international visitors, honorary degrees, and considerable prosperity. He died at Cambridge in 1882.

Unlike other poets of the time, Longfellow had a power with which to create myths - figures and situations that would become part of American lore: *Paul Revere's Ride, The Courtship of Miles Standish, The Song of Hiawatha, The Village Blacksmith, Evangeline, The Wreck of the Hesperus.*

It is unclear why this nonpolitical poet sits in his chair at one of Washington's busiest intersections, except that his statue had to be put somewhere. The Longfellow Memorial Association gave it to the country in 1909. The poet's granddaughter unveiled it at the dedication.

MARTIN LUTHER

Thomas Circle at 14th Street and Massachusetts Avenue, in front of the Luther Memorial Church

Martin Luther was the founder of the 16th-century Reformation and is called the father of Protestantism.

Luther was born in 1483 at Eisleben, Saxony. He attended the U. of Erfurt, later studied law. While walking with a friend, talking about the relationship between man and God, his friend was struck dead by lightning. Luther switched from law to religion. He was ordained in 1507, received a doctorate, traveled to Rome. He was shocked by corruption in the Church. Too, his studies led him to believe forgiveness of sin and salvation could be achieved by faith in Christ alone, not by good deeds and not through Church practices like confession and indulgences.

In 1517, Luther posted 95 of his theses on the door of the church at Wittenberg where a representative of the pope was collecting revenues. These were meant to be points for discussion, but copies rapidly spread throughout Europe, and Luther was charged with heresy. By 1520, Luther completed three books containing his views - inviting German princes to reform the Church, attacking the papacy and the theology of sacraments, and stating his position on good deeds. The Church excommunicated him, and he was banned from the empire.

Luther translated the bible into German. He wrote pamphlets, catechisms, hymns, commentaries - over 100 volumes. With others he organized evangelical churches in the German territories, abolished confession and private mass, let priests marry, abandoned convents and monasteries. He married a former nun, and they raised six children. By 1530, many theologians, princes, and city councils subscribed to Luther's positions. In 1546 when Luther died at Eisleben, he left behind a Protestant movement that quickly spread throughout the Western world.

The bronze statue of Luther was cast in Germany, a duplicate of one in Worms. It was donated by the Martin Luther Society of New York and erected in 1884 on the 400th anniversary of Luther's birth. Over 5,000 people attended the unveiling - and saw: First, the American flag that covered the statue froze and wouldn't come off. Then, during the singing of Luther's hymn *A Mighty Fortress Is Our God*, the platform holding all the dignitaries collapsed.

JOHN MARSHALL. (See also **John Marshall Park.**)

On the west terrace of the U.S. Capitol.

The chief justice is shown seated by sculptor William Story, son of Joseph Story, one of Marshall's colleagues on the court. There's a duplicate from the same mold in front of the Philadelphia Museum of Art.

Statues

GEORGE MCCLELLAN

Connecticut Avenue at Columbia Road, N.W.

Maj. Gen. George Brinton McClellan sits on his horse atop a decorated pedestal on the hill at this intersection. Contest winner Frederick MacMornie's statue was created and exhibited in Paris, then dedicated at this site in 1907.

McClellan is known as the procrastinating general that President Lincoln had to remove from command. But he was much more than that: McClellan was born in Philadelphia in 1826. He graduated from West Point, and as an engineer, was with Gen. Scott in the Mexican War. Afterwards, he taught at West Point, then studied European military systems. Among improvements from the studies was a new cavalry saddle known as the McClellan saddle. In 1857 McClellan resigned his commission to become vice president of the Illinois Central Railroad, then president of part of the Ohio and Mississippi Railroad.

McClellan returned to the military at the start of the Civil War and commanded the Department of the Ohio, clearing western Virginia of Confederates. President Lincoln picked him to command the Army of the Potomac and defend Washington. He was a brilliant organizer, administrator, and trainer, and had small successes, but at the same time, worried Lincoln by being too cautious. Lincoln replaced him in 1862. Some say that he was temperamentally unfit for high command, others that he was denied victories by political interference.

In 1864, the Democratic Party nominated McClellan for president. He opposed emancipation of the slaves and wished to continue the war, although the party platform called for war's end. McClellan garnered 1.8 million to Lincoln's 2.2 million votes. On election day, he resigned his commission. He spent three years abroad, took on the task of being chief engineer at the New York City docks, and finally was elected governor of New Jersey. He died at 59 in 1885.

GEORGE GORDON MEADE

Pennsylvania Avenue, between 3rd and 4th Streets, N.W.

George Meade was born in Cadiz, Spain, in 1815. He graduated from West Point in 1835 and served as a lieutenant in the Second Seminole Indian War in Florida, but then resigned to work as an engineer. He rejoined the Army in 1842, served in the Mexican War, and made captain in 1856. When the Civil War broke out in 1861, Meade was commissioned a brigadier general of volunteers in charge of a group helping build the defenses around Washington.

Under Gen. McClellan, Meade led a brigade in battles at Mechanicsville, Gaines' Mill, and Frayser's Farm, where he was wounded. He recovered and fought in the Second Battle of Bull Run. When Gen. Joe Hooker was wounded at Antietam, Meade took over the 1st Corps. He was promoted to major general and given command of the 5th Corps, which he led successfully at Chancellorsville. When Hooker resigned, Meade was given command of the Army of the Potomac.

Meade's great military achievement was his victory over Gen. Robert E. Lee at the Battle of Gettysburg, fought just three days later, July 1-3, 1863. This was a major victory, accomplished in a command new to him, with hastily assembled forces, at a place not of his choosing. Meade and his army went on to fight at Petersburg and Appomattox. At the end of the war, Meade was made a major general in the regular Army, and then commanded the Military District of the Atlantic, headquartered in Philadelphia. He died there in 1872.

In his statue, Gen. Meade stands, surrounded by allegorical figures of courage, fame, loyalty, progress, energy, chivalry, and the wings of war. It was a gift from the Commonwealth of Pennsylvania to honor his victory at Gettysburg.

ALBERT PIKE
3rd and D Streets, N.W.

Pike's statue was donated by the Masons. It shows him standing, holding his book about Freemasonry. Below him is the goddess of Masonry holding the banner of the Scottish Rite.

Albert Pike was born in Boston in 1809. He dropped out of school, wrote poetry (e.g., a Confederate version of *Dixie*), went West, taught school in Arkansas, joined the staff of the *Arkansas Advocate* and soon owned the newspaper, studied law and became a lawyer, then commanded a troop in the Mexican War. His travels made him an Indian expert, and during the Civil War, he was made a Confederate brigadier general commanding the Indian Territory. But he criticized Jefferson Davis, was arrested for insubordination, and retired for most of the war. Afterwards he was pardoned by President Johnson and returned to practicing law, this time in Memphis and Washington.

Meanwhile Pike had become a Freemason. He was elected Sovereign Grand Commander of the Supreme Grand Council, Southern Jurisdiction, of the Scottish Rite Masons. He held that position for 32 years. He spent years rewriting the rituals of the order and published its *Morals and Dogma of the Ancient and Accepted Scottish Rite of Freemasonry*.

Pike died in Washington in 1891. His will said he should be cremated and his ashes sprinkled among the trees in front of the Scottish Rite Temple. Instead, the temple council had him buried in Georgetown. In 1915, the new temple (at 16th and S Streets, N.W.) was opened, and in 1944, Pike was moved to a crypt inside. It is said he haunts the building, looking for his trees. Maybe he can take consolation in being the only Confederate general with a statue in Washington.

Statues

CASIMIR PULASKI

Pennsylvania Avenue and 13th Street, N.W.

The park formed by Pennsylvania Avenue and E, 13th, and 14th Streets, in front of the National Theater, is called Freedom Plaza. Its main statue is the one to Count Casimir Pulaski.

Pulaski was born in Lithuania in 1748, studied law, served in the Polish army. In 1769, he joined an uprising against the king. He commanded insurgents until 1771, when he failed in an attempt to capture the king. He was outlawed in the country and fled to France. There he met Benjamin Franklin and volunteered his services to the American cause. Franklin gave him a letter of introduction to George Washington - as well as money for his trip. His subsequent actions weren't particularly successful: He fought at Brandywine, then commanded a battalion of cavalry but resigned after a dispute with other officers. Congress made him a brigadier general and gave him an independent corps of cavalry that became known as Pulaski's Legion. He was a courageous leader, inspired his troops, and recorded several victorious assaults against the British. But his troops were defeated in New Jersey, were inactive for long periods, and suffered another defeat in South Carolina. He was commanding cavalry at Savannah, GA, in 1779, when he was wounded. He died two days later. He is buried in Savannah.

His large statue was erected in 1910. It shows him atop his horse and dressed in the Polish uniform he preferred over his Continental Army one.

JEAN ROCHAMBEAU. (See also **Rochambeau Bridge.**)

In the Southwest corner of Lafayette Park.

Jean Baptiste Donatien de Vimeur de Rochambeau was born in France in 1725 and educated for the priesthood, but entered the army at 16. In 1780 France sent him in command of 6,000 men to aid America in its fight for freedom against the British. He and his army joined Gen. Washington in the victorious march on Yorktown, and Rochambeau was present at Cornwallis' surrender there in 1781.

When Rochambeau returned to France he was made governor of Picardy and Artois, and later was made a marshal. He commanded an army for French revolutionists, but resigned because of their cruelty, then was imprisoned and barely escaped the guillotine. Napoleon recognized his service to his country and gave him a pension. He died in 1807.

In Lafayette Park he wears his Continental Army uniform. Around his statue are symbols of France aiding America and Liberty defending an embattled eagle. The statue was dedicated by President Theodore Roosevelt and unveiled by the Comtesse de Rochambeau in 1902, with members of the Rochambeau and Lafayette families looking on.

FRANKLIN DELANO ROOSEVELT

Original memorial is on Pennsylvania Avenue at 9th Street, N.W., in front of the National Archives. New one is in West Potomac Park.

Franklin Delano Roosevelt was born in Hyde Park, NY, in 1882. He attended Harvard University. He was considered handsome and athletic. In 1905 he married his cousin, Anna Eleanor Roosevelt, given away at the wedding by her uncle, Theodore Roosevelt. Young Roosevelt then went to Columbia Law School, but left when admitted to the bar and joined a Wall Street law firm. His handling of small-claim cases made him sympathize with the poor. In 1910 as a Democrat he used an old Maxwell car to campaign in Republican farm territory and got elected to the state senate. In 1912, he backed Woodrow Wilson. As an award he was named assistant secretary of the navy. In 1920, his name and liberal image got him the vice presidential nomination under Ohio Gov. James Cox, but they lost to Warren Harding.

In 1921, at his summer home on Campobello Island in New Brunswick, Canada, Roosevelt was stricken with poliomyelitis and lost use of his legs. He decided to stay in public life. In 1924, he nominated New York Gov. Alfred E. Smith for president. Smith didn't get the nomination until 1928, then persuaded Roosevelt to run to replace him as governor. Smith lost the election to Herbert Hoover, but Roosevelt won. His governorship was full of social-welfare measures. He cultivated a presidential image, using advisors like neighbor Henry Morganthau and labor expert Frances Perkins. Roosevelt secured the 1932 nomination over Smith, and because the Great Depression made Hoover vulnerable, promised Americans a "New Deal" and won the presidency.

On the eve of his inauguration, the banking system collapsed as depositors withdrew savings that banks had tied up in long-term loans. Roosevelt declared, "The only thing we have to fear is fear itself." He closed the banks, got Congress to pass emergency legislation, in a week provided cash for the banks to reopen, and held his first "fireside chat," asking Americans to quit hoarding cash. They responded, and the crisis passed.

Roosevelt's New Deal included abandonment of the gold standard, aid to farmers and federal control of surpluses (AAA), funds for relief and public works (WPA), expanded government regulation of business (NRA), unprecedented redistribution of earnings through excess profit and income taxes, and advantages to labor in organizing and bargaining. Also, it provided guaranteed income for retired people (Social Security), unemployment insurance, cheap electric power (TVA), and a youth conservation corps (CCC). All this caused large deficit spending. While enlarging the role of government, Roosevelt often did so by administratively creating "emergency" agencies. The Supreme Court finally declared much of the New Deal unconstitutional. In 1937, Roosevelt tried to increase size of the court and pack it with liberals, but conservatives succeeded in stopping the plan.

Roosevelt held news conferences almost weekly, addressing the American people in a folksy manner. He appeared completely in charge. For re-election, he easily beat Alfred Landon in 1936, defied tradition for a third term over Wendell Willkie in 1940, and defeated Thomas Dewey in 1944 for a fourth term. In the process, he converted the Democratic Party into the majority one by his appeal to urban, labor, and minority voters.

In 1941 Japan's attack on Pearl Harbor and Germany's declaration of war drew the U.S. into World War II. Roosevelt and Winston Churchill, Britain's prime minister, determined over-all Allied strategy. Roosevelt met with heads of Allied states at Casablanca, Quebec, Teheran, Cairo, and Yalta. In 1945, exhausted, at his Warm Springs, GA, spa for a vacation, he died.

In 1955 Congress authorized a Roosevelt memorial. Roosevelt asked that if people insisted on a memorial that it be plain and no larger than his desk. Accordingly, in 1965 a simple desk-sized marble block with plaque was dedicated in front of the National Archives. It is not in keeping with his wish that the new Roosevelt Memorial, dedicated in 1997, covers an area larger than three football fields, contains enough stones to build an 80-story building, and includes nine sculptures, waterfalls, reception center, and gift shop.

THEODORE ROOSEVELT

On Roosevelt Island in the Potomac River, just north of Roosevelt Bridge and accessed from northbound George Washington Parkway

"Teddy" Roosevelt was born in New York City in 1858. He was so frail he didn't attend school but instead had tutors. He was determined to overcome his weakness, and his family provided him a gym and even a horse. He traveled in Europe, then at 14 up the Nile. He first showed his interest in natural history by returning with a collection of birds, given to the Smithsonian Institution.

At 18 Roosevelt entered Harvard, went on to Columbia Law School. He tired of law, got elected to the state legislature, served as speaker. But he got discouraged and left political life. On Valentine's Day in 1884 his young wife of four years died, and so did his mother. Depressed, he retired to family ranches in South Dakota, then toured Europe. He met a childhood friend and married again. They lived at Oyster Bay, Long Island. They eventually had four sons.

President Harrison named Roosevelt to the Civil Service Commission in 1889, where he served for six years and cleaned up appointments. It brought him national fame. He was made New York City police commissioner in 1895, again cutting evil from government. President McKinley appointed Roosevelt secretary of navy. He immediately strengthened the navy so when the Spanish-American War began in 1898, the navy was ready. He helped organize a regiment of volunteers, and the Rough Riders were born. Roosevelt became their colonel.

After the war Roosevelt was more popular than ever. New York elected him governor. This time he tackled big business - and made enemies. To get rid of him, his party made him vice-presidential nominee under McKinley for the 1900 election. But in 1901 McKinley was assassinated, and Roosevelt unexpectedly became president. Over two terms, he struggled against big business interference in politics ("trust-busting," he called it), enlarged the navy, passed a pure food bill, enlarged and protected national forests in the west, established the departments of commerce and labor, and established a census bureau. He obtained territory in Panama for building a canal. He served as a go-between to bring about settlement of the Russo-Japanese War. He received the Nobel Peace Prize.

After his terms ended, he went big-game hunting in Africa. Specimens he collected were given to the Smithsonian. Still a popular speaker, he went on the lecture circuit. In 1912, amid a split in the Republican Party, he became the presidential nominee of a new Progressive (Bull Moose) Party, but was defeated by Woodrow Wilson. So he went off on another journey, to Brazil. The climate was too much, and he became quite ill. Over the next few years, his strength weakened. He died in his sleep in 1919 at his home at Sagamore Hill, NY.

Roosevelt's memorial is on what used to be Analostan Island, home of Gen. John Mason, son of Virginia patriot George Mason. Mason's island home was often visited by George Washington and Thomas Jefferson. The Masons moved to Fairfax in 1834 and by 1937 their home was torn down. The island was purchased by the Theodore Roosevelt Memorial Association. It took until 1961 to agree on the memorial's design. Nature trails cross the island, and at their center is a plaza with a 17-foot statue of Roosevelt. Nearby are engraved his ideas about nature, mankind, youth, and government. He stands with his right arm raised. He's not waving. It's just a typical pose for this energetic speaker.

BENJAMIN RUSH

On the grounds of the Naval Bureau of Medicine and Surgery at 23rd and E Streets, N.W.

This hilly site always was a military center. In 1800 Marine Corps headquarters were here, and in 1843 the first Naval Observatory was built on top of the hill. In the 1930s the Naval Hospital, Medical School, Dental School, Dispensary, and similar institutions affecting naval medical care were all centered here. The statue of Dr. Rush was erected by the American Medical Association in 1904 and dedicated with President Roosevelt looking on.

Benjamin Rush was born in Byberry, PA, in 1746. He graduated from Princeton and obtained his doctorate from the University of Edinburgh. In 1769 he became professor of chemistry at the College of Philadelphia, first such chair in America. He represented Pennsylvania in the Continental Congress and signed the Declaration of Independence. From 1776 to 1778 he served as surgeon general. In the 1780s he wrote to abolish slavery and capital punishment, advocated public schools, attacked evils of liquor, advocated a modern penal system, opened the first public health clinic, helped found Dickinson College. From 1789 until 1813 he was professor of medicine at the University of Pennsylvania. He was one of the first to note that mosquitoes were prevalent when outbreaks of yellow fever occurred. He initiated shock therapy for the mentally ill. For 16 years, he was treasurer of the U.S. mint, appointed by President Adams. In the late 1790s, Rush came under attack in the press for his medical and political beliefs. Rush sued, and the supreme court of Pennsylvania awarded him damages in a landmark case that defined the line between freedom of the press and physicians' rights of practice. He died in Philadelphia in 1813.

JOSE DE SAN MARTIN

Virginia Avenue and 20th Street, N.W.

Jose de San Martin, "Knight of the Andes" and "Liberator of the South," was born in 1778 in the Argentine village of Yapeyu where his father was royal governor. He went to Madrid to be educated, and at 11 enrolled in the Spanish army, spending 20 years in active service, some against Portugal and in Africa.

In 1812 San Martin returned to Argentina and was made governor at Mendoza near the mountain passes to Chile. San Martin viewed himself as a military leader, not a political one, and he offered his services to the independence movement and its revolutionaries. He became determined to liberate Argentina by striking at the citadel of Spanish power - Peru. In 1817 he led soldiers across the mountains - a rugged 17-day march - surprised the enemy armies in Chile, and brought independence to that country. He was offered the presidency, but declined it in favor of one of his chief lieutenants, Bernardo O'Higgins. By 1820 San Martin had created a navy so as to send troops into Peru. In a year, Lima was freed, and Peruvians hailed San Martin as "Protector of Peru." In this position, San Martin expelled Spanish citizens, abolished slavery, and reformed the systems that depended on Indian labor.

It was now time to combine forces with Simon Bolivar to plan the future of South America. The two met twice, alone, at Guayaquil in 1822. One meeting was 30 minutes, the other five hours. No one knows what transpired - obviously no agreement was reached. San Martin was dejected, and a month later resigned his protectorship and his military command. He went to Europe and remained in self-exile there until his death at Boulogne, France, in 1850. His body was returned to the cathedral in Buenos Aires in 1880.

The Argentine people honor San Martin as one of their great leaders. His statue is a copy of one in Buenos Aires. Among its inscriptions is "His name, like Washington, represents the American ideal of democracy, justice, and liberty."

ALEXANDER SHEPHERD. (See **Shepherd Park.**)
Indiana Avenue and 4th Street, N.W.

Alexander Shepherd was the 19th century political "boss" credited with making Washington a city and at the same time blamed for bankrupting it. After his death in 1902, city residents raised funds for his statue, which was dedicated in 1909 and placed at Pennsylvania Avenue and 14th Street. It stood at that prominent spot until 1979, when Freedom Plaza was built. At this writing, the statue stands in the city's auto impoundment lot next to the Blue Plains sewage-treatment plant. Its movement has been approved to this new location between the Municipal Building and D.C. Superior Court, where the first city hall stood, but some residents are arguing for a still more prominent place.

WILLIAM TECUMSEH SHERMAN
Pennsylvania Avenue, on the square at 15th and E Streets

Sherman was born in 1820 in Lancaster, OH. He was named Tecumseh after the Shawnee Indian chief, whom his father admired. At 9 when his father died, he was adopted, and his foster mother added the William. Through his foster father's influence he was appointed to West Point, graduating in 1840. In 1850 he married his foster sister. He found his early Army life "dull, tame" and resigned. He tried banking, law, finally teaching at a state military academy in Louisiana.

When the Civil War broke out he commanded a brigade at the First Battle of Bull Run (Manassas), where his troops were routed by Confederates. He was promoted by President Lincoln to brigadier general, sent to Kentucky, and failed again, so badly that he was thought insane and was known as Crazy Sherman. Under Gen. Grant, Sherman was brilliant at the Battle of Shiloh. He became a major general. He played a major role in the capture of Vicksburg, held the flank at Chattanooga, pushed his troops to Knoxville to save Union forces there. When Grant became commander of all Union armies, Sherman took command in the South. He started his march to Atlanta in May 1864 and captured the city in September, then marched to the sea, ravaging the countryside and taking Savannah "as a Christmas gift." In 1865, he headed north but found little opposition before Gen. Lee surrendered and the war ended.

When Grant became president, Sherman became general in chief of the army, a post he held for 14 years. Sherman was popular in the North, with broad views on public affairs. He was hated in the South because of his destruction of much of Georgia. In 1884 a move was made to draft him for president. He answered with his famous "I will not accept if nominated, and will not serve if elected." He died in New York City in 1891.

Sherman's monument is big. He sits on a horse on a pedestal on a raised plaza. There're Peace, War, tablets of his generals and his march through Georgia, mosaics naming his battles, and soldiers representing infantry, cavalry, artillery, and engineers. The site was chosen because Sherman stood on it when reviewing returning Civil War troops in 1865.

TARAS SHEVCHENKO

P Street between 22nd and 23rd Streets, N.W.

Taras Shevchenko was born a serf at Kiev in 1814. He had a passion for reading, poetry, and drawing, so his master had him trained. He got introduced to Ukrainian writer Hrebinka whose library was put at his disposal, and new friends purchased his freedom. He enrolled at the Petersburg Art Academy. His first collection of poems in 1840 brought him fame. More poems followed, some ballads, others distinguished by folklore elements, nostalgia for the Cossack era, visions of Ukraine's heroic past, abhorrence of injustice, even Christian themes. Shevchenko protested against oppression, called attention to political prisoners in the Siberian mines, denounced Peter I and Catherine II for crimes against the Ukrainian people, called to the people to fight for freedom - all via his poems, with their folk-song rhythms, then-new vocabularies, imagery, passion, and ideas. He's considered the creator of the Ukrainian literary language.

In 1846, Ukrainian intellectuals formed a secret brotherhood to advocate union of all Slavs with independence and equality for each nation. Shevchenko joined. The brotherhood was denounced, and Shevchenko was imprisoned. After ten years, he was released, but was never again free from police surveillance. He died in 1861.

His statue was sponsored by Ukrainian-Americans and dedicated in 1964. President Eisenhower did the unveiling, and 100,000 people looked on.

FREDERICH VON STEUBEN

In the Northwest Corner of Lafayette Park

Baron Frederich William Augustus von Steuben arrived in America in 1777. He had served in the Seven Years' War and had been a general staff officer in the Prussian army and aide-de-camp to Frederick the Great. He came to Gen. George Washington at Valley Forge with a letter of introduction from Benjamin Franklin. With his knowledge of Prussian military training, organization, and administration, he was able within weeks to mold American recruits into a force equal in training and discipline to the British - a remarkable military feat. And von Steuben spoke no English! He was made a major general and took part in the siege at Yorktown. After leaving the army in 1784, he became an American citizen. He was granted 16,000 acres in New York by the state and a pension by Congress. He died in 1794. He is honored in Lafayette Park with a statue that includes a woman and child depicting America honoring von Steuben and a youth and warrior symbolizing military instruction. The statue was dedicated by President Taft in 1910.

ROBERT A. TAFT

Just Northwest of the Capitol, across Constitution Avenue and between 1st Street and New Jersey Avenue, N.W.

The eldest son of President William Howard Taft, Robert was U.S. senator from Ohio from 1932 until his death in 1953. He was a conservative, opposing President Roosevelt and his New Deal policies, ultimately earning the title, "Mr. Republican," and eventually campaigning for the Republican nomination against the more liberal Dwight Eisenhower in the 1952 election. Taft's memorial is a 100-foot 27-bell carillon, with his 11-foot statue at its base.

DANIEL WEBSTER

At Scott Circle, Massachusetts Avenue and 16th Street, N.W.

Daniel Webster was a great orator - ambitious, tall, with resonant voice. He was often compared with enormous natural wonders like Niagara Falls. At the same time, humility was not one of his virtues, and he was always in debt.

Webster was born at Salisbury, NH, in 1782. He graduated from Dartmouth, studied law, was admitted to the bar in 1805. Drawn to politics, he served from New Hampshire in the House of Representatives from 1813 to 1817. He opposed the War of 1812, voted against war taxes, defeated a draft bill. In the Dartmouth College case, his stand for its charter and against state control of the college won at the Supreme Court. In 1823 he returned to the House, representing Massachusetts, and in 1827 was elected to the Senate.

In 1830 he gave his most famous speech, "A Reply to Hayne." It was 73 pages long. South Carolina Sen. Robert Hayne had defended states rights by his theory that states could nullify federal laws and refuse to obey them. Webster answered, saying the constitution had created a single, unified nation. His speech ended with the phrase "Liberty and Union, now and forever, one and inseparable."

In 1836, Webster ran for president, later campaigned for William Henry Harrison and was rewarded by being made secretary of state. He negotiated with Britain a settlement for the boundary of Maine. In 1845 he returned to the Senate where he opposed the Mexican War and admission of Texas to the Union. He again had presidential ambitions, but Zachary Taylor won nomination and election. As the question of slavery arose Webster supported Henry Clay's Compromise of 1850. His sponsorship of the bill probably postponed civil war for a decade. When Millard Fillmore succeeded Taylor as president, Webster again became secretary of state. His health began to fail, and he died in Marshfield, MA, in 1852.

Webster's statue shows him making his reply to Hayne. It was commissioned by Stilson Hutchins, founder of *The Washington Post*, who dedicated the statue in 1900 and gave it as a gift to the federal government.

JOHN WESLEY. (See also **Francis Asbury**.)

Outside the Wesley Theological Seminary at 4400 Massachusetts Avenue, N.W.

The Wesley name was made famous by two of the family's 19 children, John and Charles. John was born in England in 1703. His father was a rector, his mother daughter of a minister - herself one of 25 children. John studied at Oxford and Christ Church, was elected fellow of Lincoln College, and was ordained in 1728. At Oxford, Charles founded a Holy Club of men interested in spiritual growth, and John became a participant. In 1735, both Wesleys accompanied James Oglethorpe to the new colony of Georgia. John's church views were rigid and aroused such opposition that he had to return to England. Once back, he had a religious conversion centered on the belief that one could gain salvation by faith in Christ alone. John emulated George Whitefield, who had mounted a horse to preach to humble folk in the open, and became an itinerant preacher. He organized his followers like the Holy Club of his Oxford days, and they became known as Methodists, for their systematic program for conversion - a "method to their madness." By 1739 he was establishing Methodist societies throughout the British Isles. He married, but continued ordered living until he died in 1791. Charles went on to become perhaps England's greatest hymnist, writing over 5,000 hymns, among them "Hark, the Herald Angels Sing."

The Wesley statue is a copy of a sculpture at Wesley Chapel in Bristol, England. It is a gift from English Lord Rank, himself a Methodist. It shows Wesley on horseback, bible in hand.

JOHN WITHERSPOON

Connecticut Avenue at N Street, N.W.

Witherspoon was born near Edinburgh, Scotland, in 1723. He obtained a divinity degree from Edinburgh University in 1743, and as a pastor, he became known as leader of the conservative group of the Presbyterian Church. In 1768 he accepted the presidency of the College of New Jersey, now Princeton, a position he held until his death in 1794. He represented New Jersey in the Continental Congress and was the only clergyman to sign the Declaration of Independence. During the Revolution, he helped with foreign relations and finance. After the war, he helped organize the Presbyterian Church in the U.S.

Witherspoon's statue was dedicated by the Witherspoon Memorial Association in 1909. He stands with bible in hand, looking out of place at this busy intersection. There's a reason: Originally he was in front of the National Presbyterian Church. In 1966 the church was moved to Nebraska Avenue, N.W. Presbyterians want the statue moved to the new church site, but government officials say it can't be moved without an act of Congress and besides, Witherspoon's reputation as a patriot is sufficient to leave him in place.

STREETS

There are hundreds of streets in the city, so why these few here? Because they are the main routes in and out of the city. Because they have names of fascinating people and far-away places. Because three are ones specially named at the oft-visited Lincoln Memorial and at the Holocaust Museum. Because streets downtown that interrupt the grid of lettered, numbered, and state-named streets are rare and unusual. And because in an already published compilation of the origins of Washington's street names, two of the most traveled arteries - Kenilworth Avenue and the Whitehurst Freeway - are unexplained and a third - Benning Road - is credited to the wrong person. The book is *George Washington Never Slept Here* by Amy Allotta and published by Bonus Books, Inc., Chicago, IL, in 1993. It's the first compilation of city street name origins and presents the stories behind hundreds of them.

HENRY BACON DRIVE

From the Lincoln Memorial, past the Vietnam Veterans' Memorial, to Constitution Avenue

This one-block drive bears Henry Bacon's name, because he designed the Lincoln Memorial. He was born in Watseka, IL, in 1866. He attended the University of Illinois and received a scholarship that led to studies in Europe. In the late 1800s, he was with McKim, Mead, and White, architects, until he formed his own partnership of Brite and Bacon. After 1902, he practiced alone. Bacon championed the classic Greek style of architecture, as is clearly seen in his 1922 Lincoln Memorial. He collaborated with sculptor Daniel Chester French in over 50 memorials. Bacon died in New York City in 1924.

BENNING ROAD

Running from Maryland Avenue, N.E., across the Anacostia River, past Kenilworth Avenue and East Capitol Street, S.E., and into Maryland

This main District artery takes its name from William Benning who had land holdings in the area. Benning was born in Amelia County, VA, in 1771. He arrived in the Washington area in 1794, bought 33 acres on the east side of the Anacostia River just north of the navy yard, and built his home there. He also owned a wooden toll bridge across the river. In 1814, it was burned by the British, but in 1820, it was rebuilt. The bridge was known as Benning's Bridge, and the road from Washington to the area was known as Benning's Road. In 1827, Benning moved to E Street, N.W. He was a successful businessman and a member of the board of directors of the Bank of Washington. After his death in 1831, his wife continued to operate the bridge for another ten years.

BLADENSBURG ROAD

Running northeast into Maryland from its start at the intersection of Florida and Maryland Avenues and Benning Road, N.E.

This main District road passes the National Arboretum and Mt. Olivet Cemetery. It ends toward the town of Bladensburg, MD. The town was laid out in 1742 and took its name from Thomas Bladen, then the governor of Maryland.

DWIGHT D. EISENHOWER FREEWAY. (See **Eisenhower Theater.**)

I-395, from the Potomac River east to Pennsylvania Avenue

As this elevated interstate highway cuts through the District of Columbia, it is known as the Southwest/Southeast Freeway. In 1990, on President Eisenhower's 100th birthday, its name was formally changed by the District government. A year later, Congress approved the change. Today, eight years after that, the Eisenhower Freeway is still called by its old name by almost everyone.

FOXHALL ROAD

Running between MacArthur Boulevard and Nebraska Avenue, N.W.

This road is named for foundry owner Henry Foxall. His name was misspelled on the first street sign erected and has never been corrected.

Foxall was born in Mammouthshire, England, in 1758. He became superintendent of iron works in Dublin, Ireland. He was also a lay minister. In 1797 he came to Philadelphia. From 1800 to 1815, he was owner of a foundry in Georgetown making cannons, shot, wheels, etc., many of which were used in the War of 1812. He also served as minister of the Methodist Church in Georgetown and gave ground and funds for the Foundry Methodist Church in Washington. (That name came only partly from Foxall's foundry - Methodist John Wesley's first church in London was the Foundry Church.) Foxall built additional churches downtown and at the Navy Yard. He got involved in politics, and from 1821 to 1823, served as mayor of Georgetown. In 1823, he returned to visit England and died there.

DANIEL FRENCH DRIVE. (See also **Abraham Lincoln.**)

From the Lincoln Memorial past the Korean War Memorial to Independence Avenue

This one-block drive bears French's name, because he was sculptor of Lincoln's statue inside the Lincoln Memorial. Daniel Chester French was born in Exeter, NH, in 1850. He attended Massachusetts Institute of Technology for a year, then studied briefly in New York and Florence. When 23, he received his first commission and created the Minute Man statue, which established his reputation. The statue became a symbol of American patriotism, and was the one used on defense bonds, stamps, and posters of World War II. His large body of work consists mainly of American rather than classical subjects. His statue of Lincoln is typical. In Washington, he also designed the Butt-Millet and Dupont fountains. French died in Stockbridge, MA, in 1931.

KENILWORTH AVENUE

The extension of Anacostia Freeway north of East Capitol Street and on to the Maryland state line where it becomes the Washington-Baltimore Parkway

At the turn of the century, Allen W. Mallery developed a subdivision in the northeast tip of the District and named it for the ancient English town and castle made famous in Sir Walter Scott's *Ivanhoe*. In 1901, the Kenilworth Citizens Association was founded, and Mallery served as its first president. A 1925 brochure, "Rare Water Lilies" by aquatic gardens founder W. B. Shaw lists his address simply as Kenilworth, Washington, D.C. And a 1940 *Indianapolis Star* article describes "Kenilworth, D.C., a picturesque village." Although the "village" no longer exists per se, the northern part of the avenue runs through where it used to be.

MACARTHUR BOULEVARD

Running northwest from Canal Road, N.W., past the Georgetown Reservoir through the Palisades neighborhood and into Maryland

This boulevard, originally Conduit Road (because the city's water supply ran under it) was renamed for military leader Douglas MacArthur. He was given the honor in 1942 while leading World War II troops in the Pacific.

MacArthur was born in Little Rock, AR, in 1880. He graduated first in his class from West Point in 1903. A series of engineering assignments and one as an aide to President Theodore Roosevelt introduced him to the Philippines. During World War I, MacArthur commanded the 42nd (Rainbow) Division in France. Afterwards he was superintendent at West Point, where he expanded the curriculum, raised standards, and bettered the athletic program. He held two more Philippine commands. In 1928, he headed the U.S. Olympic Committee.

In 1930, MacArthur became chief of staff and a full general. It fell to him to expel the Bonus Army (World War I veterans marching for their promised bonus) from Washington, for which he got a lot of criticism. But he operated the army effectively throughout the Great Depression, considering lack of appropriations. In 1935, he was made military advisor to the Philippines, and a year later, the Philippine president named him field marshal of the Philippine army, a position he held until 1941. In 1937 MacArthur retired.

In 1941 when World War II was imminent, MacArthur was recalled by President Franklin Roosevelt. He led a skillful defense against the invading Japanese in the

Philippines on Bataan and Corregidor until moving to Australia, where he became supreme Allied commander in the Pacific. In 1942, he launched a counteroffensive in New Guinea. It took until mid-1945 to drive the Japanese out of the Southwestern Pacific and the Philippines. MacArthur was promoted to five-star rank. In September, he accepted the surrender of Japan, then from 1945 to 1951, directed the Allied occupation of Japan, introducing reforms in land distribution, disarmament, and a liberal constitution.

In 1950, when North Korean troops invaded South Korea, MacArthur was named supreme United Nations commander. His troops stopped the enemy advance near Pusan. He then conducted a brilliant amphibious landing at Inchon and moved the enemy back to the Manchurian border. The enormous Chinese army then entered the war, driving back into South Korea by mid-1951. MacArthur called for aggressive action, including bombing of Chinese bases in Manchuria, but his superiors disagreed. President Truman charged MacArthur with insubordination and relieved him of command. MacArthur returned to the U.S. In 1952 conservative Republicans tried to nominate him for president. He lived in New York City and frequently spoke on public issues. He died in 1964.

RENO ROAD

The extension of 34th Street running north between Wisconsin and Connecticut Avenues to Western Avenue and the Maryland state line

Reno Road took its name from Fort Reno, a nearby Civil War fort named for Maj. Gen. Jesse Lee Reno. Reno, NV, also bears his name.

Reno was born at Wheeling, WV, in 1823. In 1846, he graduated from West Point and served in the War with Mexico. He returned to West Point where he taught mathematics. He had assignments concerning artillery on the ordnance board at Washington Arsenal, on border and coast surveys, and as commander of the arsenal at Mt. Vernon, AL. By 1860, he was a captain. In 1861, he became a brigadier general of volunteers, and commanded a brigade and later division under Gen. Ambrose Burnside in North Carolina. In 1862 he became a major general and fought at Manassas, Chantilly, and then at South Mountain, where he was killed.

SUITLAND PARKWAY

The extension of South Capitol Street running southeast across the Anacostia River and into Maryland

The parkway passes Suitland, MD, named for Col. Samuel Taylor Suit, who lived in the area from 1834 to 1888 and was a state senator.

RAOUL WALLENBERG PLACE

The section of 15th Street between Independence and Maine Avenues, between the Holocaust Museum and the Tidal Basin

This place honors the Swedish diplomat credited with saving as many as 100,000 Jews during World War II.

Wallenberg was born in Stockholm in 1912. He traveled widely and was proficient in several languages. In 1935 he graduated from the University of Michigan, then worked in South Africa and Palestine, later managed an export-import business in Stockholm.

In 1944 in Budapest, Wallenberg became an attaché in the Swedish mission. He distributed fake Swedish passports and identification papers to thousands of Jews who would otherwise have been sent to death camps, and hid others in buildings under Swedish custody. In 1945, after the Soviet army reached the city, he left Budapest by car with two Russian officers to meet with Soviet officials. He was never seen again. The Soviets denied any knowledge, but in 1957, the Soviet government reported that Wallenberg had died in prison in 1947. Yet, in 1971, an international committee concluded that he was still alive. In 1981, an act of Congress made Wallenberg an honorary American citizen - only Winston Churchill had been given that honor before. In 1983, this street was given his name.

WHITEHURST FREEWAY

Elevated expressway at the base of Georgetown, running east from the Key Bridge at M Street to K Street, N.W.

This was Washington's first elevated highway. It's named for Captain H. C. Whitehurst, director of highways for the District from 1930 until his death in 1948.

Whitehurst was born in Richmond, VA. He graduated from Virginia Tech in 1906. In World War I he served as a combat engineer officer. Later, he headed construction at Wilson Dam in Alabama. In 1926, as a captain, he was assigned to the District Engineer Commissioner's office. In 1929 he resigned to enter private industry, but instead was talked into heading D.C.'s road development. Under his administration, underpasses were built at Scott and Thomas Circles, Dupont Circle was constructed, K Street was elevated, the Calvert Street Bridge over Rock Creek and the Pennsylvania Avenue Bridge over the Anacostia were built, the Sousa Bridge and 14th Street bridges were completed, and District roads increased from 550 miles to over 1,000. The plan for the "sky road" south of Georgetown that now bears his name was his own. The freeway was completed in 1949. Whitehurst's four-year-old granddaughter cut the ribbon to open the road.

THEATERS AND AUDITORIUMS

Washington is not just a political center, but a cultural one. In addition to visiting memorials, museums, or galleries, a visitor or resident is likely to attend some event in a theater, auditorium, or similar facility. And that place is likely to be named for someone. The John F. Kennedy Center for the Performing Arts contains the Eisenhower Theater. The Library of Congress presents concerts, readings, films, and lectures in its Coolidge Auditorium, Whittall Pavilion, Mary Pickford Theater, and Mumford Room. The Smithsonian Institution presents performances and talks in its Baird and Meyer auditoriums, movies in its Langley Theater, and shows in its Einstein Planetarium. Here are over 20 stories behind those and other names of the most frequently mentioned theater facilities in the city.

ARENA STAGE. (See also **Kreeger Theater** and **Fichandler Stage.**)
6th and M Streets, S.W.

Arena Stage was formed in 1950, a pioneer of theater-in-the-round and one of the first regional repertory companies. The original part of the present building was constructed in 1961 with an in-the-round theater. It could not be called a theater, though, because city building codes required a theater to have a proscenium arch and a fire curtain. Hence its "stage" name.

Arena Stage now comprises the Kreeger Theater, Fichandler Stage, and Old Vat Room. The Kreeger Theater was added in 1971, a gift by David Lloyd Kreeger. Fichandler Stage is named for Arena's founder, Zelda Fichandler. For years before the present building, the organization staged its plays in the hospitality hall/ice room of the old Heurich Brewery, which stood where the Kennedy Center is. Someone referred to it as "the old vat." Thus the origin of the Old Vat Room.

BAIRD AUDITORIUM. (See also **The Smithsonian Building** and **Joseph Henry.**)
In the Museum of Natural History, Constitution Avenue at 10th Street, N.W.

This auditorium, main site for many Smithsonian programs, bears the name of Spencer Fullerton Baird, second secretary of the Smithsonian. Baird was born in 1823 in Reading, PA. He attended Dickinson College when he was only 13, obtained B.A. and M.A. degrees, and was later appointed professor of natural history there. In an era in which there were few museums and no laws protecting wildlife, those interested in natural history depended on their own collections. When he was 16, Baird started daily walks up to 40 miles in length, kept details in a journal, and skinned and preserved his own animal and bird specimens.

Baird's wife was daughter of the inspector general of the U.S. Army, and with Joseph Henry's approval, Baird circulated a letter to Army personnel requesting that specimens be sent to him as an agent of the Smithsonian. In 1850, Baird was appointed assistant secretary of the Smithsonian, and by that time, the Smithsonian held 6,000 specimens from 26 Army expeditions and naturalists around the world. Under Baird's administration, the Smithsonian's specimen collections grew dramatically. Baird compiled descriptions of birds, set standards for classification, expanded knowledge of fishes as well, developed the marine laboratory at Woods Hole, MA. From 1871 he headed the U.S. Commission of Fish and Fisheries. Upon Henry's death in 1878, Baird became Smithsonian secretary, a post he held until his own death at Woods Hole in 1887.

CARTER BARRON AMPHITHEATER

Just off 5500 16th Street , N.W., in Rock Creek Park

Theater executive Carter Tate Barron was born in Clarkesville, GA, in 1905. He graduated from Georgia Tech in 1927. He managed the Metropolitan Theater in Atlanta when it was converted for talking pictures, later managed Atlanta's prime theaters, the Capitol and Fox. In 1934 he became manager for Loew's Washington theaters, then manager of Loew's five-state Eastern Division. In 1942 he became Metro-Goldwyn-Mayer's Washington representative. Barron was subsequently active in the Washington community - and in Democratic politics. For examples: He served as president of the Washington Board of Trade, in 1942-45 co-chaired the amusement division of the War Bond Campaign, and was vice chairman of the National Capitol Sesquicentennial Commission. He chaired the entertainment committee for President Roosevelt's birthday balls and provided entertainment for the 1940 National Democratic Convention. He chaired the entertainment committee for President Truman's inauguration.

Carter Barron Amphitheater was built in 1950 to celebrate the capitol's sesquicentennial. Upon Barron's death the same year, it was named for him. For almost 20 years, the "theater under the stars" hosted Broadway musicals, ballets, and performers of all kinds. After the 1968 civil rights riots, audiences pretty much abandoned it. Now it is used only occasionally.

CARMICHAEL AUDITORIUM

In the Museum of American History, Constitution Avenue at 14th Street, N.W.

The auditorium bears the name of Leonard Carmichael, psychologist, educator, and seventh secretary of the Smithsonian Institution. Carmichael was born in Philadelphia in 1898. He graduated from Tufts College in 1921, obtained his Ph.D. from Harvard, returned to Tufts for a Sc.D. He taught psychology at Brown and Princeton universities. While at Brown he published the first use on humans of the electroencephalograph. He taught at Harvard, Radcliffe, and Clark, and became dean at Rochester. He then served as president of Tufts from 1938 to

1952. During World War II, he directed the National Roster of Scientific and Specialized Personnel, recruiting and assigning scientists to projects like atomic energy and radar. He was a scientific author, received many honorary degrees, and held prominent positions in numerous professional organizations.

Carmichael was named secretary at the Smithsonian in 1952. He was an effective and politically astute manager. He saw the old Patent Office Building acquired to house the Collection of Fine Arts and Portrait Gallery. He oversaw what is now the Museum of American History. President Eisenhower authorized it in 1955, just after Carmichael's arrival, and President Johnson dedicated it in 1964, just before Carmichael left. It is the auditorium in this building that bears his name. Carmichael became vice president for exploration and research of the National Geographic Society in 1964. He died in Washington in 1973.

COOLIDGE AUDITORIUM

In the Jefferson Building, 1st Street, between East Capitol Street and Independence Avenue, S.E.

This 500-seat auditorium is named, not for the former president, but for Elizabeth Sprague Coolidge. It is the main facility for performances within the Library of Congress.

Mrs. Coolidge was born in Chicago in 1864. She married Frederic Coolidge, an orthopedic surgeon. She began to write music in the 1890s, but in her thirties had to stop as her hearing began to fail. Instead, she became one of the great patrons of music. She was the founder in 1918 of the Berkshire Festival outside Pittsfield, MA. In 1925 she created the Elizabeth Sprague Coolidge Foundation at the Library of Congress to provide for music festivals, concerts, and prizes for original chamber music compositions. The Library had no provision for receiving such a gift and no trustees to run a foundation, so an act of Congress was needed. It paved the way for subsequent private gifts to the Library. Mrs. Coolidge particularly encouraged composition and performance of music too unique or expensive to be ordinarily undertaken. Works thus commissioned include Benjamin Britten's String Quartet No. 1, Howard Hanson's Four Psalms, Gian Carlo Menotti's The Unicorn, the Gorgon, and the Manicore, and Aaron Copland's Appalachian Spring. Mrs. Coolidge also presented the Library with the auditorium necessary for such activities, so it bears her name.

Mrs. Coolidge made other similar philanthropies: She gave buildings (Sprague Hall at Yale is named for her), established musician pension funds, instituted a medal for eminent services to chamber music, gave thousands for scholarships, and contributed greatly toward cultural activity in Europe. In turn, she was the recipient of numerous degrees and awards, among which were the French Legion of Honor and the Order of the Crown of Belgium. Mrs. Coolidge died in 1953.

EINSTEIN PLANETARIUM. (See also **Albert Einstein.**)
In the National Air and Space Museum, Independence Avenue and 7th Street, S.W.

Shows in the planetarium explore the universe, space, and astronomy. It is named for Albert Einstein, one of the greatest theoretical physicists. Einstein was the man who first united theories of space and time and for whom the entire universe was his laboratory.

EISENHOWER THEATER. (See also the **John F. Kennedy Center for the Performing Arts.**)
In the John F. Kennedy Center for the Performing Arts

In 1954, Congress authorized a "National Cultural Center" to be in Washington, and in 1958, it set aside 17 acres of West Potomac Park as the location. Public support did not materialize until the death of President Kennedy and until his name was attached to the center. But because the original authorizations had been made by President Eisenhower, his name was given to the theater in the Center.

Dwight D. Eisenhower was born in 1890 in Denison, TX, and grew up in Abilene, KS. In 1915 he graduated from West Point. The next year he married Mamie Doud. Early assignments included the Battle Monuments Commission under Gen. Pershing and administrative assistant to Army Chief of Staff Douglas MacArthur. He attended Command and General Staff School, graduating first in his class. He grew a reputation as a first-rate organizer and trainer of men.

When the U.S. entered World War II, Eisenhower was assigned to Army Chief of Staff George C. Marshall. In 1942 he was sent to Britain as U.S. commander in Europe and later that year commanded the invasion of North Africa. It was followed in 1943 by invasions of Sicily and Italy. In 1944 he was named supreme commander (five-star general) for the invasion of France. On June 6, 1944, "D Day," Allied forces invaded Normandy in a landing on a scale never equaled in military history. In ten weeks, the Germans were driven from France. In less than a year, war in Europe was over. Eisenhower wrote his memoir of the conflict, *Crusade in Europe*. He became president of Columbia University. In 1950, fearing Soviet invasion of Europe, President Truman named him to head the North American Treaty Organization (NATO) to protect Europe.

In 1952, the popular Eisenhower was urged by both parties to run for president, chose the Republicans, and after an "I Like Ike" campaign, overwhelmed Illinois Gov. Adlai Stevenson. He was easily elected a second time. During most of his administration Democrats controlled Congress, and domestically Eisenhower had to be a middle-of-the-roader. He tried to balance the budget, keep inflation down, provide efficient government, boost free markets. He twice signed civil rights acts. His biggest achievement was creation of the interstate highway and St.

Lawrence seaway systems. In foreign affairs he stopped the Korean War, concluding a truce but also ending it without victory. In 1954 he refused to send troops to aid France in Indo-China (later Vietnam). He provided a tough stand against communism, created the CIA and stopped China from taking over Taiwan.

Eisenhower is remembered as a military man and statesman, but he was also a supporter of the arts. He not only encouraged a national cultural center, but was the first president to promote legislation for restoration of Ford's Theater. He participated in the ground breaking ceremony for New York's Lincoln Center. He made musicales - 24 in all - a regular feature of state dinners at the White House.

In 1955 Eisenhower had a heart attack, in 1957 a stroke. In 1960 he was still popular, but his health precluded running again. Had he chosen to do so, he couldn't have: the 22nd Amendment had taken effect, making him the first president unable to seek a third term. In 1961 he retired to his farm in Gettysburg, PA, where he resumed writing. He died in 1969.

FICHANDLER STAGE

In Arena Stage, 6th and M Streets, S.W.

Zelda Diamond Fichandler was born in Boston, raised in Washington. Her father was a physicist, and she studied Russian at Cornell University. One of her Russian professors suggested she'd be better at drama. She married economist Thomas Fichandler in 1946, but in 1950 she got her M.A. degree in drama at George Washington University. It was then that she and Edward Mangum, one of her GW teachers, co-founded Arena Stage. She, Tom, and Mangum created a square acting area in an old burlesque-movie house on Mt. Vernon Square. Mangum left after a year, but Zelda and Tom presented dozens of plays for five years. Zelda often directed. They then moved to the old Heurich Brewery, using its hospitality and ice-storage rooms as theater space. Arena then took a major step forward: it raised $1 million and was able to build its own building - the in-the-round theater that now bears the Fichandler name. In 1970 Zelda received an L.H.D. degree from Hood College. She lectured and taught at Boston University, Carnegie Tech, GW, and the University of Texas. She still occasionally directs.

FORD'S THEATER

511 10th Street, between E and F Streets, N.W.

This building has not had a happy history, until the last 25 years or so. In 1859, the original building - the First Baptist Church - was abandoned when its congregation merged with another. John T. Ford had managed theaters in Philadelphia and Baltimore, and realizing the need for one in Washington, bought the church and converted it. The new theater opened in 1861. On December 30, 1862, it burned down. Ford rebuilt it, this time more elaborately, and the theater was recognized as one of the finest in the country, only to be the site of Lincoln's assassination on April 14, 1865. Afterwards the War Department held the theater until June. Ford tried to reopen, but public opinion opposed, and the government again took over the building and prohibited its use as a theater. It was used mainly for records storage until 1893, when three floors collapsed, killing 22 clerks and injuring 68 others. By 1932, the theater housed the Osborn Oldroyd collection of Lincolniana, which he had gathered over 60 years. In 1964 Ford's theater was authentically rebuilt to its appearance on the night of the assassination, and reopened for performances to the public.

GILBERT H. GROSVENOR AUDITORIUM

In National Geographic Society Headquarters, 1600 M Street, N.W.

This auditorium is the scene of films and lectures by photographers, explorers, scientists, travelers, authors, and other noteworthy members of the National Geographic Society. The Society was formed in 1888 by Gardner Greene Hubbard. After his death in 1897, his son in law, Alexander Graham Bell, took it over, but it had only a thousand members and was in debt. One of the Society's lecturers had been Dr. Edwin A. Grosvenor, professor of history at Amherst, whose twin sons had just graduated there. Bell offered a staff position to whichever son might be interested. Gilbert Grosvenor liked the idea (he also liked Bell's daughter, Elsie May) and was hired in 1899. In his first year, membership doubled - and Grosvenor and Elsie May were married. In January 1905, with the *National Geographic Magazine* still struggling, Grosvenor lacked sufficient text to publish, so substituted eleven pages of photographs of Lhasa, Tibet, accompanied only by captions. Membership suddenly jumped. The *Geographic* with its combination of photos and text was on its way to success.

Gilbert Hovey Grosvenor has born to American parents in Istanbul, Turkey, in 1875. He became editor in chief of the *Geographic* in 1903 (a position he held for over 50 years), president of the society in 1920, and chairman of its board in 1954. He wrote articles and books on numerous expeditions including Peary's to the North Pole. He was the recipient of many honors, doctorates, and awards, and geographic features in many parts of the world bear his name. He died at the Grosvenor estate in Braddeck, Nova Scotia, in 1966.

Ever since Bell's decision to hire Gilbert, Grosvenors have been connected with the Society. The current chairman of the board, Gilbert M. Grosvenor, is the fifth family member to serve in that capacity.

HARTKE THEATER

On Harewood Road, on the campus of Catholic University

The theater is named for Fr. Gilbert Vincent Hartke, Dominican priest who founded Catholic University's Department of Speech and Drama and built it into one of the major theater programs in the nation.

Theaters and Auditoriums

Hartke was born in Chicago in 1907 near a pre-Hollywood film studio. When he was 6, he was acting in two-reelers, and by eighth grade, he was set on a career in show business. But he was also drawn to the Church, attended Providence College, and joined the Order of Preachers (Dominicans), where he thought his dramatic skills could be best used. He was ordained in 1936 and came to Catholic University. He organized a department to improve speech, produce plays, and develop playwrights. After World War II Hartke found a left-over military theater at the naval base in Norfolk, bought it for a dollar, and had it hauled to the campus and reassembled. It served as the school's first theater for 20 years - until its roof caved in on Ash Wednesday, 1967. That resulted in a new 590-seat $2 million theater to be built three years later - the Hartke Theater.

What Knute Rockne was to Notre Dame, Fr. Hartke was to Catholic University and its drama program. During his life about 600 plays were produced, and 2,500 students went through his program. Several have succeeded: Jerome Ragni, co-author of *Hair*, Mart Crowley who wrote *The Boys in the Band*, John Pielmeier, author of *Agnes of God*, and Jason Miller, Pulitzer Prize winner for *That Championship Season.* Actor Jon Voight got his start at CU, as did TV's Ed McMahon. In 1949, Hartke created the National Players, a professional theater company of drama graduates that played throughout the U.S. and Europe, at military installations, even in China. In 1962, Olney Theater, now Maryland's state theater, was given to Hartke by its former owner. Still another offshoot of Hartke's summer stock programs is the St. Michael's Playhouse in Burlington, VT. Helen Hayes, a native Washingtonian and friend of Hartke's, made her last stage appearance at the Hartke Theater in 1971.

Hartke retired in 1974 to become professor emeritus, but he remained the guiding force behind CU's drama program until his death in 1986.

JOHN F. KENNEDY CENTER FOR THE PERFORMING ARTS
2700 F Street, N.W., between New Hampshire Avenue and the Potomac River.

In 1954, Congress authorized a "National Cultural Center." In 1958, it set aside 17 acres of West Potomac Park. Public support never materialized. But in 1963, in the aftermath of President Kennedy's assassination, when his name was attached to the center, worldwide support and contributions suddenly appeared. The Kennedy Center opened in 1971. It houses the Opera House, Concert Hall, Eisenhower Theater, Terrace Theater, Theater Lab, American Film Institute movie theater, a performing arts library, gift shop, three restaurants, and three levels of parking. It is the official memorial to the president in Washington.

John Fitzgerald Kennedy was born at Brookline, MA, in 1917. He went to private schools, studied at the London School of Economics, went to Princeton but left because of illness, and in 1940 graduated from Harvard. He had hurt his back playing football and in 1941, at the start of World War II, was turned down by the Army. He was later accepted by the Navy. As a lieutenant (JG), Kennedy commanded a PT (torpedo) boat in the Solomon Islands that was rammed and sunk by a Japanese destroyer. He saved his crew, but he was thrown onto the deck further injuring his back, and after an operation, was discharged. He decided on a political career and returned to Massachusetts.

In 1946 James Curley left his House of Representatives seat to become mayor of Boston. Kennedy replaced him, eventually serving three terms. In 1952, he defeated Henry Cabot Lodge, Jr., to enter the Senate. In 1953 he married Jacqueline Bouvier. In 1954 and 1955 he had to undergo additional operations on his back. While recuperating he kept busy by writing about acts of courage by U.S. senators; the resulting book, *Profiles in Courage*, won a Pulitzer Prize. By 1956, Kennedy almost got the vice-presidential nomination away from Sen. Estes Kefauver. In 1958 he was re-elected to the Senate, and in 1960 defeated Sen. Hubert Humphrey for the presidential nomination. In a television debate, he appeared more statesmanlike than Vice President Richard Nixon and went on to win the presidency. It was close - his margin out of 62,000,000 votes was only 119,000. Kennedy was the youngest ever elected and the first Roman Catholic.

Kennedy promised sweeping "New Frontier" legislation similar to President Roosevelt's, but once in office offered more cautious ideas. Most of it was ignored by the Republican Congress. He did manage to increase substantially the space program, with a goal of "a man on the moon by the end of the decade." He established the Peace Corps. He and his wife hosted the world's best entertainers at the White House. But in 1961, he received a major setback: A force of anti-Castro Cubans, directed by the U.S. Central Intelligence Agency, was to invade Cuba at the Bay of Pigs. This had been planned before Kennedy took office, and he let it proceed, but modified the plan and limited American support. The invasion failed. Kennedy defied Soviet attempts to get the Allies out of Berlin. But the Soviets responded by erecting a wall between East and West. Kennedy's most important act came a year later, when he successfully demanded the Soviet Union dismantle its missile bases in Cuba.

In 1963, Kennedy went to Texas on a speech-making tour and took part in a parade in Dallas. An assassin fired shots, killing the president and wounding John Connally, Texas governor, who was riding with the Kennedys. Before the day was over, police arrested Harvey Lee Oswald for the murder. In 1964 a seven-man commission under Chief Justice Earl Warren reported that Oswald was the gunman and that there was no evidence of a conspiracy. In 1979, a House assassinations committee, after two years of work, concluded that Oswald *was* part of a conspiracy and that it may have included members of organized crime. Controversy over Kennedy's death continues today.

KREEGER THEATER. (See also **Arena Stage.**)
In Arena Stage, 6th and M Streets, S.W.

David Lloyd Kreeger was one of Washington's most important patrons. He gave money, but he also gave his time and expertise. He was born in New York City in 1909. He graduated magna cum laude from Rutgers in 1929, then did so again from Harvard Law School. He became an editor of the *Harvard Law Review*, but in 1934, came to Washington as a senior attorney with the Agriculture Department. He later worked in the Interior and Justice departments until 1946. A friend he had helped financially told him of a company for sale that was trying to sell insurance by mail. Banks wouldn't finance the purchase. So Kreeger raised the money privately. Kreeger and the subsequent Government Employees Insurance Co. (GEICO) managed to make him, his partners, and his friend wealthy. He became its senior vice president, general counsel and director in 1957, president in 1964, chairman and CEO in 1970, and honorary chairman in 1979. He was also a director of Crestar Bank and president of his own philanthropic foundation. He earned honorary degrees and over 20 national and international awards and decorations. He died in 1990.

Kreeger had a fervor for the arts. He was an amateur violinist and art collector. He was once called "a one-man band for the arts." His house on Foxhall Road contained a concert hall, three underground galleries, and a pool-side sculpture garden. At one time or another he was chairman or president of the National Symphony, Washington Opera, and Corcoran Gallery. He was a donor to dozens of organizations and causes. He endowed the concertmaster chair of the National Symphony and the Kreeger Creativity Awards at Catholic University. He gave money for buildings: the Kreeger Music Building at American University, Kreeger Auditorium at the Jewish Community Center in Rockville, MD, the theater at Rutgers named for his parents, and the Kreeger Theater at Arena Stage.

LANGLEY THEATER. (See also **Baird Auditorium.**)
In the National Air & Space Museum, Independence Avenue at 6th Street, S.W.

The museum's five-story theater that shows spectacular IMAX movies is named for Samuel Pierpont Langley.

Langley was born in 1834 in Boston and as a young man worked as a civil engineer and architect. He was appointed assistant at Harvard Observatory in 1865, director of the Naval Academy Observatory in 1866, and director of the Allegheny Observatory in Pittsburgh in 1867. For twenty years he served as professor of physics and astronomy at Western University of Pennsylvania in Pittsburgh and became an internationally recognized astrophysicist. He sketched sunspots, invented the bolometer for measuring tiny temperature differences, and discovered radiation beyond previously known limits.

Upon the death of Spencer Baird in 1887, Langley was named secretary of the Smithsonian Institution. He broadened its scope and created its astrophysical observatory. In 1896 he successfully flew two crafts that weighed about 25 pounds - the first sustained flights by engine-driven heavier-than-air craft - demonstrating that manmade mechanical flight was practical. During his administration, the National Zoo was established. And the Smithsonian was found by a court to be the qualified recipient of Harriet Lane Johnston's (President Buchanan's niece) bequeathed collection of paintings, making a national gallery inevitable. Langley served as secretary until his death in 1906.

LINCOLN THEATER

1215 U Street

The Lincoln Theater (named for the 16th U.S. president) was a grand movie palace, built in 1921 to offer first-run movies that black audiences could not see downtown. Indeed U Street was once called "Black Broadway," the center of black entertainment and culture in the city. The 1600-seat theater with its 38-foot wide stage also offered stage acts. In the late 1920s, a dance hall, called the Colonnade ballroom, was added at the rear, and the biggest names played there: Lena Horne, Louis Armstrong, Fats Waller, Bessie Smith, the Mills Brothers, Count Basie. The theater thrived until the 1950s when desegregation allowed blacks to attend theaters elsewhere. The Colonnade was torn down, the theater closed. But in 1994 Francine and Jeff Cohen purchased the theater, there were fund-raisers by the Black Repertory Theater and others, and a $9 million renovation by the city that enabled the theater to reopen and once again present stage shows.

LISNER AUDITORIUM

At 21st and H Streets, N.W., on the campus of George Washington University

Abram Lisner was born in Waldorf, Sachen Meinengun, Germany, in 1855. He arrived in the U.S. when he was 13. Too nervous to attend public school, he was tutored privately. He went to work for an older brother in New York and learned the merchandising business. He arrived in Washington in the late 1800s, and his fortune was made by the early 1900s as owner and president of the Palais Royal department store. Unusually capable in business management, he was once known as the "best businessman south of New York" by the country's largest dry goods firm. He was also "intensely a citizen of Washington," generous in gifts to various organizations, yet leading a secluded life especially per Washington standards. He became associated with George Washington University, received an honorary M.A. degree from there in 1918, and served on its board of directors. A talented musician and fond of the theater, he donated funds for construction of GWU's six-floor library, then left money in his will for the auditorium that bears his name. Lisner died in 1937. The auditorium was completed and opened in 1941.

MEAD AUDITORIUM
In Studio Theater, 1333 P Street, N.W.

In 1997, Studio Theater named one of its two auditoriums the Mead, for Gilbert and Jaylee Mead. The Mead Family Foundation has given funds to numerous Washington theaters, arts, and educational groups, and gave $400,000 to Studio Theater for its recent renovation.

Gilbert's grandfather was the founder of Consolidated Papers, one of the country's largest paper manufacturers, and from which the family's fortune comes. But for more than 20 years, the Meads lived in Greenbelt, MD, and worked at Goddard Space Flight Center, Gilbert as a geophysicist and Jaylee as an astronomer. Both hold doctorate degrees. They met on the job, and were married in 1968. In 1971, the Meads joined a group for Goddard employees called MAD (for Music And Drama). Gilbert, an accomplished musician, served as a musical director and conductor, while Jaylee produced some shows and appeared on stage in others. Upon retirement, in 1992 they moved to Washington.

EUGENE AND AGNES E. MEYER AUDITORIUM. (See also **Freer Gallery of Art.**)
In the Freer Gallery of Art, on the South side of the Mall, Jefferson Drive, at 12th Street, S.W.

This 300-seat auditorium is used for programs of the Freer and Sackler galleries and for Smithsonian musical events. It was named in honor of a gift from the Eugene and Agnes Meyer Foundation of more than $1 million to renovate and equip the facility.

Eugene Meyer had three careers and was distinguished in all of them. He was born in Los Angeles in 1875. He graduated from Yale, spent a year in his father's banking house, Lazard Freres, in New York, then struck out on his own. For 16 years he was active in financing and development of the oil, copper, steel, and auto industries. A success in business, he decided on public service. He came to Washington in 1917 to serve under President Wilson and remained to serve under Presidents Harding, Coolidge, Hoover, Roosevelt, Truman, and Eisenhower. He was first chairman of the Reconstruction Finance Corporation, governor of the Federal Reserve Board, and first president of the World Bank. In 1933 he bought *The Washington Post* at auction and became a newspaper publisher. He grew its circulation, purchased and incorporated the competing *Times Herald*, and made *The Post* the most widely read paper in the capital. Meyer died in 1959.

Agnes Ernst was born in New York in 1887. She graduated from Barnard College in 1907 and became the first women reporter on the old *New York Morning Sun*. After a year studying in Paris, she wrote her first book, on

Chinese painting. In 1910, she married Eugene Meyer. She continued writing; for example, during the 1940s wrote *Journey Through Chaos*, the most comprehensive report on social conditions in wartime America. In 1944, she and her husband set up their foundation for donation of funds to community service, arts and humanities, and projects concerning health and education. But Agnes Meyer's connection with the Freer Gallery went further than just the donation: In 1913 she had met Charles Freer at an exhibition of Chinese paintings in New York. Their mutual interest established a bond between them. She visited Freer in Detroit, and they visited dealers together. So high was the esteem in which Freer held the Meyers, that in his will, he named them as two of only five people whose gifts of objects could be accepted in the gallery. After his death and the subsequent opening of the gallery, Agnes Meyer served as a director, was instrumental in the arrangements of objects, and served as advisor to the staff.

MUMFORD ROOM

On the 6th Floor of the Madison Building, Independence Avenue between 1st and 2nd Streets, S.E.

Lawrence Quincy Mumford (1903-1982) was Librarian of Congress for 20 years, from 1954 to 1974. Although the Library serves Congress, its librarians are appointed by the president. Mumford, appointed by President Eisenhower, is the only one to have held a professional library degree. Mumford expanded the Library's roles, particularly its bibliographic activities and foreign acquisitions, expanded minority hiring, successfully stopped President Kennedy's attempt to transfer the Library to the executive branch, initiated automation efforts, and began the study that resulted in the Library's third building, the Madison Building. The room that bears his name in that building is used for lectures, presentations, and demonstrations.

MARY PICKFORD THEATER

On the 3rd Floor of the Madison Building, Independence Avenue between 1st and 2nd Streets, S.E.

Gladys Marie Smith, later known as Mary Pickford, was born in Toronto, Canada, in 1893. As a child she performed on stage, and made her Broadway debut when only 14. In 1909, D.W. Griffith hired her for a small film part, and she rapidly became a star, usually playing a sentimental teenager. Such movies included *Tess of the Storm Country* (1914), *Rebecca of Sunnybrook Farm* (1917), *Pollyanna* (1920), and *Little Lord Fauntleroy* (1921). In 1920, she married film star Douglas Fairbanks, and their home, Pickfair, in Beverly Hills was a center for Hollywood social life. Once sound was added to motion pictures, she played more mature parts. In 1929, she won an Academy Award for *Coquette*. In 1935, she wrote an autobiography, *My Rendezvous with Life*. In 1936, the Fairbanks were divorced, and a year later Mary married actor Buddy Rogers. She died in Santa Monica in 1979.

Theaters and Auditoriums

The Library of Congress' Madison Building houses its film collection, and its main theater for showings is its 64-seat Mary Pickford Theater. A plaque at the entrance states, "The theater honors the film actress and producer, pioneer of the nation's democratic art - America's Sweetheart, 1893-1979." Another states "World's First Super Star of the Cinema."

SYLVAN THEATER

On the Washington Monument grounds near Independence Avenue and 15th Street, N.W.

Alice Pike Barney was a local social and artistic leader, playwright, painter. She presented an allegorical tableau at the Washington Monument in 1915, and 10,000 people attended. It was at her suggestion that an outdoor theater be built on the grounds. The theater was established two years later, and she gave it the name of Sylvan Theater. The first six performances there were of Barney's own plays. Today the theater hosts concerts and plays during the summer.

Alice Pike Barney was born in 1861, daughter of a millionaire Cincinnati distiller, who built Cincinnati's first opera house. When 17, she became betrothed to newspaperman Henry Stanley, but while Stanley was in Africa searching for Dr. Livingston, she was pressured into marrying an Ohio banker, Albert Barney. She took up art, was associated with James McNeill Whistler and Carolus Durand, and had exhibitions in New York, Paris, and London. Her sketch of Whistler is well known, and she did portraits of Alice Roosevelt Longworth and George Bernard Shaw. When Albert died in 1914, he left her an estate of $5 million. She came to Washington where she built a home, a copy of a Venetian palace, and entertained artists, statesmen, intellectuals, and the socially select. She became well known for her escapades, too. One was when she did a nude sculpture of her daughter and placed in on the front lawn, shocking the neighborhood. She later moved to Los Angeles where she founded the Theater Mart for young actors and playwrights, won the Drama Critics Award for her play, *The Lighthouse*, and produced a ballet at the Hollywood Bowl. Barney died in Hollywood in 1931. She's buried in Dayton, OH.

WARNER THEATER

13th and E Streets, N.W.

Unlike most places in this book, the theater is not named for a local person, but as one might guess, for the Warner Brothers film company.

The theater was built in 1924 and opened the following year. It was to be called the Cosmopolitan, but its name was quickly changed to the Earle when it was discovered that the original was too long to fit on the marquee. The Earle was named for its treasurer, former Governor Earle of Pennsylvania. It was called "the perfect theater" and major stars of vaudeville played there. In the 1940s, Warner

Brothers made the Earle into its Washington showcase for its new film releases, along with stage shows. By 1945, the stage shows were dropped completely. In 1947, its name was changed to the Warner. It also served as home for Arthur Godfrey's first radio broadcasts. Riots in Washington in 1968 killed downtown night life, and in the early 1970s, the theater closed. In 1977 it had a brief revival as a rock music hall, then in 1978, after a major renovation, it reopened once again as a legitimate theater.

WHITTALL PAVILION

In the Jefferson Building, 1st Street, between East Capitol Street and Independence Avenue, S.E.

Gertrude Clark Whittall (1867-1965) was one of the Library of Congress' major patrons of music and literature. She moved to Washington in 1934 and presented to the Library five Stradivarius instruments. She then established a foundation to support chamber music concerts at which the instruments could be played. Concerts are frequently played in this garden pavilion bearing her name.

In 1941 her gift was expanded so the Library could acquire manuscripts of European composers. That collection now includes manuscripts of dozens of composers from Bach to Weber, the largest collection of Brahms manuscripts outside Vienna, and special collections of materials from Paganini and Mendelsson.

WASHINGTON HIMSELF

George Washington deserves a chapter by himself. After all, the city is named for him and its most famous monument is dedicated to him. Most Americans learned about him in school and, if that was some time ago, remember only a few facts about him. He got known as "Father of His Country" only after a fabulous career, so here's his story once again.

GEORGE WASHINGTON

George Washington was born in 1732 on his father's plantation on the Potomac River. He grew up near Fredericksburg, VA. As a child, he had no formal education. His father died when he was 11, leaving his mother and five other children in poverty. His half brother, Lawrence, inherited the estate called Mount Vernon (named after British Admiral Edward Vernon under whom Lawrence had served) and took George there. Nearby was Belvoir, estate of the Fairfax family into which Lawrence had married. Lord Fairfax liked George, and it was there that George learned the courtliness that later impressed others.

In 1748 Lord Fairfax sent a surveying party beyond the Blue Ridge Mountains. George went along as an assistant, and upon his return, obtained a license and became a public surveyor. In 1752, Lawrence died, his wife died two months later, and George inherited Mount Vernon.

During the 1750s, both Britain and France tried to occupy the Ohio valley. The French ordered the English out. The Virginia governor made Washington a major and sent him to Fort Le Boeuf near Lake Erie 500 miles away with word that the French should move out instead. Of course they refused. Washington was made lieutenant colonel and sent with 700 men to claim to the valley. He attacked a party of French and killed their leader. The French cried assassination and responded. Washington quickly built an earthen fort, called Fort Necessity, but was defeated. The incident precipitated the French and Indian War.

The following year, General Edward Braddock, with Washington as aide-de-camp, led a force against the French. Washington was so sick with fever that he rode into battle on a pillow instead of a saddle. Four bullets went through his coat, and two horses were shot from under him. Yet he helped carry the mortally wounded Braddock from the field. Despite the defeat, Washington's fame spread, and he was promoted to colonel and made commander of Virginia's troops.

Washington with small bands of volunteers held back Indian invaders all along the Virginia frontier, and when joined with British soldiers in 1758, entered Fort Duquesne just after the French had left it. The place was renamed Pittsburgh after British statesman William Pitt.

From 1759 to 1775, Washington farmed at Mount Vernon. He married widow Martha Custis and became guardian of her two children. He had none of his own.

The British took Boston. The colonies prepared for action. Washington made a speech and said, "I will raise one thousand men, subsist them at my own expense, and march, myself at their head, for the relief of Boston." When a congress of the colonies was called in 1775, the speech was recalled, and the Bostonians proposed Washington as commander in chief. So Gen. Washington headed the army - one from 13 colonies, each of which thought itself independent. Washington spent most of his time begging for soldiers, supplies, and united action.

The Bostonians seized Bunker Hill, losing the battle but damaging the British, who still held downtown Boston. When Washington arrived he bluffed the British until March 1776, then seized strategic heights. The British could not defend Boston and pulled out. Washington moved to New York City where he correctly thought the British would attack next. They did - with 400 transports, 32,000 soldiers, 30 ships, and 10,000 seamen. Washington had 8,000 troops. He was defeated at Long Island, could not hold New York City, moved to White Plains, finally retreated to Philadelphia and across the Delaware. By this time, he had only 3,000 men. They were so ragged, he had to beg for clothes. He pledged his own fortune to persuade soldiers to re-enlist. He was now the one person holding the army - indeed the colonies - together.

Christmas night 1776 saw Washington cross the Delaware and capture an outpost at Trenton. He took 800 prisoners. It gave encouragement - a Christmas present - to the colonies. He lost another battle at Trenton but won at Princeton and gained such a position at Morristown that the British withdrew from New Jersey. The French were impressed enough to declare war on England (albeit for their own selfish reasons) and send volunteers. The winter of 1777-78 was spent at Valley Forge. Subsequent battles for the next three years were fought to a standstill. Then, in 1781, France sent a fleet toward Virginia and cornered Gen. Cornwallis at Yorktown. Washington moved his army accordingly, and Cornwallis surrendered. The British realized they would never win the war, and began peace meetings in Paris. The peace process took another two years during which Washington kept the army together. The Treaty of Paris was finally signed in 1783. The British marched out of New York City and Washington marched in. He called his officers together one last time at Fraunces' Tavern and disbanded the army. This final military act was extraordinary: In other countries such a supreme general could have set up a dictatorship. He simply returned to Mount Vernon, from which he had been absent seven years, to farm.

The colonies, now states, struggled under Articles of Confederation, and a movement was started to call a constitutional convention. It met in 1787. Washington was made chairman, and it was his leadership that enabled the constitution to be drafted despite many arguments. It took another two years before enough colonies accepted it and an election could be held. Washington was chosen president and inaugurated April 30, 1789. The nation was finally the United States of America.

When Washington took office, there were no departments, staffs, or offices. He and Vice-President John Adams constituted the entire executive and judicial government. It took inspired creative effort along with successful planning and action to create a workable government. But the remarkable achievement of Washington as president is that he and his aides were able to construct foundations so good that the government of the country has rested on them ever since.

Congress set up departments, and Washington appointed the first cabinet: Henry Knox, war department; Alexander Hamilton, treasury; Thomas Jefferson, state; Samuel Osgood, postmaster general; and Edmund Randolph, attorney general. Sound currency and paper money were created, taxes were levied, nationwide banking was set up, and patent law was put in place. A federal court system was designed, so well that its features survive today: judicial districts grouped into circuits, plus a supreme court with a chief and associate justices. Foreign policy was made, and despite problems with Britain and France, war was avoided. The new country prospered and grew.

Washington was re-elected for a second term, then refused a third, a tradition broken only once and now stated in the 22nd Amendment of the Constitution. He returned to farming at Mount Vernon - but not for long. It looked like England and France might unite to fight the United States, and Washington was called back as commander in chief. The prospect of war diminished, and Washington once again returned to Mount Vernon. In 1799 he rode through his estate on horseback during a snowstorm, caught cold, developed a sore and swollen throat, and never recovered. He died only a few months before the city bearing his name was officially opened. He is buried next to his wife at Mount Vernon.

THE CITY OF WASHINGTON. (See also **Pierre L'Enfant**.)

The original capital of the new United States was New York City. Its permanent site is the result of the Compromise of 1790. Alexander Hamilton, advocate of a strong central government, wanted the federal government to assume the war debt left by the states. Thomas Jefferson, advocate of states rights, feared such central power. Besides, such a decision would benefit rich northerners; southern states had already paid their war debt. Bargaining over dinner one evening, the two made an agreement: Jefferson agreed to federal assumption of the state debts and Hamilton would support a capital in the South. Also, Congress would meet in the country's most cosmopolitan city,

Philadelphia, for the next ten years while a 10-mile square elsewhere would be selected and ceded to the federal government.

The site chosen was along the Potomac River. Washington himself took charge. He had previously surveyed the area. Some wanted the location above Great Falls to prevent attack from the sea. Washington wanted it below the falls so that a commercial port could develop. In 1791 Washington named three commissioners who were to select the site and oversee its development. Two days later he asked Congress to amend the law, because he had selected the site himself. After grumbling, Congress made the change.

Next, Washington selected as surveyor Andrew Ellicott, whose family had founded Ellicott City, MD, and who had the best surveying and sighting equipment in the country. Ellicott in turn was assisted by Benjamin Banneker, a self-educated black farmer. While they surveyed the 10-mile square area, Washington named Pierre L'Enfant as chief engineer for the city. He had just redesigned New York City Hall where Washington had been inaugurated.

L'Enfant saw first Jenkins Hill (now Capitol Hill) as "a pedestal awaiting a monument." Pennsylvania Avenue would be the city's principal ceremonial street and would run straight from Congress' home to the President's House one mile away. He planned avenues 160 feet wide radiating from squares to be crowned with heroic sculptures plus a grid of streets broken by broad boulevards. He planned the Mall, to be landscaped like the formal gardens of Europe.

The commissioners began design competitions for the Capitol and the President's House. It was the commissioners along with Thomas Jefferson and James Madison who gave the name of Washington to the new city in 1791. They wrote to L'Enfant, "We have agreed that the federal district shall be called 'The Territory of Columbia' and the federal city 'The City of Washington.'" They had no authority to do this, but no one ever questioned the action. So Washington himself knew the city would someday bear his name. He modestly continued to call it Federal City. It would then take decades for the city to shed its forests, swamps, and muddy trails, and to build significant buildings. But the work was underway.

THE WASHINGTON MONUMENT

On The Mall, between Constitution and Independence Avenues, next to 15th Street, N.W.

A monument in honor of Washington was first considered in 1783 by the Continental Congress. Pierre L'Enfant selected the site, just about where the present monument stands. But no action was taken for 50 years. In 1833, a Washington National Monument Society was formed, collected funds, and approved a design. Congress granted authority for a monument, and on July 4,

1848, the cornerstone was laid. The trowel used in 1793 by Washington for the cornerstone of the Capitol was used.

The original monument design, by architect John Mills, called for a circular building with columns and a place for statues of presidents and heroes. On top was to be an obelisk. By 1854 the base had been begun, but the Civil War stopped work. In 1876 President Grant approved an act for the Engineer Corps to complete the monument. In 1880 work resumed on the shaft; the idea of the building below was dropped. Marble from the same Maryland site as the original was used, but it came from a different stratum and has weathered to a different shade, so that the original base and newer top portion of the monument can be clearly seen today. The monument was dedicated on Washington's birthday in 1885, and it was opened to the public in 1888.

The monument is 555 feet high. Its base is 55 feet on each side, tapering to 34 feet at the top. Inside is a stairway of 50 landings and 898 steps (and there's an elevator). Along the steps are 250 carved stones and plaques presented by individuals, societies, cities, states, and nations.

GEORGE WASHINGTON STATUE

On the Washington Cathedral grounds just off Wisconsin, Cathedral, and Mount St. Alban Avenues, N.W.

There's a rather odd, equestrian statue of Washington near the south side of Washington Cathedral. The sculptor was Herbert Hazeltine, known for animal figures as well as portraits. This 1959 statue is bronze, but has been finished completely in satin gold leaf. The horse's unusual eyes are glass. The face of Washington was copied from a portrait by Rembrandt Peale owned by the Cathedral. The horse is actually Man-O'-War, reportedly one of Hazeltine's favorites.

GEORGE WASHINGTON UNIVERSITY

Surrounding the area near I and 20th Streets, N.W.

Washington gave fifty shares of his Potomac Canal Company stock to help finance a school. It was founded, in 1821, as Columbian College. At its first commencement ceremonies in 1824, attendees included President Monroe, former president John Quincy Adams, the Marquis de Lafayette, Henry Clay, and John C. Calhoun. The school boasts several firsts including the city's first medical school in 1825, the country's first journalism class in 1869, and the first foreign service school in 1898. The school changed its name in 1904 to honor its initial benefactor.

WASHINGTON CIRCLE

Pennsylvania Avenue, N.W., where New Hampshire Avenue and 23rd and K Streets intersect

On the circle, Lt. Gen. George Washington is shown atop his horse doing battle with the British. Washington sits calmly, while his horse looks terrified of the explosions around them. In 1853 the statue of Andrew Jackson was placed in Lafayette Park and proved so popular that Congress finally took action on a similar one for George Washington. The same sculptor, Clark Mills, was hired. The Washington statue was unveiled and placed at its present location in 1860.

BIBLIOGRAPHY

This book was compiled over a five-year period, and many sources were used: several encyclopedia, specialized dictionaries, numerous government pamphlets, and dozens of uncredited clip files. In addition to those and to the two books cited in the text, here are some of the articles and major books used as references.

Applewhite, E.J., *Washington Itself*, Alfred A. Knopf, New York, 1989

Beatty, Morgan, *Your Nation's Capital*, Farrar, Straus and Cudahy, New York, 1956

Becker, Ralph E., *Miracle on the Potomac, The Kennedy Center from the Beginning*, Bartleby Press, Silver Spring, MD, 1990

Bergheim, Laura, *The Washington Historical Atlas*, Woodbine House, 1992

Bryce, James, *In the Nation's Capital*, speech delivered before the Committee of One Hundred on the Future Development for Washington, D.C., February 27, 1913

Cameron, Robert, *Above Washington*, Cameron & Company, San Francisco, 1979

Catton, Bruce, *The American Heritage Picture History of the Civil War*, American Heritage/Bonanza Books, New York, 1982

Civil Engineering Landmarks of the Nation's Capital, Committee on History and Heritage of the National Capital Section, Association of Civil Engineers, Washington, DC, 1982

Conaway, James, *The Smithsonian: 150 Years of Adventure, Discovery, and Wonder*, Smithsonian Books, Washington, 1995

Cooling III, Benjamin Franklin, and Owen II, Walton H., *Mr. Lincoln's Forts - A Guide to the Civil War Defenses of Washington*, White Mane Publishing Co., Shippensburg, PA, 1988

Decatur House, The National Trust for Historic Preservation, Washington, D.C. (Undated)

Downtown Urban Renewal Area Landmarks, National Capital Planning Commission, Washington, D.C., 1970

Bibliography

Eskew, Garnett Laidlaw, *Willard's of Washington*, Coward-McCann, Inc., New York, 1954

Estell, Kenneth, ed., *The African American Almanac*, 6th Edition, Gale Research Inc., Detroit, 1994

Evelyn, Douglas E., and Dickson, Paul, *On This Spot*, Farragut Publishing Company, Washington, D.C., 1992

Federal Writers' Project, Works Progress Administration, *Washington City and Capital*, Government Printing Office, Washington, D.C., 1937

Fitzpatrick, Sandra, and Goodwin, Maria R., *The Guide to Black Washington*, Hippocrene Books, Inc., New York, 1990

Forman, Stephen M., *Guide to Civil War Washington*, Elliott & Clark Publishing, Washington, D.C., 1995

Goode, James M. *Best Addresses*, Smithsonian Institution Press, Washington, D.C., 1988

Goode, James M., *Capitol Losses*, Smithsonian Institution Press, Washington, D.C. 1979

Griffin, Mark G., and McCloskey, Ellen M., *Lily Spandorf's Washington Never More*, Grew Publishing Company, Washington, D.C., 1988

Highsmith, Carol M., and Landphair, Ted, *Library of Congress, America's Memory*, Fulcrum Publishing, Golden, CO, 1994

Holman, Doree Germaine, *Old Bethesda*, Franklin Press, Gaithersburg, MD (Undated)

Jacob, Kathryn Allamong, *Capital Elites*, Smithsonian Institution, Washington, D.C., 1995

Kenny, Hamill, *The Placenames of Maryland, Their Origin and Meaning*, Maryland Historical Society, Baltimore, MD. 1984

Locke, Elizabeth L. F., "Exploring the Grosvenors," *Town & Country*, February 1988

McClellan, Phyllis I., *Silent Sentinel on the Potomac, Fort McNair, 1791-1991*, Heritage Books, Inc., Bowie, MD, 1993

Bibliography

Meyer, Agnes E., *Out of These Roots*, Little, Brown, and Company, Boston, 1953

Miller, Fredric M., and Gillette, Howard, Jr., *Washington Seen, A Photographic History, 1875-1965*, Johns Hopkins University Press, Baltimore, 1995

O'Brien, Robert, *Marriott, the J. Willard Marriott Story*, Deseret Book Company, Salt Lake City, 1977

Offutt, William, *Bethesda, A Social History*, The Innovative Game, Bethesda, MD, 1995

Olszewski, George J., *Franklin Park*, U.S. Department of Interior, National Park Service, Washington, D.C., 1970

Olszewski, George J., *Lincoln Park*, U.S. Department of Interior, National Park Service, Washington, D.C., 1968

Origins and *Origins II*, Neighborhood Planning Council, Washington, D.C., 1975-6

Peter, Grace Dunlop, and Southwick, Joyce D., *Cleveland Park*, Cleveland Park Community Library Committee, Washington, D.C., 1958

The Presidents and Their Wives, National Souvenir Center, Washington, D.C., 1967

Prominent Personages of the Nation's Capital, Washington Times Co. (Source Book), Washington, D.C. (Undated)

Pusey, Merlo J., *Eugene Meyer*, Alfred A. Knopf, New York, 1974

Richards, David, "Curtain Up! Write the Check!," *The Washington Post*, June 1, 1997

Ringle, Ken, "Smithsonian: The Greatest of the Mall," *The Washington Post*, August 10, 1996

Ross, Betty, *Museum Guide to Washington D.C.*, Americana Press, Chevy Chase, MD, 1992

Rush, Bryson B., *Footnote Washington,* EPM Publications, McLean, VA, 1983

Seale, William, *The President's House*, White House Historical Association, Washington, D.C., 1986

Slauson, Allan B., *History of the City of Washington - Its Men and Institutions*, The Washington Post, c. 1903

Smith, Kathryn Schneider, *Washington at Home, An Illustrated History of Neighborhoods in the Nation's Capital*, Windsor Publications, Inc., 1988

Special Collections in the Library of Congress, Annette Melville, ed., Library of Congress, Washington, D.C., 1980

Struck, Doug, "A Tribute to FDR and His Generation," *The Washington Post*, April 9, 1997

Thomas, Henry, and Thomas, Dana Lee, *Living Biographies of Religious Leaders*, Blue Ribbon Books, New York, 1946

Thorlby, Anthony, ed., *The Penguin Companion to European Literature*, McGraw-Hill Book Company, New York, 1969

Treasure, Edna H., *The Origin, Growth, and Development of the Lucy Webb Hayes National Training School Including Sibley Memorial Hospital*, The Catholic University of America Press, Washington, D.C., 1943

Van Dyne, Larry, "The Making of Washington," *The Washingtonian* magazine, November, 1987

Wallace, Richard, and Carr, Marie Pinak, *The Willard Hotel, An Illustrated History*, Dicmar Publishing, Washington, D.C., 1986

Weeks, Christopher, *AIA Guide to the Architecture of Washington, D.C.*, The Johns Hopkins University Press, Baltimore, 1994

Wheeler, Linda, "Boss Shepherd"s Exile Will End," *The Washington Post*, January 10, 1997

Who's Who in Washington, 1934-35, Stanley H. Williamson, ed., Ransdell, Inc., Washington, D.C.

Who Was Who in America, Vol. 3, Marquis Who's Who Inc., Chicago, 1960

Worth, Fred L., *Strange and Fascinating Facts about Washington, D.C.*, Bell Books, New York, 1988

INDEX

The people names that follow are names commemorated in the city and those of people who helped create the city and its memorials. Names italicized are those of places to which no person name directly corresponds. These are indeed "the names of Washington."

Adams, Henry 69
Adams, John 24
Adams, John Quincy 55
Adas Israel 53
Addison, Thomas 41
Alexander, Archer 68
Aligheri, Dante 107
Ames, G. A. 39
Anacostia 56
Analostan Island 133
Anderson, Larz, III 46
Apex Building 25
Archbold, Anne 12
Arena Stage 144
Artigas, Jose Gervasio 82, 101
Asbury, Francis 102

Bacon, Henry 126, 139
Baird, Spencer Fullerton 54, 144
Ballou, Frank Washington 93
Banneker, Benjamin 9, 161
Barber, Amzi L. 61
Barlow, Joe 60
Barney, Alice Pike 156
Barron, Carter Tate 145
Barry, John 102
Barsotti, Carlo 107
Bartholdi, Frederic 37
Beall, George 59
Beall, Ninian 48, 59
Bell, Alexander Graham 54, 70, 80, 93, 149
Bellair 56
Belt, Joseph 57
Benning, William 139
Bethune, Mary McLeod 46, 102
Blackstone, William 104
Bladen, Thomas 140
Blair, Francis Preston 66
Bleak House 63
Bliss, Robert 48
Blount, Henry 48
Blue Plains 66
B'nai B'rith 50
Bolling, Raynal Cawthorne 44
Borglum, Gutzon 22
Bolivar, Simon 88, 103, 134
Brady, Matthew 67
Brent, Robert 56
Brooks, Jehiel 56
Brown, Bernice 55
Brown, Samuel 61
Buchanan, James 104
Bunshaft, Gordon 50
Burke, Edmund 105
Burleith 57
Burnham, Daniel 43
Burr, Aaron 117
Buzzard Point 91
Bryce, James 9
Butt, Archibald Wallingham 37, 84

Cannon, Joseph Gurney 26
Cardozo, Francis 94
Carmichael, Leonard 145
Carnegie, Andrew 17
Carroll, Daniel 42, 91
Carroll, John 105
Case, Francis 3
Cavanaugh, John 21
Cedar Hill 47
Center Market 41
Chain Bridge 3
Chevy Chase 57
Churchill, Winston 106
Clay, Henry 4
Cleveland, Stephen Glover 57
Cluss, Adolph 54

Cohen, Francine and Jeff ... 153
Columbus, Christopher ... 38
Congressional Cemetery ... 66, 83
Cooke Henry ... 63
Coolidge, Elizabeth Sprague ... 146
Coolidge, John Calvin ... 94
Cooper, Anna Julia ... 10
Corcoran, William Wilson ... 47, 52, 77
Cornell, Florence ... 55
Cret Paul ... 68
Custis, Martha Parke ... 79
Cutts, Richard ... 51

Dallas, George ... 48
Dante ... 107
Davidson, Samuel ... 12
D. C. Stadium ... 71
Dean, Julian ... 58
Decatur, Stephen ... 48, 102
Demonet, Jules ... 67
Dirksen, Everett M. ... 26
Douglass, Frederick ... 3, 47
Dumbarton Oaks ... 48
Dunbar, Paul Laurence ... 85, 95
Dupont, Samuel Francis ... 10, 39

Eastern Market ... 41
Eckington ... 58, 86
Ebbitt, William E. ... 76
Einstein, Albert ... 108, 147
Eisenhower, Dwight D. ... 140, 147
Eliot, Charles ... 43
Ellicott, Andrew ... 9, 161
Ellington, Edward Kennedy "Duke" ... 3, 96
Emancipation Monument ... 68
Emmet, Robert ... 109
Ericsson, John ... 82, 109

Farragut, David G. ... 11
Fichandler, Zelda ... 144, 148
Flannery, Lot ... 126
Fletcher, Joseph ... 68
Foggy Bottom ... 59
Folger, Henry Clay ... 68
Ford, Gerald Rudolph ... 26
Ford, John T. ... 84, 148
Forrestal, James Vincent ... 27
Foxall, Henry ... 140

Franklin, Benjamin ... 12, 109
Freer, Charles Lang ... 49, 154
Frelinghuysen, F. T. ... 10
French, Daniel Chester ... 11, 37, 111, 126, 140
Friendship Heights ... 41
Fountain Square ... 12
Funk, Jacob ... 59

Gadsby, John ... 48
Gales, Joseph ... 58
Gallatin, Abraham Alfonse Albert .. 110
Gallaudet, Thomas Hopkins ... 97, 111
Gallaudet, Edward Miner ... 97, 111
Galvez, Bernardo de ... 111
Garfield, James Abram ... 12, 112
Georgetown ... 59
Gerry, Elbridge ... 67
Gibbons, James ... 113
Gilbert, Benjamin ... 64
Glover, Charles ... 12, 60
Hillandale ... 13
Gompers, Samuel ... 13, 113
Gordon, George ... 59
Grant, Hiram Ulysses S. ... 13, 114
Greene, Nathaniel ... 115
Greenleaf, James ... 91
Grosvenor, Gilbert Hovey ... 149
Guerin, Jules ... 126

Hains, Peter Conover ... 92
Hahnemann, Christian Friedrich Samuel ... 116
Hale, Nathan ... 116
Hamburgh ... 59
Hamilton, Alexander ... 111, 116
Hancock, Winfield Scott ... 117
Hart, Philip Aloysius ... 28
Hartke, Gilbert Vincent ... 149
Haupt, Enid Annenberg ... 69
Hay, John ... 69
Hayes, Lucy Webb ... 79
Hazeltine, Herbert ... 162
Henderson, Mary ... 16
Henry, Joseph ... 54, 118
Heurich, Christian ... 49
Hirshhorn, Joseph H. ... 50
Holmeade Manor ... 61
Hoover, Herbert Clark ... 28

Index

Hoover, John Edgar....................29, 67
Howard, Oliver Otis.......................... 97
Hoxie, Vinnie.................................. 11
Hubbard, Gardiner Greene........ 70, 149
Humphrey, Hubert Horatio 30
Humphreys, A. A. 45
Hutchins, Stilson 110

Iowa Circle 14

Jackson, Andrew 118
Jefferson, Thomas 31, 119
Joan of Arc.................................... 121
Jones, John Paul............................. 122
Juarez, Benito................................ 123

Kahlert, Marion............................... 67
Kalorama 60
Kendall, Amos............................56, 97
Kenilworth 70, 141
Kennedy, Edgar............................... 71
Kennedy, John Fitzgerald 150
Kennedy, Robert F. 71, 123
Key, Francis Scott..............................4
Key, Philip Barton 65
King, Martin Luther, Jr.................... 72
Klutznick, Philip and Ethel 50
Knox, Henry.................................... 46
Knox, John Jay................................ 61
Kosciuszko, Tadeusz...................... 123
Kreeger, David Lloyd 144, 152
Kutz, Charles W. 4

L'Enfant, Pierre Charles 42, 160
Lafayette, Gilbert 13, 124
Lamond, Angus............................... 60
Lane, Harriet 104
Langdon, Andrew.......................60, 61
Langdon, LeDroit............................ 61
Langley, Samuel Pierpont 152
Langston, John Mercer.................... 73
Latrobe, Benjamin........................... 67
LeDroit Park 61
Library of Congress 24, 31, 32
Lincoln, Abraham . 14, 51, 68, 125, 153
Lisner, Abram 153
Little, Malcolm................................ 14
Livingston, Edward 48
Logan, John Alexander 14

Long Bridge 4
Longfellow, Henry Wadsworth 126
Longworth, Nicholas........................ 31
Lovell, Joseph 66
Luther, Martin 127

MacMornie, Frederick.................... 128
Madison, Dolley........................ 32, 51
Madison, James 32
Malcolm X 14
Mallery, Allen W. 141
Mangum, Edward........................... 148
Marriott, J. Willard 73
Marshall, John 15, 127
Marshall, Thurgood......................... 33
Mason, George 5
Mason, John 133
Mayflower Hotel 74
MacArthur, Douglas....................... 141
McClellan, George Brinton 128
McKinley, William 98
McLean, John R. 41
McMillan, James 74
McNair, Leslie J. 44
McPherson, James Birdseye 16
Mead, Gilbert and Jaylee................ 154
Meade, George Gordon.................. 128
Mellon, Andrew W. 39
Meridian Hill Park.......................... 16
Mestrovic, Ivan 121
Meyer, Agnes Ernst and Eugene..... 154
Millet, Francis Davis.................. 37, 84
Mills, Clark 119, 163
Mills, John 162
Mills, Robert 67
Morgan, Thomas P. 55, 64
Morton, Levi P. 78
Mount Pleasant 61
Mt. Vernon Square 17
Mumford, Lawrence Quincy 155
Murdock, John................................. 41
Murrow, Edward R.......................... 17

Newlands, Francis Griffith 39
Nassif Building 33

Oak View 57
Octagon House.........................75, 88
Old Ebbitt Grill 76

Old Vat Room 144
O'Neill, Thomas Philip, Jr. 33
Offutt, Henry Wootton 41
Owen, Robert Latham 18, 81

Pei, I.M. 43
Perkins, Frances 34, 86
Pershing, John Joseph 18
Peter, Robert 16
Peter, Thomas 79
Peter's Hill 16
Petersen, William 51
Petworth 61
Phelps, Seth Ledyard 99
Phillips, Duncan 51
Pickford, Mary 155
Pierce, Isaac 76
Pike, Albert 87, 129
Platt, Charles 49
Potomac 76
President's Park 13
Pulaski, Casimir 130
Push-Ma-Ha-Ta 67

Randle, Arthur E. 19, 61
Rawlins, John Aaron 19, 85
Rayburn, Samuel Taliaferro 34
Reagan, Ronald 34
Red Top 57
Reed, Walter 45
Reno, Jesse Lee 142
Renwick, James 52, 54
Riggs, George Washington ... 47, 60, 76
Rios, Ariel 25
Ripley, Mary Livingston 78
Ripley, Sidney Dillon 52, 77
Rochambeau, Jean de 5, 130
Roosevelt, Franklin Delano 87, 131
Roosevelt, Theodore 132
Rush, Benjamin 133
Russell, Richard B. 35

Sackler, Arthur M. 52
Saint-Gaudens, Louis 43
San Martin, Jose de 134
Scott, Winfield 20
Scott Square 16
Seward, Olive Risley 21
Seward, William H. 20
Seymour, George 116
Shaw, Robert G. 62
Shaw, W. B. 70, 141
Shepherd, Alexander
  Robey 63, 81, 135
Sheridan, Philip H. 21
Sheriff, Levi 58
Sherman, William Tecumseh.... 22, 135
Shevchenko, Taras 136
Shoemaker, Albert 41
Shoreham Hotel 78
Sibley, William J. 78
Small, Albert and Lillian 53
Smithson, James Macie 53
Sousa, John Philip 5, 67
Spingarn, Jack Elias 99
Stanton, Edwin McMasters 22
St. Elizabeths Hospital 78
Steuben, Frederich von 136
St. Jerome 121
Stoddert, James 41
Stone, William James 61
Story, William 127
Strauss, Oscar Solomon 40
Studio Theater 154
Suit, Samuel Taylor 142
Sumner, Charles 54
Switzer, Mary E. 36
Sylvan Theater 156

Taft, Robert A. 137
Taft, William Howard 6
Takoma Park 64
Tayloe, Benjamin 81
Tayloe, John 61, 75
Temple Heights 64
Tenally, John 64
Thomas, George H. 22
Thompson, James 91
Thornton, William 75, 79
Threlkeld, Henry 57
Tidal Basin 79
Totten, Joseph G. 42
Tudor Place 79

Union Station 43
Uniontown 56

Index

Van Ness, John Peter 43
Volta Bureau 80

Walker, Albert 23
Wallenberg, Raoul 143
Ward, Artemas 23
Wardman, Harry 69, 80
Walker, Allen E. 74
Warner, B. H. 17, 61
Warner Theater 157
Warren, Monroe, Sr. 71
Washington Barracks 44
Washington, George 83, 158ff
Washington, Margaret Murray 99
Watergate 80
Waterson, George 67
Webster, Daniel 137

Weldon, Felix de 104
Welsh, Kevin J. 7
Wesley, John 102, 138
Western Market 41
Westmoreland Circle 23
Whitehurst, H. C. 143
Whittall, Gertrude Clark 157
Willard, Henry Augustus, *et al* 89
Williams, Arland D., Jr. 7
Wilson, John 90
Wilson, Woodrow 7, 54
Winder, William 36
Witherspoon, John 138
Woodley 65
Woodson, Howard Dilworth 100

Young, Whitney Moore, Jr. 8